Rethinking Third Places

Rethinking Third Places

Informal Public Spaces and Community Building

Edited by

Joanne Dolley

Cities Research Institute, Griffith University, Queensland, Australia

Caryl Bosman

Griffith School of Environment and Science, Griffith University, Queensland, Australia

Edward **Elgar**
PUBLISHING

Cheltenham, UK • Northampton, MA, USA

Published by
Edward Elgar Publishing Limited
The Lypiatts
15 Lansdown Road
Cheltenham
Glos GL50 2JA
UK

Edward Elgar Publishing, Inc.
William Pratt House
9 Dewey Court
Northampton
Massachusetts 01060
USA

A catalogue record for this book
is available from the British Library

Library of Congress Control Number: 2018967911

This book is available electronically in the **Elgar**online
Social and Political Science subject collection
DOI 10.4337/9781786433916

Printed on elemental chlorine free (ECF)
recycled paper containing 30% Post-Consumer Waste

ISBN 978 1 78643 390 9 (cased)
ISBN 978 1 78643 391 6 (eBook)

Typeset by Servis Filmsetting Ltd, Stockport, Cheshire
Printed and bound in the USA

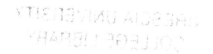

Contents

Figures

Tables

Contributors

Sara Alidoust (PhD, B.Arch, M.Arch) is a seniors living development researcher/advisor. She is engaged in both the industry and research, related to designing and planning for the aging population. Her research includes the links between public health, environmental sustainability and urban planning. She is interested in investigating the particular needs of different groups of society, especially older people in design, planning and policy making.

Sarah Baker is a Professor of Cultural Sociology at Griffith University. Her books include *Community Custodians of Popular Music's Past: A DIY Approach to Heritage* (Routledge, 2017), *Teaching Youth Studies Through Popular Culture* (ACYS, 2014), *Creative Labour: Media Work in Three Cultural Industries* (Routledge, 2011) and *Curating Pop: Exhibiting Popular Music in the Museum* (Bloomsbury, 2019).

David Beynon is an Associate Professor at the University of Tasmania and a practicing architect. His research involves investigating the social, cultural and compositional dimensions of architecture and urban environments, the role of architecture in processes of urban renewal, migration and cultural change, and the adaptation of architectural content and meaning through motifs, rituals and form in Australia and Asia. Publications on this research include *Digital Archetypes: Adaptations of Early Temple Architecture in South and Southeast Asia* (with Sambit Datta, Ashgate Publishing, 2014).

Caryl Bosman is an Associate Professor in Urban and Environmental Planning at Griffith University. She has received numerous accolades for teaching excellence, including two Australian National awards. Her current research interests focus on the scholarship of learning and teaching, histories of planning and placemaking, with a focus on heritage, and the provision of housing for an aging population. She has worked in architectural practices in South Africa, London and Adelaide and taught in both architectural and planning degree programmes.

Elizelle Juaneé Cilliers is a Professor and Chair of the Urban and Regional Planning Department of the North West University in South Africa, and leader of the research programme on Sustainable Planning, Development and Implementation. She is a registered Urban Planner at the South African Council for Planners and member of the International Society of Urban and Regional Planners. She is on the Editorial Board of the *Journal for Town and Regional Planning* and host of a weekly Environmental Radio talk in South Africa.

Jez Collins is the Founder and Director of the Birmingham Music Archive C.I.C., a cultural and creative arts organisation that captures, documents and celebrates the musical culture of Birmingham and develops associated projects such as exhibitions, tours, talks, youth and community focused projects and broadcast media (films and radio). Collins was previously employed at Birmingham City University as the Keeper of the Archive and as a Researcher in their Centre for Media & Cultural Research. He holds an MA in Creative Industries and Cultural Policy and his work has been widely published in academic and popular press publications. Collins is also a co-Director of Un-Convention C.I.C., a Trustee of the National Jazz Archive, a member of the Advisory Board for the Community Archives & Heritage Group and sits on the Heritage Committee panel for the Birmingham Civic Society.

Joanne Dolley is a doctoral student and member of the Cities Research Institute at Griffith University. Her research focuses on the community aspect of community gardens through a particular lens of third place to explore how community gardens contribute to building social capital. Her Masters research explored opportunities to teach literacy and numeracy through school garden programmes. Joanne was part of a team awarded a University of Southern Denmark/Griffith University collaborative research grant titled, 'Planning for age friendly cities: Urban allotments and healthy aging'.

Simone Driessen is a lecturer and researcher in the Media and Communication Department of Erasmus University Rotterdam. Her PhD focused on the affordances of mainstream popular music in the everyday life of aging audiences. In several empirical cases, she studied how a particular generation explains and legitimises the consumption and appreciation of music from its recent past in different contexts. She lectures on media entertainment, fandom, mediatisation, and global communication in the Bachelor of Communication and Media.

Leila Mahmoudi Farahani is a Research Fellow at Centre for Urban Research, RMIT University, working as a member of the Clean Air and Urban Landscape Hub. She conducts industry and government-funded research in monitoring and evaluating public and green spaces, with a particular focus on how the built environment and physical structure of neighbourhoods impact residents. She has practised as an architect and urban designer. Her research interests include greening, public life studies, liveability, sustainable urban development, sociocultural studies and environmental psychology.

Simone Fullagar is Chair of the Physical Culture, Sport and Health research group at the University of Bath, UK and Adjunct Professor at Griffith University, Australia. As an interdisciplinary sociologist, Simone undertakes research across the areas of embodiment, health, mental health and physical culture/sport using material-discursive theories. She is currently completing a book on the sociocultural context of women's recovery from depression with Wendy O'Brien and Adele Pavlidis.

Gordon Holden is an Emeritus Professor at Griffith University where he was the Foundation Head of Architecture. He is an architectural and urban design education leader, having initiated, structured and directed several programmes across four Universities in three countries. Gordon is the 2010 recipient of the Australian Institute of Architects Award the 'Neville Quarry Architectural Education Prize' for outstanding leadership in architectural education. He researches, publishes and teaches in architectural and urban design history, theory and practice. A main interest is in sustainable urban placemaking.

Lauren Istvandity is a Postdoctoral Research Fellow at Queensland Conservatorium Griffith University. Her expertise lies in the areas of music heritage and memory studies. Recent and upcoming publications include *The Lifetime Soundtrack: Music and Autobiographical Memory* (Equinox, forthcoming), *Curating Pop* (with Sarah Baker and Raphael Nowak, Bloomsbury, forthcoming) and the co-edited collection *Routledge Handbook to Popular Music History and Heritage* (with Sarah Baker, Catherine Strong and Zelmarie Cantillon, 2018).

Do Own Kim is a doctoral student at the Annenberg School for Communication and Journalism, University of Southern California and a Korea Foundation for Advanced Studies (KFAS) fellow. She is interested in both humanistic and social scientific approaches to mediated communication, culture, and technology. She is particularly interested in the impact and implications of new media technologies in user engagement and cultural practices.

Kathy Lloyd is a Senior Lecturer at Griffith University. Her research focuses on the relationship between leisure and community quality of life; women, physical activity and psychological well-being and how physical activity interventions impact on women's persistence in physical activity. More recently her research has explored the relationship between urban form and liveability with a focus on the experiences of women, social change and the role of public space as a site of sociability.

Wendy O'Brien is an interdisciplinary sociologist with research interests including the following areas: mental health, women's well-being, liveability, feminism, active embodiment, emotional geographies, volunteers in sport and communities of practice in higher education. She has presented papers at international conferences and published research papers and book chapters in these areas.

Daniel O'Hare is Associate Professor Urban Planning and leader of the Built Environment group in the Faculty of Society and Design, Bond University. He holds a PhD and MA in Urban Design from Oxford Brookes University, UK and a Bachelor of Town Planning from University of NSW. His earlier professional practice was in the community and government sectors. Danny's long-term research interest is the transformation of coastal tourism areas into sustainable city regions. He is passionate about urban design for transit-supportive walkable cities.

Catherine Strong is a Senior Lecturer in the Music Industry programme at RMIT in Melbourne. Among her publications are *Grunge: Music and Memory* (2011), and *Death and the Rock Star* (2015, edited with Barbara Lebrun). Her research deals with various aspects of memory, nostalgia and gender in rock music, popular culture and the media. She is currently Chair of IASPM-ANZ and co-editor of *Popular Music History* journal.

Dmitri Williams is an Associate Professor at the USC Annenberg School for Communication and Journalism. His research focuses on the social and economic impacts of new media, with a focus on online games. He was the first researcher to use online games for experiments, and to undertake longitudinal research on video games. He studies the psychology of online populations using data science and large-scale analytics. His work has been featured in most major media outlets.

Geoff Woolcock is a Senior Research Fellow at the University of Southern Queensland's Institute for Resilient Regions and Adjunct Associate Professor at both Griffith and QUT. He works with a diverse range of public and private sector organisations helping develop whole of community outcome measures for a variety of social interventions, particularly in socio-economically disadvantaged communities. He has 30 years community-based research experience nationally and internationally, across the community service sectors, and has co-published more than 150 peer-reviewed papers and community reports. Geoff is a frequent public speaker and commentator about building child-friendly communities.

Foreword

I introduced the notion of a 'Third Place' in 1989, in the hard-cover edition of *The Great Good Place*.[1] That book and the concept of the third place came about after I was first introduced to life in a modern American suburb. Earlier I held a position at the University of Nevada in the city of Reno. Life there was easy with a block and a half walk to campus, two blocks to a grocery store, and a walk of three blocks put me downtown among the casinos and restaurants.

From Reno, I moved to Pensacola, Florida as a charter member of the newly-founded University of West Florida and, for the first time in my life, I lived in an automobile suburb. In Reno, I had parked my car out back and watched it gather dust as I had little need for it. Now I needed the car every day of the week and for everything. The use-value of my neighborhood (things available on foot) was zero. There were sidewalks but nothing to walk to, and that 'place on the corner' where earlier generations met and got to know one another had been zoned out; living in a community for single-use zoning had killed any hope of it.

After several weeks of shuttling back and forth between the two small worlds of home and work, I got lucky. Regularly driving past Krell's bakery, I noticed through its several picture windows, the same group of men sitting at the counter every morning. By my third visit I was one of the gang. One morning Roby was outside putting a new alternator in my car while I was inside enjoying my coffee. Buck had a big tree that needed to come down, an easy job for me and my chainsaw. Gene's son became my 'yard man.' These few examples suggest the practical gains of third place involvement, apart from the daily conversation and laughter in good company – the major benefit. My residential neighborhood offered nothing, but Krell's made up for it.

In a long life, I've had many third places but it was Krell's, more than any of them, that struck me with their importance. It was living in the sterile world our planners have created that brought the message home. In 2001, I followed the original book with a reader in which 20 authors

---

[1] Ray's forthcoming book is called *The Joy of Tippling*. Ray explains that the book 'encourages a moderate consumption of alcohol which brings people together in happy communion and promotes a livelier form of conversation.'

detailed a variety of places serving to bring people together beyond the confines of home and work.

The present volume zeroes in on the widespread problem of loneliness in urban centers; a problem that city planners seem never to understand nor address. Among several new approaches to third place planning are the effects of technological advances, the need for child-friendly places, the development of community gardens, and the role of music. It pleases me greatly that this book is the product of two women, for if ever a field needed more women, and needed them badly, it is urban planning.

Ray Oldenburg
March 2018

Acknowledgments

We are grateful for the assistance provided by our Editors, Barbara Pretty and Katy Crossan, in preparing this book. We would also like to thank Ray Oldenburg for his generous contribution to the project.

Caryl and Joanne

And thanks Adrian Wilkinson, Rose Pascoe, and Joan and Clive Dolley.

Joanne

1. Rethinking third places and community building

Caryl Bosman and Joanne Dolley

INTRODUCTION

Ideals of community as produced by many planning discourses – in Australia, the UK and America – in the 2000s are not dissimilar to their historical forbears. Most remain associated with aspirations to 'the good life', a more caring, sharing, connected and united world (Freie 1998). An imagined gemeinschaft village life is still a popular image of 'community': small scaled, place-based, face-to-face relationships, self-contained, self-governing and self-referential. However, the unquestioned belief that physical planning can create ideals of community and provide the necessary ingredients for 'the good life' is no longer axiomatic. The often simplistic interpretation of 'community' has meant social and cultural difference has not always been recognised and everyday life patterns have been largely regulated by the 'master' plan. We argue that the values attributed to ideals of community have been re-invented, re-produced and re-inscribed, over the course of the twentieth century as universal and unquestionable 'truths'. This chapter maps some of the planning techniques and rationalities that underpin these 'truths'; 'truths' that ultimately affect the planning and development practices that comprise many contemporary city landscapes and in particular in the case of this book, third places.

This first chapter introduces the concept of third place and establishes a critical platform for understanding the relations between place and community. The chapter concludes with an outline of the book structure. The chapters in this book highlight the importance of third places and how they can be incorporated into urban design to offer places of interaction – promoting togetherness in an urbanised world of mobility and rapid change; frequently cited causes for the demise of community and the decline in social health and well-being. The book chapters analyze a diverse array of spaces identified as third places, authored by scholars from different disciplines and from different countries around the world.

RETHINKING THIRD PLACE

In 1989 the sociologist, Professor Ray Oldenburg, released the influential book *The Great Good Place: Cafes, Coffee Shops, Community Centers, Beauty Parlors, General Stores, Bars, Hangouts, and How They Get You Through the Day*, in which he described his concept of third place. Third place is a concept which identifies places which are not home (first place) or work (second place), but are 'informal public gathering places' (Oldenburg 1997 p. 6). They are neutral places which provide opportunities for people to meet and interact and to develop a sense of belonging to place (Oldenburg 1999). Oldenburg (1989) attributes eight distinguishing characteristics in defining or identifying third places:

1. Neutral ground or a common meeting place.
2. Levellers or places that encourage, and are inclusive of, social and cultural diversity.
3. Places that are easy to access and accommodate various sedentary and active activities.
4. Place champions or regular patrons.
5. Low profile and informal places.
6. Places which foster a playful atmosphere.
7. A home away from home.
8. A place where conversation is the primary activity.

Third places are as relevant at the end of the second decade of the twenty-first century as they were 30 years ago. Urbanisation and its associated problems and solutions, and in particular the effect on community relations, remain 'hot topics'. Loss of community and sense of place is often identified as a problem by social researchers. Oldenburg (1997 p. 7) wrote: 'Life without community has produced, for many, a life style consisting mainly of a home-to-work-and-back-again shuttle. Social well-being and psychological health depend upon community'. One conceptual place where community building occurs is the third place. In a time of rapid urbanisation, with a UN projection that 75 per cent of the population will be living in cities by 2050, there is a critical need to revisit third place as a possible contribution to easing increasing levels of anxiety and loneliness and thereby contributing to the health and well-being of individuals and communities (Hollis 2013; Jacobs 1996; Firth et al. 2011; Putnam 2000).

There has been a great deal of interest in the concept of third place. A 2018 Google Scholar search on Oldenburg's 1989 book found it cited in 2634 articles. Oldenburg published his second third place book *Celebrating The Third Place: Inspiring Stories about the 'Great Good Places' at the*

Heart of Our Communities (2001) at the turn of the century. The book is a collection of 19 essays which tell stories by proprietors and patrons about successful businesses in the USA which have purposely incorporated third place in their physical planning and urban design schemes. These include a shopping centre, tavern, restaurant, coffeehouse, garden shop and a bookstore. Both of Oldenburg's books continue to inspire research across a broad range of locations and in a variety of theoretical frameworks. For example, authors have incorporated the third place concept into the design of aged care facilities; many have explored new types of third places such as libraries, parks and other non-commercial public places; and others have investigated cyberspace and social media in terms of third places. For example, Mele et al. (2015) found that wet markets in Singapore are a good example of third places, facilitating casual and regular social interactions between local residents across ethnicities, gender and socio-economic status. Jones et al. (2015) discovered that fast food outlets act as effective third places bringing together ethnically diverse customers, facilitated by their predictability and ubiquity. There are ever new places which can be added to the list of third places, including the camaraderie which is evident in smoking zones in the countries with limited public spaces for smoking; or the height of popularity of the game of Pokemon Go, where everyone from school children to adults with child-like wonder traipsed through churchyards, building foyers, parklands using their mobile devices searching for place-based electronic creatures.

Third places are important because they act as 'mediation between the individual and the larger society' and increase neighbourhood sense of belonging and community (Oldenburg 1999 p.xxix). Numerous social researchers suggest that everyday incidental interactions of third places improve relationships between neighbours; decrease loneliness and isolation; improve the perception of safety; build social capital and create a sense of place (Oldenburg 1999; Thompson and Maggin 2012; Galdini 2016; Vincent et al. 2016).

PLANNING FOR COMMUNITY: HISTORICAL LEGITIMISATIONS

This section highlights particular sites in which ideals of community were/ are employed as planning techniques, with the intention to produce specific outcomes and achieve particular economic ends – disciplined, docile subjects and collectives. We draw attention to Ebenezer Howard's Garden City; Frank Lloyd Wright, Raymond Unwin and Charles Reade's versions of the same; New Urbanist interventions and Eco-Village promulgations primarily to suggest some of the historical precedencies that many urban planning discourses re-produced as more-or-less 'truthful', 'normal' and 'good'. In addition, by including references to some of the 'heroic' patriarchal planning histories – Howard, Wright, Unwin and Reade – it is not our intention to re-inscribe, what Leonie Sandercock refers to as totalising modernist narratives. Rather, following Sandercock the revisiting of these histories is to 'recover, to make visible, these stories that have been rendered invisible' (Sandercock 1998 p. 5). It is pertinent to consider the planning context and historical ideals of community as the context for third places. As Oldenburg explained, 'American planners and developers have shown a great disdain for those earlier arrangements in which there was life beyond home and work' (Oldenburg 1989 p. 18). This leads to Oldenburg's description of third places as 'those gathering places where community is most alive and people are most themselves' (Oldenburg 1989 p. 40).

Garden City Emergences

One of the most enduring and influential planning treatises that sought to construct the site of 'community' as civil, moral and good was Ebenezer Howard's Garden City model. Howard (1850–1928) drew from a wide range of literature and ideas of the late nineteenth century to address issues arising from the mass migration of rural dwellers to city centres. Through planning and design of self-contained and self-governing Garden Cities, linked by rapid transport routes, Howard sought to provide the accessibility and sociability of the city together with the healthiness of country life. In his book *To-morrow: A Peaceful Path to Real Reform* the Garden City is given as being aligned with nature, offering social opportunities, ample recreation areas that are readily and easily accessible to all residents, a healthy inexpensive lifestyle, clean air and water, well paid employment opportunities, sound investment potential, and the freedom of individuality within the context of 'community' co-operation (Hall and Ward 1998). It was thus fully inclusive. Howard's aim, according to Jane Jacobs, 'was the creation of self-sufficient small towns, really very nice towns if you were docile and had no plans of your own and did not mind spending your life among others with no plans of their own' (Jacobs 1972 p. 27). The Garden City is given as the epitome of 'the good life'; an ideal rather than a lived experience. In this model all residents are disciplined, docile and obedient subjects and there is no dirt, poverty, illness, or disease. Notwithstanding, Howard did acknowledge the existence of individuals who required specialised care. He notionally allowed for a lunatic asylum sited within the greenbelt bounding the Garden City.

Howard's Garden City 'community' included a range of people from industrial capitalists to low paid labourers and the political structure of the Garden City was based upon equality, mutual consensus, sharing and fairness. The boundaries of the Garden City are restricted and fixed by the feasibility of all members to participate in a mutual communicative process, so limiting the number of people who can live within the city. Also, membership of the collective is only ascribed to those who actively and physically participate. Those who choose not to participate or are unable to, are alienated or deemed to be deviant. The Garden City model, thus delineates the included 'us' from the excluded 'them' and determines what is 'ours' and what is 'theirs'.

At the same time that Howard was experimenting with his Garden City model, the American architect Frank Lloyd Wright (1867–1959) was arguing for a city planning approach that reflected and embodied democracy and the modern world. Wright's utopian vision for 'Broadacre City', as with Howard's Garden City, emerged at a time of social dis-ease, with the 'ills' of capitalism and overcrowding being the primary impetus for city planning practices of the day. Wright's planned city, as with some of his contemporaries – in particular the Swiss/French architect, Le Corbusier – was largely premised on the belief that physical planning practices could produce the greatest happiness for the greatest number. Thomas Osborne and Nikolas Rose (1999 p. 747) argue that Wright's model city – as with Corbusier's versions – was a governmental space: 'in the sense that the construction of this organic social city and the normal citizen who will inhabit it functions as the regulative ideal of a range of programmes and initiatives within which the normal citizen is the social citizen of what [has been called] "healthy social communities"'.

As did Howard, Wright too sought to create an urban environment that would facilitate healthy and happy subjects, achieved through planning techniques that deployed ideals of community. Wright's Broadacre City, as the title implies, was a merging of city life and country values. Wright sought to establish 'community' through the provision of extensive farm and recreational areas, pollution free factories, local schools, a range of houses to cater for a cross-section of the population, and an inclusive local government structure. Wright argued for an organic architecture that responded to local topographies, climates, and functions. Like Howard, Wright recognised the importance of modern technology rather than harking back to the Middle Ages for his imagery, as some of his English contemporaries – Raymond Unwin in particular – were advocating. Wright's model city boldly embraced modern ideology, the car and manufactured standardised components. By the 1960s, however, these Modernist town planning techniques and practices were being criticised for producing a 'low grade, uniform environment from which escape was impossible' (Mumford 1991 p. 553). This criticism was reiterated in the 1990s by the New Urbanists – as argued below – who blamed Modernist planning practices for the demise of 'community' and all that pertains to 'the good life'. Oldenburg (1989 p. 180) describes the effects as: 'The planners and developers continue to add to the rows of regimented loneliness in neighborhoods so sterile as to cry out for something as modest as a central mail drop or a little coffee counter at which those in the area might discover one another.'

In Britain, Modernist town planning techniques and practices were mostly portrayed in the post World War Two re-workings of Howard's Garden City model, renamed 'New Town'. The early New Towns were government incentives with a focus on public housing and employment opportunities, although not always within walking distance as with Howard's model. This new version of the Garden City sought to address issues arising from the post war period: affordable housing for returning war veterans, the growing use of the motor vehicle, and the fashionable shopping mall. Oldenburg (1989 p. 282) noted the post World War Two period as a turning point for an 'informal public life' as people retreated to their homes and corner stores and cafés have 'fallen to urban renewal', replaced by freeways and modern infrastructure.

Although New Town planning techniques were influenced by and reflected contemporary (late 1940s–1950s) trends and technologies, at the same time they largely drew upon and re-produced Howard's early 1900s city-in-the-country model. New Towns were sited in rural areas and as such were promoted for their country lifestyle; a 'more balanced and complete community life' (Freestone 1989 p. 227). Many New Town planners looked to a past romanticised ideal of village life to create an essentially urban 'community'. In these instances ideals of community were invoked to depict nostalgia for the 'good old days'. The historically imagined, gemeinschaft ideals of community that the planners were promoting, however, seemed no longer applicable or possible. The changes in lifestyles and trends in the late 1950s and 1960s suggested many people did not have the same connection to place that traditional village life relied upon. Increased mobility during this time, higher wage opportunities, and changes in gender roles and technology – and therefore labour requirements – often meant fundamental changes to many urban living patterns. Oldenburg (1989 p. 285) noted, 'Segregation, isolation, compartmentalization and sterilization seem to be the guiding principles of urban growth and renewal.'

As with Howard and Wright's city planning models, New Town ideals of community were to be achieved primarily through the provision for a range of houses to cater for a range of people. Unlike some of the nineteenth-century social mix planning techniques – that co-located working and middle class housing – the planning of New Towns relied on the social and physical segregation and ranking of blue and white collar workers. B.J. Heraud (1968 p. 35) argues that there was a supposition held by many New Town planners that, exposure to a 'mixed environment' would 'enlarge people's horizons and so benefit society as a whole'. In addition, Mark Peel (1992 p. 25) suggests that there was a general belief among many planners, at the time, that New Towns 'if planned properly, could still produce valued social outcomes–social mix, neighbourhood community, and village-like social relationships'. This achievement was flawed from the outset given the differences between the spontaneous and irregular characteristics of village layouts and the planned and controlled New Town landscapes. As N. Dennis (1968) points out, village life revolved around an overlapping and complex web of everyday relationships with people who were generally known and named. New Town planning, however, involved a group of new residents who did not necessarily know each other or have anything in common. It could be argued that this set of circumstances cries out for informal meeting places. Oldenburg (1989 p. 286) discusses the challenges of 'trying to enjoy life amid a badly designed environment' and suggests that 'grass roots efforts are the best hope for creating enjoyable urban habitats'. Several chapters in this book discuss grass roots efforts to create a sense of community, in particular, Chapter 7 which looks at music archives and Chapter 8 on community gardens.

By the 1980s, the commitment of the Australian government (and the British government) to New Town programmes was dwindling. This was partly the result of increased migration, demographic and lifestyle shifts and changes in modes of government. The withdrawal of the government from direct involvement in the planning and development of new residential areas opened opportunities for private enterprise intervention.

Village Idyll

Although Howard did not fully realise his Garden City dream, his work was the impetus for others who believed they could instigate social reform through planning for ideals of community. Raymond Unwin (1863–1940), having resigned as Howard's Garden City architect, remoulded Howard's model in line with his own ideology. Unwin focused more on middle class residential commuter suburbs. He drew heavily on the Arts and Crafts Movement of John Ruskin and William Morris and turned to the Middle Ages for his imagery and ideals. This bias was encapsulated in his book

Town Planning in Practice first published in 1909. In effect, through specific town planning practices Unwin sought to regulate everyday life of the individual, in accordance with particular ideals of community, an argument which is taken up a little later.

For Unwin, village life encapsulated 'the good life' and ideals of community. The village was a site of both social and aesthetic value; social in terms of bringing together a group of like-minded people, with similar values and interests, and aesthetic in the sense of place creation. Unwin believed that through the use of local building materials and practices, residents would establish an identity and a sense of belonging to place. This common identity he argued established 'community', as people shared common ties and memories. Unwin's concept of 'community' is thus closely aligned with gemeinschaft relationships. Here, 'community' is consigned to being rural as opposed to urban. It is associated with belonging rather than alienation, communality rather than individualism and the traditional rather than the modern. The urban versus rural dialectic is played out in a direct and blatant fashion. Howard sought to sift the qualities associated with 'the good life' from both poles in his Garden City model, while Unwin drew almost exclusively from the rural pole. In Unwin's argument for a 'new form of community that would rise up out of the land, clear, clean, honest and alive' (Unwin 1994 p. xxi), place-based relationships and imagined, 'golden age' values are re-inscribed.

Unwin sought to rationalise, re-organise and rank the largely incremental and spontaneous planning practices that informed village life in pre-industrial England. He stated that (Unwin 1901 p. 93):

> It is the crystallisation of the elements of the village in accordance with a definitely organised life of mutual relations, respect or service, which gives the appearance of being an organised whole, the home of a community, to what would otherwise be a mere conglomeration of buildings.

This attempt by Unwin, to create a 'new form of community' by developing low density residential 'villages' for like-minded people, has been criticised for propagating suburban sprawl and reinforcing social polarisation. As we will demonstrate, many current planners and developers also promulgated village planning techniques and practices as a means to produce ideals of community.

Unwin's village model emerged in the antipodes and found its way to South Australia through Charles Reade (1880–1933). Reade was commissioned by the South Australian government to design a garden suburb as a model example of latest planning practice. The new fully planned village, now known as Colonel Light Gardens, contrasted with existing suburban development which was largely haphazard and subject to opportunists and laissez-faire practices. Australian suburban development had emerged in opposition to the slums; the 'dense, dirty, unnatural, disorderly and disease ridden, vs [the] open, clean, natural and healthy' (Davison 1993 p. 3). Reade traded heavily on this imagery in his argument for the village model. Reade's model was underpinned by and realised through the implementation of planning techniques pertaining to ideals of community.

Like Howard and Unwin, Reade attempted to plan a residential setting that would be manifest through largely utopian images of docile and happy 'community' subjects. Reade's village model represented a healthy environment, an enclave for white nuclear families, a moral and upright 'community', stability, conformity and a sound financial investment (Freestone 1989 pp. 84–85). The Australian suburbs have historically been socially exclusive places, home only for those who could afford to move from the dense and overcrowded cities to embrace the country lifestyle which suburbia promised.

Urban Villages[1]

Much of the recent (1990s–2000s) planning rhetoric about the re-creation of villages and re-establishing of 'communities' is essentially about a lifestyle that is walkable. In these discourses a walkable lifestyle is promoted as being one that fulfils and sustains everyday needs within the locality, so reducing the need to use non-renewable resources. In these new villages, the government of everyday life is through practices of social interaction, through physical mobility (walking or cycling) and local travel. The Modernist planning techniques regulated behaviour through motorised travel and many Modernist planners argued that this mode of travel liberated the individual. Liberation and 'freedom' are now construed in relation to physical mobility. Through planning practices that emphasise pedestrian propinquity, individuals are 'liberated' from the car and from the negative impacts of suburban landscapes. Howard's Garden City model too, allegedly, offered residents 'freedom' to walk to places of employment and places of recreation. This focus is reiterated in the New Urbanists discourses: passive social contact, proximity and appropriateness of space.

The New Urbanist Movement was established in the early 1990s by a group of American architects and its proponents believe it 'is poised to become the dominant real estate and planning trend of . . . [this] century' (Steuteville 2000). The New Urbanist Movement (largely operated

---

[1] The term 'urban village' was popularised by HRH The Prince of Wales in the 1980s.

through private enterprise practices) has had a significant impact on some
of the planning policies, legislation and projects set up by the American
Federal Department of Housing and Urban Development (HUD). The
movement is described as a reworking of traditional neighbourhood
ideology for the social environment of the 1990s (Fulton 1996). Heidi
Landecker (1996) likens the movement to a new religion with prophets
(founders Peter Calthorpe, Elizabeth Plater-Zyberk and Andres Duany),
a Bible (*The New Urbanism: Toward an Architecture of Community* ed.
Peter Katz) and thirteen commandments given to regulate planning and
development practices. New Urbanist development practices have been
primarily taken from Unwin's *Town Planning in Practice* first published in
1909 and Clarence Perry's 'Neighbourhood Unit' of 1929.

New Urbanist discourses claim to address the 'ills' of Modernism and
the 'evils' of conventional suburban planning of the 1930s and 1940s.
Modernist architects, such as Le Corbusier and Frank Lloyd Wright, are
blamed for the demise of 'vital communities' by privileging private over
public spaces, focusing on the motor vehicle and instigating segregation
policies (Calthorpe 1994 p.xv). The Modernists, Vincent Scully (1994)
laments, killed the traditional city and everything that pertained to
'the good life': 'community', 'correctness' and 'humanness'. Many New
Urbanists consider American suburbia to be a landscape that largely
inhibits experiences of 'the good life' – ideals of community and gemeinschaft relationships. Suburbia is depicted as being lonely and isolated,
without public spaces to gather informally; a place where children grow
up unbalanced, without any understanding of traditional (gemeinschaft?)
values, morals or social responsibilities (Audirac 1999). As Oldenburg
(1989 p.282) described, 'Adolecents spend more time in shopping malls
than they do in any place beyond home and school. The duel degree is in
consumership and passivity'. In response to the view of suburbia, many
New Urbanists argue for a return to a cherished national icon, 'that of
a compact, close-knit community' (Katz 1994 p.ix) achieved through
comprehensive, historically founded, more-or-less 'truthful' planning
techniques.

As such, the New Urbanist ideology remains within a Modernist agenda.
The Modernists too believed that by the design of physical infrastructure
particular social patterns could be created or influenced. For them it
was through the dominance of car travel and the development of tower
blocks. The New Urbanists seek to achieve the same end through a return
to traditional village life. Both argue for the creation of 'community'
(however defined) achieved through planning and built form as the means
to cure the contemporary 'ills' of society. While the Modernists sought to
achieve their end through the celebration of new technology and affirming

their belief in the future, the New Urbanists look to a romanticised past (a pre-capitalist, pre-industrial, pre-motorised era) for their realisation of 'community' (Audirac and Shermyen 1994).

For the New Urbanists, it is the fundamental qualities of small country towns or villages that they wish to emulate, rather than city urbanity. Peter Calthorpe gives the key New Urbanists planning determinates as being 'pedestrian scale, an identifiable centre and edge, integrated diversity of use and population and defined public space' (Calthorpe 1994 p. 122). These 'post-suburban' developments are proposed to include the urban advantages of employment, civic, commercial and retail opportunities coupled with the rural advantages of clean air, healthy lifestyles and open public spaces. These qualities the New Urbanists state – as did Howard – are essential for 'restoring functional, sustainable communities' (Steuteville 2000).

In keeping with Howard's Garden City model and the subsequent derivatives, the New Urbanists' claim for 'community' also includes a variety of house types and styles for a range of life stages and incomes. The New Urbanist Charter (Congress for the New Urbanism 1998) states 'Within neighborhoods, a broad range of housing types and price levels can bring people of diverse ages, races, and incomes into daily interaction, strengthening the personal and civic bonds essential to an authentic community.' The difference between the earlier city/town/village planning models and the New Urbanists models rest in private enterprise interests. Ideals of community become a commodity only for those who can afford them.

The rationalities of government underpinning these new 'fully planned communities' are no longer fuelled by aspirations of social reform for the poor. Rather, they are influenced by market forces, where ideals of community are commercialised and sold as a commodity for profit. Any remnant of social reform embedded in these rationalities applies only to those who can afford it. Andres Duany and Elizabeth Plater-Zyberk suggest that middle-class home owners reduce the number of cars per family, in order to set back the higher costs of living in a New Urbanist development. They state 'No other action of the designer can achieve an improvement in the availability of housing for the middle class comparable to the sensible organization of a good neighborhood plan' (Duany and Plater-Zyberk 1994 p. xix).

In arguing for a new (or not so new) pattern of urban development the New Urbanists assume that the majority of Americans are inherently unhappy and dissatisfied with suburban life: a large allotment, detached house, back yard, privacy and car reliance. Some research suggests however, that suburbia fosters positive relationship networks because residents tend to be of similar life stages; for example, young families, families with teenagers or retirees.

The use of ideals of community as planning techniques – be they espoused by New Urbanists or others – has ethical implications in that planners become implicated in regulating and moulding behaviour patterns to certain ends: collective cohesion, interaction, sharing, supportive networks, membership and personal investment. Ideals of community utilised as planning techniques also assumes that individuals have a predisposition for neighbourly interaction, irrespective of personal histories, incomes and beliefs. In addition, they assume that residents will be happy to reduce or moderate their use of the car in an environment that is not always conducive to the economic journey. Oldenburg (1989 p. 286) refers to informal public life of the past as the 'triumph of the space user over the space planner – we simply took over establishments and spaces created for other purposes. What is revolutionary about our new environment is its unprecedented resistance to user modification.'

'Sustainable' Villages

More recently a new village product has entered the housing market. This fully planned product, or Eco Village, is designed in accordance with accepted sustainability principles; most commonly: recycling, solar power and rain water retention infrastructures. Many Eco Village discourses re-inscribe New Urbanist planning techniques in a bid to create ideals of community. Hugh Barton (2000 p. 11) defines an Eco-Village as 'an attractive, convivial and healthy place that balances privacy with community and local provision with city access'. As do the New Urbanists, Eco-Village discourses also argue for ideals of community as produced through an assemblage of urban and rural lifestyle rhetorics. Similar to Unwin and Wright's theorisations, identity with place is to be achieved through practices of planning and architecture, which are to respond to the local climate, topography and landscape. The model for these contemporary villages suggests they are located in country areas and include a range of employment opportunities to cater for all skill levels. Eco-Village proponents also argue for residential diversity – a range of house sizes and styles and diversity of people, from across the full spectrum of the population – as a planning technique essential for the production of 'sustainable communities'. It is through the practices of planning and architecture that, Alison Gilchrist (2000 p. 150) suggests, ideals of community become 'inextricably linked to sustainability'.

Eco-Villages are also resource inclusive developments with a focus on pedestrian propinquity; in that schools, retail, commercial and civic amenities are provided for, in conjunction with residential accommodation. Like the New Urbanists, the assumption underpinning Eco-Village planning techniques is that the provision of local amenities and an emphasis on pedestrian propinquity will produce friendly verbal interaction and local networks will be established. Importantly, this 'sustainable' village model is based upon efficient networks of activities and travel within and between villages, so eliminating the need for a privately owned motor vehicle, and traditional village values apply: gemeinschaft relationships and 'the good life'.

Eco-Villages, as with previous schemes, have been criticised for ignoring the existing pattern of contemporary life. Taylor (2000 p. 28) suggests that a 'new' model of development is not what is required to achieve the desired and much debated ecologically sustainable – and we would add 'community' formation – goals. Rather, planners, architects and other urban theorists need to work within the given fabric of modern urban life if any significant change is to be realised. Goals need to be realistic rather than based on utopian ideals of social mix and ideals of community. Peter Hall and Colin Ward (1998 p. 121) suggest this involves, among other things, equally top-down State regulations and bottom-up local approaches. In our positioning of third place, this book acknowledges both these governmental modes of producing place and community networks. This historical background provides the rationale for the variety of planning and design contexts within which third places exist (or don't exist) and in which grass roots actions of the residents can create third places.

STRUCTURE OF THE BOOK

The book explores the virtual and geographical understanding of place and community through the lens of third places. The first six chapters focus on theoretical and broad concepts of third place for example: rethinking third place and community (this chapter); feminist perspectives; life stage perspectives: older age and child friendly; and urban design and safety considerations: green planning and eyes on the street. The final five chapters focus on specific examples of third places: community museums; community gardens; cyber space; public transport and sidewalks.

In Chapter 2, 'Feminist Perspectives on Third Places' Simone Fullagar, Wendy O'Brien and Kathy Lloyd apply a feminist perspective to third place, concluding that women require third places that are both physically and socially transparent, that is, safe spaces. This chapter questions normative urban design assumptions often associated with white middle class male views. The feminist perspective was not included in Oldenburg's early work largely because the prevailing assumption of the time was that feminine space related to the home (first place). Fullagar et al. identify how third places facilitate or constrain women's right to the city. The focus on feminism in this chapter also highlights links between third place and transgender and non-binary identities. It also points to ways of thinking about gendered experiences relating to class, sexuality, culture, age and ability. Building upon Oldenburg's conception of third places as places where people interact, the authors discuss third places as more than human, places where people also interact with plants, animals and urban infrastructure. The chapter concludes with an acknowledgement that third places are essentially good and they call for more work to be done to create places that are inclusive for everyone and which allow all people to exercise their right to the place.

Chapter 3 builds on concerns of gender and third places to focus on the latter stages of a life. Sara Alidoust and Caryl Bosman analyse third places in terms of the contributions they can make to promoting social health for many people over the age of 65. Ageing populations are world-wide phenomena and there is general acknowledgement that urban design and planning principles, including the provision of third places, need to recognise and support active and healthy ageing agendas. Accessibility of amenities is critical in achieving these agendas. The chapter concludes by arguing for the planning of transport and third place interventions in sprawling suburban landscapes, to allow older people more opportunities to be socially connected.

The other end of the lifecycle continuum is taken up in Chapter 4 by Geoff Woolcock in his chapter on child-friendly third places. Geoff investigates third places in relation to how child friendly they are, using South Bank Parklands in Brisbane, Australia as a case study. He unpacks the significance of built and natural third places in the health and well-being of children and young people. Woolcock paints a disturbing picture of childhood obesity, inactivity and social disconnectedness and argues for the importance of well designed third places that, 'not only welcome children but also establish social and psychological connections that stimulate learning and ultimately, active civic participation'. The chapter provides the traits of effective child-friendly third places including opportunities for unstructured, challenging, adventurous (but safe) play.

Elizelle Juaneé Cilliers' chapter, Chapter 5, seeks to demonstrate the value and role of planning in creating and recreating public spaces which are third places; neutral places which provide opportunities for people to meet and interact and to develop a sense of being a part of a place. To do this she identifies a number of design elements to support the provision and reclaiming of third places in contemporary urban contexts. Through different approaches to planning (place-making, green planning and lively planning) she establishes an evidence-based framework using five international, best-practice case studies to develop third places. The chapter concludes with a global challenge 'to change life, we must first change spaces into third places'.

In keeping with the urban planning/design theme, in Chapter 6 Gordon Holden draws on Jane Jacobs' 'Eyes on the Street' to examine the role of third place in improving perceived safety. Holden focuses on the multidimensional and interconnected aspects of perceived and actual safety within the context of third places in neighbourhoods. He discusses the complexities surrounding the concept of neighbourhoods and the positive arguments for 'eyes on the street' in urban environments as means to create perceived and actual zones of safety. Holden proposes that third places contribute to 'eyes on the street' and therefore safety because these places act as nodes, attracting public participation and interaction. Through the use of four case studies on the Gold Coast, Australia he explores the presence or absence of third places within the context of recorded crime in those places. He concludes that third places may well contribute significantly to both the perception of and actual safety of a place and lower crime rates.

The remaining chapters in the book look at particular sites as third places. The concept of third place also includes places that foster hobbies and collective networks as in the theme of Chapter 7: 'Understanding Popular Music Heritage Practice Through the Lens of "Third Place"'. Lauren Istvandity, Sarah Baker, Jez Collins, Simone Driessen, and Catherine Strong draw from different case studies ranging from do-it-yourself archiving, digital archives, walking tours, and pop music reunion tours to build a convincing augment for the value and currency of alternative third places in urban areas. Baker, in particular, points to the value of community archives and museums as third places which foster social health and can prevent an increase in social isolation among older single adults. In the same chapter Collins posits third places in the virtual online space. This new variety of third place, she argues, allows 'individuals [to] come together online, forming communities dedicated to creating, populating, sustaining and celebrating alternative popular music histories'. The final section of this chapter focuses on tours as third places. Strong's thesis is built around 'how the physical space of urban environments plays a role in how popular music is remembered'. She argues that walking tours are inherently third places. Driessen considers how 'the reunion concert tour of heritage music acts as a site where aspects of third place are enacted'. In this understanding of third place, the reunion concert venue becomes a temporary third place.

Chapter 8, by Joanne Dolley is entitled 'Third Places and Social Capital: Case Study Community Gardens'. This chapter explores the literature on community gardens and the author's recent research which investigated community gardens against third place characteristics in a range of locations in Australia and Denmark. All of the case study community gardens exhibited most or all of the eight third place characteristics and some were particularly effective third places. The theoretical framework used for this research project is social capital and more specifically, Granovetter's 'weak ties'. The chapter gives examples of ways in which community gardens can act as third places. The findings provide insights for better design of third places and the design of community gardens, where building social capital and sense of community is a goal.

Dmitri Williams and Do Own Kim's chapter, 'Third Places in the Ether Around Us: Layers on the Real World', focuses on the third places which exist beyond the 'physical realm' to non-physical spaces made possible through technology. They approach the topic through theories utilised in the study of computer-mediated communication, in particular the concept of 'layering' of multiple online and offline environments. Williams and Kim outline the strengths and weaknesses of virtual places over real-world places. They identify aspects of virtual space which enhance third place interactions by cutting through barriers of socio-economic status and physical attributes. However, the authors caution on the use of filter bubbles, which feed us interactions with like-minded people, isolating our social connections somewhat like a gated community – possibly Oldenburg's 'worst nightmare'. Williams and Kim also draw attention to new technology blurring the edges between first, second and third places, for example, as social media interrupts work, work emails edge into home life, and third place virtual games take place at home. The chapter concludes that as we move into an 'ever-more technologically mediated future', technology has potential to provide third places to anyone anywhere, but just as physical architecture influences human behaviour, it is important to consider the design of the social 'architecture' of online spaces.

Chapter 10 focuses on public transport as a third place. Daniel O'Hare 'considers whether the public transport commute, historically a linear experience between the workplace and home, can be a third place rather than a soulless shuttle to be bracketed with "work" as the opposite to "home"'. O'Hare examines the changing nature and form of work and he links this to the design of cities and the experience of commuters' journeys. He posits that many young adults today (2018) are choosing not to drive and consequently the use of public transport, active modes of travel and third places are flourishing. Public transport is continually shaping and reshaping the level of passenger interaction, with in-vehicle design and waiting areas (station/stop) designs either facilitating or limiting certain types of interactions. The use of mobile technology means many public transport users can connect to virtual communities and so transform the travel journey into a third place. The chapter ends with a call for a greater recognition of public transport as a third place to be 'enjoyed rather than endured' and that well-designed and managed public transport contributes to people-centred cities.

The final chapter, Chapter 11, by Leila Mahmoudi Farahani and David Beynon, focuses on streets as sites of third place activity. By analysing the unobtrusive video footage of interactions which occur along several commercial streets in the City of Greater Geelong, Victoria, it was determined that sidewalk cafés and restaurants, shops and interaction zones such street crossings act, in varying degrees, as third places. Their methodology of video analysis of the use of space and their depiction of findings through diagrams provides a unique level of detail of third place interactions. Using their data and referring theoretically to Lefebvre's ideas on meanings in space, they are able to comment on what makes a vital, active streetscape and propose design features which can enhance the design of third places.

CONCLUDING THOUGHTS

Third places are neutral, open places which act as levellers to bring together local residents of different ethnicities, ages, genders, socio-economic status, education levels and interests. Third places are sites of diversity where everyone is welcome, free to come and go and feel comfortable. Third places can play an important role in improving social interactions in neighbourhoods. Ray Oldenburg, the creator of the concept, listed many examples of third places, such as parks, cafés and piazzas, where people could meet informally. This chapter provides the historical and current urban planning context in which third places reside. This book is a timely exploration of the role of third place in building relations of community in a modern highly urbanised mobile society.

REFERENCES

Audirac, I. (1999) 'Stated preference for pedestrian proximity: An assessment of new urbanist sense of community', *Journal of Planning Education and Research*, 19(1): 53–66.

Audirac, I. and Shermyen, A.H. (1994) 'An evaluation of neotraditional design's social prescription: Postmodern placebo or remedy for suburban malaise?' *Journal of Planning Education and Research*, 13(3): 161–173.

Barton, H. (2000) 'Conflicting perceptions of neighbourhood'. In Barton, H. (ed.) *Sustainable Communities*. London: Earthscan, pp. 3–17.

Calthorpe, P. (1994) 'The region'. In Katz, P. (ed.) *The New Urbanism: Toward an Architecture of Community*. New York: McGraw-Hill, pp. xi–xvi.

Congress for the New Urbanism (1998) 'Charter of the new urbanism'. Available: www.cnu.org (accessed 3 December 2018).

Davison, G. (1993) 'The past and the future of the Australian suburb'. In Coles, R.C. (ed.) *Urban Research Program*. Canberra: Research School of Social Sciences, Australian National University, pp. 1–26.

Dennis, N. (1968) 'The popularity of the neighbourhood community idea'. In Pahl, R.E. (ed.) *Readings in Urban Sociology*. London: Pergamon, pp. 74–92.

Duany, A. and Plater-Zyberk, E. (1994) 'The neighborhood, the district and the corridor'. In Katz, P. (ed.) *The New Urbanism: Toward an Architecture of Community*. New York: McGraw-Hill, pp. xvii–xx.

Firth, C., Maye, D. and Pearson, D. (2011) 'Developing "community" in community gardens', *Local Environment: The International Journal of Justice and Sustainability*, 16(6): 555–568.

Freestone, R. (1989) *Model Communities: The Garden City Movement in Australia*. Melbourne: Thomas Nelson Australia.

Freie, J.F. (1998) *Counterfeit Community: The Exploitation of Our Longings for Connectedness*. Maryland: Rowman & Littlefield.

Fulton, W. (1996) 'The new urbanism challenges conventional planning', *Land Lines*, September 8(5).

Galdini, R. (2016) 'Placemaking as an approach for innovative urban renewal practices: Community gardens in Berlin', *International Review of Sociology*, 2016: 1–21.

Gilchrist, A. (2000) 'Designing for living: The challenge of sustainable communities'. In Barton, H. (ed.) *Sustainable Communities*. London, Earthscan, pp. 147–159.

Hall, P. and Ward, C. (1998) *Sociable Cities: The Legacy of Ebenezer Howard*. London: John Wiley & Sons.

Heraud, B.J. (1968) 'Social class and the new towns', *Urban Studies*, 5: 33–58.

Hollis, L. (2013) *Cities Are Good for You: The Genius of the Metropolis*. London: Bloomsbury Publishing.

Howard, E. (1898) *To-morrow: A Peaceful Path to Real Reform*. London: Swan Sonnenschein & Co.

Jacobs, J. (1972) *The Death and Life of Great American Cities*. London: Penguin.

Jacobs, M. (1996) *The Politics of the Real World. Meeting the New Century*. London: Earthscan Publications.

Jones, H., Neal, S., Mohan, G., Connell, K., Cochrane, A. and Bennett, K. (2015) 'Urban multiculture and everyday encounters in semi-public, franchised café spaces'. *The Sociological Review*, 63(3): 644–661.

Katz, P. (1994) 'Preface'. In Katz, P. (ed.) *The New Urbanism: Toward an Architecture of Community*. New York: McGraw-Hill, pp. ix–x.

Landecker, H. (1996) 'Is new urbanism good for America?' *Architecture AIA Journal*, 85(4): 68–77.

Mele, C., Ng, M. and Chim, M. (2015) 'Urban markets as a "corrective" to advanced urbanism: The social space of wet markets in contemporary Singapore'. *Urban Studies*, 52(1): 103–120.

Mumford, L. (1991) *The City In History: Its Origins, its Transformations and its Prospects*. London: Penguin Books.

Oldenburg, R. (1989) *The Great Good Place: Cafes, Coffee Shops, Community Centers, Beauty Parlors, General Stores, Bars, Hangouts, and How They Get You Through the Day*. New York: Paragon House.

Oldenburg, R. (1997) 'Our vanishing third places'. *Planning Commissioners Journal*, 25: 6–11.

Oldenburg, R. (1999) *The Great Good Place: Cafes, Coffee Shops, Bookstores, Bars, Hair Salons, and Other Hangouts at the Heart of a Community*. New York: Marlow & Company.

Oldenburg, R. (2001) *Celebrating the Third Place: Inspiring Stories about the 'Great Good Places' at the Heart of Our Communities*. Boston: Da Capo Press.

Osborne, T. and Rose, N. (1999) 'Governing cities: Notes on the spatialisation of virtue', *Environment and Planning D: Society and Space*, 17(6): 737–760.

Peel, M. (1992) 'Planning the good city in Australia: Elizabeth as a new town'. In Coles, R.C. (ed.) *Urban Research Program*, Working Paper No. 30, pp. 1–60. Canberra: Research School of Social Sciences, Australian National University.

Perry, C. (1929) 'The Neighborhood Unit', Monograph One. Vol. 7, Regional Survey of New York and its Environs, Neighborhood and Community Planning. New York: New York Regional Plan, 1929.

Putnam, D. (2000) *Bowling Alone*. New York: Simon & Schuster.

Sandercock, Leonie (1998) *Towards Cosmopolis*. London: John Wiley & Sons.

Scully, V. (1994) 'The architecture of community'. In Katz, P. (ed.) *The New Urbanism: Toward an Architecture of Community*. New York: McGraw-Hill, pp. 221–230.

Steuteville, R. (2000) 'The new urbanism: An alternative to modern automobile-orientated planning development', *New Urban News*, 28 June 2000. Available: www.newurbannews.com (accessed 20 December 2018).

Taylor, N. (2000) 'Eco-villages: Dreams and reality'. In Barton, H. (ed.) *Sustainable Communities*. London: Earthscan, pp. 19–28.

Thompson, S. and Maggin, P. (2012) *Planning Australia: An Overview of Urban and Regional Planning*. Cambridge: Cambridge University Press.

Unwin, R. (1901) 'Building and natural beauty'. In *The Art of Building A Home*. London: Longmans Green, p. 93. Quoted in Creese, Walter (1986) *The Search For Environment: The Garden City: Before and After*. New Haven: Yale University Press.

Unwin, R. (1994) [1909]) *Town Planning In Practice*. New York: Princeton Architectural Press.

Vincent, C., Neal, S. and Iqbal, H. (2016) 'Encounters with diversity: Children's friendships and parental responses'. *Urban Studies*, 54(8): 1974–1989.

2. Feminist perspectives on third places

Simone Fullagar, Wendy O'Brien and Kathy Lloyd

INTRODUCTION

In this chapter we question the assumption that third places are neutral or inherently 'good' spaces in contemporary urban life. Drawing upon different feminist perspectives we explore how third places are conceptualised and practised in gendered ways that were rarely considered in the early work of Oldenburg (1999). We draw together literature across the fields of leisure studies, geography and urban planning, and gender studies to consider how women embody third places in different ways and the influence of representations that mediate the gendered experience of the city. As leisure researchers our interests focus on the relationship between leisure practices and the gendered context of third places that can facilitate or constrain women's 'right to the city' (Valentine 1989). At the heart of this approach is a question about how we understand the gendered power relations that shape third places with respect to their historical, sociocultural, political and economic context (Massey 2005). Different feminist theories conceptualise gender inequality and patriarchal power in different ways that offer multiple perspectives on the formation of third places and possibilities for change. We draw upon this diversity to consider the gendered assumptions informing third places, the sociality of third places for women, gendered embodiment and cultural representations as well as the gendered effects of digital technology and more-than-human third places.

THE GENDERED FORMATION OF THIRD PLACES

Feminist geographers, such as Valentine (1989 p. 389), have long argued that 'women's inhibited use and occupation of public place is a spatial expression of patriarchy'. Ortiz Escalante and Sweet (2013) also articulate how both theoretical and everyday conceptualisations of space are deeply shaped by such gender power relations that are supported by a public–private divide while also being male-centred and ethnocentric. It is reinforced by a gender dichotomy of male–female. That is, the 'public–private divide is parallel and mutually supported by parochial and conservative understandings that adhere to gender as male and female' (Sweet and Ortiz Escalante 2015 p. 1830). Not only does this dichotomous construction of space position women as 'naturally' occupying the private, domestic sphere of reproduction and care in contrast to men's entitlement to public life, it also obscures the way gender is lived in more complex and intersectional ways. The spatiality of gender relations and identity formation requires us to think about transgender and non-binary identifications, along with gendered experiences of difference related to class, sexuality, culture, age and ability. Through our focus on women's[1] experience, we take up the question of thinking with difference throughout the chapter as we understand gender to be performative – 'that is, constituting the identity that it is purported to be' (Butler 1990 p. 25). In this sense gender is an aspect of identity and social relations that we 'do' in the enactment of everyday practices, ways of thinking about cities, designing places and theorising about third places.

In thinking about the spatiality of third places we draw upon feminist theorists who think about the relationality of gendered meaning, embodied movement and knowledge production. As Massey argues, 'space does not exist prior to identities/entities and their relations'; rather, 'identities/entities, the relations "between" them, and the spatiality which is part of them, are all co-constitutive' (Massey 2005 p. 10). The gendered meanings of third places are not simply produced through women's individual actions or determined by the structural forces of patriarchial culture and insitutions. Third places are gendered through their embodied spatial practices, everyday interactions and histories that connect with the eonomic forces of global capitalism, the individualising imperatives of advanced liberalism and the persistent problems of social inequity (Massey 1994). The challenge that is evoked by Massey in this quotation involves contesting implicitly masculine assumptions about spatiality and third places, because 'we have inherited an imagination so deeply ingrained that it is often not actively thought' (Massey 2005 p. 17).

In this chapter we argue that Oldenburg's (1999) emphasis on third places in the social infrastructure of cities and the conviviality of public life tended to overlook the complex power relations that entangle gender

---

[1] We use the term women to refer to a gender category that is a matter of self-identification and subject positioning (cis and transgender). We also note the limitations of either or categories of gender for non-binary identifications.

identities within the sociocultural, political, historical and economic context of leisure practices. We explore the arguments of a number of scholars who have identified the need to move beyond the assumption that leisure cultures performed in third places are necessarily gender inclusive and equitable. For example, Johnson and Samdahl (2005) identified how gay bars can act as a third place for queer identification away from heteronormative judgement, yet they also noted the pervasiveness of misogynistic practices that excluded women. Writing about the revival of roller derby[2] as a new sport created by women for women, Pavlidis and Fullagar (2014) provide insights into how third places that are created in the name of empowerment can also serve to obscure the emotional and spatial dynamics of inclusion and exclusion between women. Refusing to simply view roller derby as a static, 'bounded' third place, Pavlidis and Fullagar (2014 p. 33) suggest that analyzing 'how the derby body is put into motion, and the affects it generates in relation to other bodies, we offer another way of thinking through the movement of gendered subjectivity as it is imagined, felt and reinvented through sport spaces'.

This way of thinking moves beyond the rather static and disembodied formulation of spatiality assumed in Oldenburg's formulation of third places and opens up questions that we will pursue about the gendered flows of power as they regulate women's leisure and create sites of challenge and resistance. Hence, Oldenburg's (1999 p. 24) claim that, 'a place that is a leveler is, by its nature, an inclusive place' requires feminist rethinking in terms of exploring how gendered power works in ways that reveal how third places can never simply be assumed as neutral or essentially 'good'.

THE VALUE OF LEISURE PRACTICES: GENDERED SOCIAL RELATIONSHIPS

Cities offer a range of third place leisure possibilities for residents and tourists. However, these leisure opportunities are not simply a matter of individual choice, they are often open to some groups and not others (Skeggs 1999). Sites for leisure are highly negotiated material and discursive spaces (Zukin 1995) where only certain citizens are able to exercise power in terms of access, recognition of identity and meaning construction. For women, the representations of space powerfully shape not only

---

[2] Roller derby has had a revival in the last decade and was started by women with a 'by the skater, for the skater' ethos. As a contact sport derby 'bouts' are played by two teams with five members on roller skates who compete on a flat track. The 'jammer' scores points by lapping the opposing team who seek to block them.

if they can access places, but also how they engage with places meant for public and civic pleasure, conviviality and belonging.

According to Johnson and Glover (2013) feminist geographers have argued the manner in which place is differentially gendered, including who owns the place and therefore who can control entry. Studies have identified a wide range of forms of ownership of space from public to private places and private–public places including pubs, bars and cafes that are open to the public yet any patron can be removed at the manager's discretion. However, increasingly, many of these places are being appropriated by the public for leisure activities so that ownership and public–private divisions have become more complex issues. For example, coffee shops and other 'third places' have now become community hubs for social interaction and this is seen to contribute to community well-being (Oldenburg 1999). As Oldenburg (1999) made clear, so-called private places such as restaurants, coffee shops, and hair salons embody places where a sizeable portion of the population now experience community. Often these are the places in which people experience their leisure in public and they are especially important for women. Meaningful positive social interactions have been identified as the precursor for social connections and the vital ingredient that creates a 'Social City' (Kelly et al. 2012). However, the third places chosen for interaction must be safe and transparent places, both physically and socially for women (Fincher and Iveson 2008). It may be the case that as Silverstone (1997) argued suburban culture is a gendered culture, so is the city in ways that often present contradictions in the name of safe sociability. For example, Skeggs (1999) noted that community programmes such as Crimewatch can work to constrain women's movement in the name of keeping them 'safe' in their homes in the suburbs.

Leisure researchers have long been interested in the sociality of third places within and beyond the city, as Yuen and Johnson (2017 p. 296) suggest, '[L]eisure settings, such as curling clubs, farmers' markets, and support groups involving workshops and social activities, have been examined as third places in the leisure literature' (Glover and Parry 2009; Glover et al. 2012; Johnson 2013; Mair 2009). Such places are often presented as gathering spaces where individuals can informally connect with family, friends, or community members. This body of literature also makes clear that such 'free choices' are undertaken within a context of multiple constraints, both explicit (e.g. available time, money, access to facilities and programmes) and hidden (e.g. cultural expectations of what is appropriate behaviour). For women in particular, leisure is very much 'constrained or enabled by patterns of work and family circumstances', for example, access to free time, income, social support, and cultural beliefs that work to both reinforce, and also disrupt private–public divisions (Brown et al. 2001 p. 132).

Aitchison (1999) noted, in an early study of women and bingo in Leeds by Dixey and Talbot (1982), the existence of gendered leisure place, the male domination of public leisure place, and the response by women of carving out a spatial sanctuary in the form of the bingo hall. Deem (1986) built on Dixey and Talbot's work by emphasising the differences between women in relation to their access to leisure and control of public leisure place and focused on the difficulties working class women, or women with young children, experienced in gaining access to leisure. For women, social encounters can occur in a range of leisure settings and guises and can be more or less bounded – that is, more or less exclusionary. Peattie (1998) emphasised the value of 'third places' – like coffee shops, community centres, bars, post offices and grocery stores – as outside-work/home sites that could offer familiarity and the opportunity for social encounters, some without cost. Examples of potential third places suggested by Fincher and Iveson (2008) that can accommodate women's financial, safety and social interaction needs include street festivals, public libraries, drop-in centres and community centres.

While these studies of how third places offer women experiences of connection and safety, gender has largely been thought of in an isolated way from other relations of power (ethnicity, class, religion, age, ability, sexuality etc.). One of the limitations in Oldenberg's (1999) work on third places is the privileging of a white, masculine and largely middle class world view that is assumed to be the 'norm' against which other racialised identities and meanings are defined or ignored. The example of pubs as visible third places highlights this point in relation to the normative assumptions about masculinity, heterosexuality and whiteness (also in terms of religions where alcohol is not consumed). In contrast, in their work on the cultural and gendered dimensions of public leisure places, Watson and Ratna (2011) draw upon the conceptual framework of intersectionality that arose out of the work of black feminists on the intensification of oppressive relations related to race, class, gender, ability, age, sexuality (on intersectionality see Cho et al. 2013). While there are ongoing debates about how intersectionality is thought in terms of marginalised and privileged identities, Styhre and Eriksson-Zetterquist (2008 p. 567) argue for a relational understanding wherein 'subject positions are not fixed and unified but fleeting and fluid identities emerging in continuously changing networks of humans, technologies and artefacts'. Watson and Ratna's (2011) study of a Bollywood festival held in a local park in northern England with a South Asian diaspora, provides a useful counterpoint for thinking through the dynamic intersectional relations that shape how a cultural festival and park interconnect as a third place. They offer a means of thinking critically about the historical, political and economic relations that shape leisure within third places as sites of negotiation over the cultural identities of groups and nations (white and South Asian Britishness). Rather than view the park festival as a 'contained' site for leisure enjoyment, they understand the porous boundaries and multiple gender relations that constitute third places as 'part of a dynamic interface between dominant discourse that positions British Asian as other and active participation in which minority ethnic identity is publicly expressed and celebrated . . . 'There was a female presence, albeit less spectacular and "in-your-face" than the manner in which some young males were behaving' (Watson and Ratna 2011 pp. 77–82). They highlight the complex interrelationships between gendered and racialised experiences within and outside the festival as young women felt both included and also marginal within shifting flows of the space. There is growing attention in research and policy on the role of third places in supporting social cohesion through informal leisure practices (parks, festivals, exhibitions) and convivial everyday relations (on parks see Neal et al. 2015). What is often missing is a more complex appreciation of how intersectional relations play out in gendered ways that often marginalise women's public participation.

THIRD PLACES THAT FACILITATE SOCIAL CONNECTION

In recent decades, the physical and social settings for creating connected and cohesive populations have been progressively eroded due to more individualised lifestyles and social networks that are not only geographically spread but also increasingly virtual (Lloyd et al. 2016) (see Williams and Kim, Chapter 9 this volume). However, third places, when conceptualised as traditional and non-traditional ways and locales can benefit women beyond initial social interaction to social connection. Son et al. (2010), for example, examined the emergence of social capital in a leisure club for middle-aged and older women and connected these outcomes to issues of individual and community health and well-being. Findings showed that not only did members make friends, interact with the broader community and gain recognition for their volunteer work, they also experienced what could be described as leisure, 'play, dress, fun and laughter' (Son et al. 2010 p. 80). These outcomes were seen to help women resist notions of ageism and give them increased leverage within the broader community. Furthermore, leisure-based volunteer experiences in a local community theatre were found to give older women a sense of personal growth that in turn benefitted the broader community (Burden 2000). These women not only developed performance and production skills, but also gained satisfaction, a sense of freedom and a sense of community. As Iso-Ahola and Park (1996) explained, beyond the physical benefits of these activities, groups form a critical part of the social 'glue' in that they provide a supportive place for sharing thoughts and feelings.

The physical spaces where community plays out have also been identified as an important aspect of third places. They not only provide the setting for meetings and interactions but also create the characteristics that are essential for people to enter these spaces including access and safety. Cheang (2002) reported on a group of Japanese American older adults in a 'third place', the fast food restaurant they frequented regularly. For this group, sociability and play were central features of their interactions but perhaps more importantly, the older adults' breakfast group created enduring relationships, a sense of community, and followed group norms. In addition, they had developed their own space inside the restaurant through their regular sessions and sense of membership. Outdoor spaces can also provide opportunities to create third places within and beyond the urban milieu. For example, Krenichyn (2006 p. 640) reported that some women found one large city park to be a 'socially intimate place and their activities there to be enriched by the presence of others, because the park was a place for bringing family, meeting friends, or encountering strangers on a regular basis'. This was a somewhat surprising finding, given the often heard representations of urban parks as dangerous and fearful places for women. Krenichyn (2006) concluded that these perceptions of trust and community interact with women's perceptions of their own safety and vulnerability in ways that construct third places as desirable or fearful locales.

Despite the central theme of meeting people that is core to the concept of the third place, Adamson and Parker (2006) argued that provision of social infrastructure is essential to mediate spatial experience. Williams and Pocock (2010) examined residents of master planned communities in Australia about the physical (e.g. buildings and facilities) and social infrastructure (e.g. formal groups and networks) provided in their living environment. Most participants indicated that superficial familiarity was facilitated by centralised facilities, recreation areas, community groups and events. However, although women were generally satisfied with these resources, new mothers in particular needed access to services, information and companionship. Importantly this included formal services and informal social groups of other mothers for social connection. In addition, a third place such as a cafe designed to accommodate pram access, a breast feeding area and nappy change facilities is important (Oldenburg and Brissett 1982). Functional and attractive places can not only benefit new mothers and families but also foster informal interaction between women who may not have other avenues of social connection. As Wearing (1995 p. 129) noted, if women 'don't see the city as a viable venue for their leisure, then they will not venture into the spaces from which they feel alienated and so they will not participate in the process of making the place a valued community resource'. It is in this way that 'third places' are particularly important to women's experiences of the city (Oldenburg and Brissett 1982).

The significance of third places for women's engagement in city life has gained greater attention in the political context of 'austerity' measures in the United Kingdom where cuts to local services have severely reduced public leisure provision from libraries, childcare, sport facilities, programmes and parks (Gilmore 2017; Jensen and Tyler 2012). Caddock (2017 pp. 69–70) identifies the effects on, and range of responses by women in different cities:

> . . .austerity is a feminist issue given its direct and disproportionate impact on women and the implicit reinforcement of wider gender roles and norms. While the gendered nature of the cuts is reflected by feminist activism in some localities such as Bristol – where in May 2015 a group of young women organized a march of thousands against austerity (Bristol Post, 2015) – within Nottingham there is a distinct feeling that wider anti-austerity campaigns such as the People's Assembly do not adequately address women's concerns and women therefore do not relate to such activism. In response, women are forming their own community groups to combat the gendered impacts of austerity by providing practical support to women affected by the cuts.

Third places, such as libraries (see Istvandity et al., Chapter 7 this volume), have been a significant focus of local activism as they are a leisure place used more often by women (and their children) and perceived to be largely safe, inclusive spaces. Yet, the meaning of such third places as self-evident sites of 'public good' have been subject to intense political contestation that is bound up with the erosion of the welfare state, individualising responsibility for cultural resources and a fundamental challenge to the equitable provision of public services (Jensen and Tyler 2012). Public parks as different kinds of third places that have been 'freely' available to women are also under threat from the withdrawal of government funds, despite research identifying their value as spaces for cross-cultural interaction (Gilmore 2017). While volunteering has been a commonly identified local solution to the closure of libraries and parks, there are significant problems with the shifting of state responsibilities onto citizens without resourcing. This is particularly the case for women whose labour is more often unpaid. These stark examples illustrate how third places are bound up with economic, political and social forces that profoundly affect opportunities for leisure and social participation for marginalised women who may be lone parents, poor, disabled and further isolated within society. Next we explore the less tangible dimensions of patriarchal power relations in terms of how the masculine 'gaze' on women and their bodies regulates choices, and how women turn that gaze upon themselves in self-limiting (and often self-protecting) ways.

(IN)VISIBLE BODIES AND MEDIATED THIRD PLACES

Writing almost three decades ago, Wekerle (1980) argued women were 'out of place' in many urban public place, such as cafes and restaurants. Several decades on Flanagan and Viliulis (2011) reiterate that these spaces and places have been constructed to create impediments that render women invisible and align with patriarchal notions of appropriate gender behaviours (Flanagan and Valiulis, 2011 p. xiii). Flanagan and Valiulis (2011 p. xii) also contend that women continue to struggle to 'assert their rightful visibility as urban citizens'. These observations extend to the third places in which women engage in interactions with others and negotiate discourses of masculine norms that render their bodies either invisible or positioned as visible in particular ways. In feminist research and scholarship women's visibility is constituted through the conceptualisation of the male gaze. Through this notion women are positioned as sexualised subjects and the object of male desire (Boyer 2012).

Media and advertising 'representations' in and around third places also work to intensify the gaze through the portrayal of sexualised or gendered images. Rosewarne (2005) argues that these images perpetuate gender roles, with men controlling space and women to be gazed upon within those spaces. These sexualised images convey the notion that women are an 'object of sexual consumption' and hence increases their sense of vulnerability (Rosewarne, 2005 p. 73). Gill (2009) writes that objectification has moved to a new phase in the 'post-feminist' context of neoliberalism where sexual subjectification is taken up as a matter of choice and empowerment (aka 'girl power'). The dramatic rise of 'raunch' culture has reworked the sexualisation of women's bodies in complex and contradictory ways (Evans et al. 2010). While seemingly offering a way for women to express agency and challenge their sexualisation, in order to be understood, 'such parodies must draw on, and thus repeat, dominant discourses of female sexuality, including objectification' (Evans et al. 2010 pp. 126–127). As Gill (2009 p. 150) argues this exercise of 'choice' can work as another form of exclusion, with only 'young, white, heterosexual and conventionally attractive' women able to access the empowerment promised. Older women, women of non-white ethnicity, different shapes and sizes, abilities and sexualities entering third places are less likely to feel any sense of ease or comfort within the visual economy of gender.

The rise of consumer culture within global capitalism is positioned as a key site through which women are urged to attain freedom, pleasure and success through exercising their right to consume and interact in coffee shops, pubs, restaurants and shopping centres (Kern 2010). Yet the third places in which women consume, such as restaurants, bars, and coffee shops remain highly gendered. Lone women dining in restaurants during the day are more likely to feel a sense of belonging than those who challenge the gendered order by dining alone at night (Lahad and May 2017). Bars are another place of social segregation where women are often vastly outnumbered by men (Bird and Sokolofski 2005). Bird and Sokolofski (2005 p. 226) also highlight that even in places such as coffee shops that do not provide 'stereotypically "masculine" symbolism', men can create a masculine domain simply by the manner in which they act. The deference afforded to men works to marginalise and objectify women (Bird and Sokolofski 2005). Bird and Sokolofski (2005) highlight that in certain instances women are able to control spaces in ways that exclude men. However, the instances of this occurring were relatively few, and socio-spatial practices in third places contribute 'to the apparent "naturalness" of a gendered order that privileges men' (Bird and Sokolofski 2005). Perhaps more importantly any challenge through 'empowerment' is reliant on individuals to enact change, hence broader changes to women's experiences of third places remains mired in a status quo.

For women who are mothers, entering third places presents another range of gendered and material challenges. Boyer and Spinney's (2016) research on mothers' journey making with prams highlights the difficulties they encounter as they attempt to move beyond domestic places into public places. Steps, small doorways, lack of lifts and public judgement of motherhood often significantly impede mothers' movements around third places. The notion of the perfect mother, caring appropriately, avoiding risks, adds a further layer of unease when considering how women feel and engage with third places. For example, women must manage their children in cafes and restaurants to ensure that their presence does not negatively impact on other patrons (Lugosi 2012). Management of breastfeeding in places such as pools or coffee shops also creates public unease which marginalises women (Boyer 2012). Interestingly, Fenster (2005) notes that young mothers often engaged with local places such as shopping centres, more intensively than before they became a mother. However, a mother's right to space has the potential to be undermined by the continued sexualisation of women, evidenced by the rise of the 'yummy mummy'.

When women are subject to the gaze of masculine power, looking can create feelings of uneasiness (Boyer 2012), and fear (Pain 2001; Kern 2010). These feelings, and particularly fear of violence, can work to restrict women's movement, in and around third places (Fairchild and Rudman 2008). Areas that may have been frequented by women during the day become ordered as male domains at night. In the night-time economy, darkness, drink spiking, alcohol consumption and women's supposed sexual availability intertwine in expected and unexpected ways (Sheard 2011). Drink spiking, in particular, has led to young women continually monitoring their drinks to ensure their safety and preclude threats of sexual violence (Brooks 2014). In their study of embodied and gendered drinking practices Waitt et al. (2011) argue that young women negotiated a range of contradictory subjectivities. They used the drinking place to assert a sense of belonging, through social relationships with other women, and assert different feminine identities. They also navigated the male gaze and discourses of safety and fear that position them accountable for unwanted attention. However, as Fileborn (2012) notes, women were more likely to blame themselves for unwanted sexual attention in licensed venues. Fairchild and Rudman (2008) also suggest that harassment by strangers in public places generated feelings of self-blame, objectification and humiliation.

In response to their sexualisation, women are asserting their right to be visible in third places in different ways. For example, an offhand comment by a police officer in Canada that women who dress like sluts were more likely to be victims of sexual assault, prompted 'Slutwalks'. These walks have spread from Canada across the globe into cities in the USA, Australia, Sweden and several other countries (Ringrose and Renold 2012). Women, and their supporters, negate notions of victimhood and male violence towards women through placards and forms of dress. Similarly, 'reclaim the night marches' protested violence against women (Staeheli and Martin 2000). Despite these attempts to claim spaces for women's needs within third places 'across time, space, and place the city has remained a patriarchal creation that strives to keep women in public as invisible as possible' (Flanagan and Valiulis 2011 p. xix).

The very materiality of third places has profoundly transformed to become highly mediated by digital technologies in ways that both open up new possibilities for women's agency, and also generate new forms of violence and sexual harassment through various forms of social media (Ringrose and Renold 2012). Exploring how digital leisure practices are gendered and third places are produced through particular platforms, requires analysis of the wider sociocultural context and micropolitics that shape how gender is negotiated in localised ways. Minahan and Cox (2007) have researched the rise of 'stitch 'n bitch' as an online/off-line formation of women's cyber culture as a third place. Digital technology affords women the opportunity to exchange resources and ideas as well as meet in groups to knit, stitch and talk (Orton-Johnson 2014). Minahan and Cox (2007) argue that desirability of such gendered places is defined in relation to women's negative responses to major political, social and technological changes that are generating a great sense of uncertainty.

GENDER RELATIONS AND MORE-THAN-HUMAN THIRD PLACES

Although Oldenburg (1999) acknowledged the importance of the city-scape in thinking about the way third places connect people spatially (street corners, facilities, indoor/outdoor buildings, parks), he did not explore more deeply how human experience is thoroughly entangled with the non-human (plants, animals, paved surfaces, objects, lighting etc.). We suggest that the conceptualisation of third places could be extended in light of more contemporary feminist approaches to thinking about city experiences as visceral, affective and more-than-human (Pink 2011; Sweet and Ortiz Escalante 2015). Waitt's (2014) exploration of young women's experiences of 'sweating' is a revealing example of how city movement, the sensory body and gendered norms are bound together in ways that shape the gendered experience of third places. For many young heterosexual women sweating evoked a visceral 'disgust' in the feminine body and had to be managed and minimised within third places (such as nightclubs and bars) that feature in the night-time economy of desire. In contrast, sweating bodies were somewhat more acceptable in sport or fitness places associated with self-improving health practices and gendered norms about body image.

Coining the term 'emplacement', Pink (2011) offers a different way of conceptualising the spatial assemblage of the city that moves beyond human centred experience and opens up new ways of thinking about how gender relations shape bodies, practices and interrelationships with non-human nature. Emplacement acknowledges the processes through which the self is moved, affected and transformed by intensities that are produced through place-events (Pink 2011). This conceptualisation is useful for thinking through third places as not simply spatial 'containers' within which human action occurs, but rather as performative leisure-events that transform embodied knowing and skill as we move and 'become part of a specific configuration, or ecology, of persons and things' (Pink 2011, p. 344).

An example from our research (Fullagar 2012; Fullagar and Pavlidis 2012) into women's experience of long-distance mass cycling events through city and rural places illustrates this more mobile, embodied and post-human notion of third places. Women's experiences of cycling with 1000 riders in a non-competitive event over nine days was often articulated in terms that forged unique gendered meanings around bike-body configurations; moving at one's own pace – sensory immersion in nature – feelings of safety riding collectively on roads – embodied capacities stretched in supportive context – clean bathrooms – new and renewed friendships – camping options – no cooking. The campsite for the event was assembled each night by volunteers and riders into a mobile third place – creating a sense of emplacement where 'the body itself is simultaneously physically transformed as part of this process' (Pink 2011 p. 347). Emplacement also evokes a sense of temporality that conceptualisations of third places often neglect. Through a different example, we can also think about how the value of non-human nature becomes visible when the spatio-temporality of third places, such as community parkrun events, are threatened with closure and reduce equitable opportunities for women's leisure. Parkrun is a free, regular community running event that successfully engages women of difference ages and abilities. Yet with funding cuts in the UK certain park authorities have tried to implement charges that have been very publicly resisted through social media, though not always successfully. Emplacement is a useful spatio-temporal way of thinking about how gender is implicated in human and non-human relations, patterns of inequality relating to access to places (cost, fear), time to engage (women's un/paid labour) and cultural histories of third places that reiterate or challenge normative gender expectations and identities.

CONCLUDING REMARKS

The third places described by Oldenberg rarely considered how these places were gendered in ways that worked to exclude women or were appropriated by women. Women's right to access spaces in the city, where they might enjoy some of the community and sociality of third places, are constrained by public–private dichotomies that reinforce masculine entitlement to public place. Thinking through the relationality and embodied spatiality of third places allows us to examine more deeply the ways in which masculine privilege is normalised and women are excluded.

For example, women's access and use of leisure places are constrained by patterns of work and family, but also by fears of safety, violence and harassment and lack of planning and infrastructure. The sexualisation and objectification of women also works to constrain how women experience third places as pleasurable or fearful sites of interaction. Powerful gender discourses work to shape how women may feel a sense of uneasiness and discomfort that hinders any sense of 'good' or social connection they may feel in such places. In addition, austerity measures that have seen a reduction in public leisure facilities, programmes and parks, and an emphasis on individualism, do little to create safe places where women can experience a sense of community.

Yet a body of feminist work highlights how women rework and reframe these places so they may enjoy them in ways not thought about in Oldenberg's conceptualisation. For example, Oldenberg's work also did not explore the materiality and entanglements of the human and non-human that affect women's experience of third places. Immersion in nature, interacting with various surfaces, plants, animals and lighting allow us to think through the material and embodied dimensions of third places. As we have suggested, Pink's (2011) notion of 'emplacement' offers a way to consider how bodies are transformed through various spatial and place-related interactions. Non-competitive events such as long distance mass cycling, where spatio-temporal boundaries are more fluid, allowed women to feel a sense of connection to both other women and their surroundings. Emplacement also makes visible the connections between spatio-temporality and non-human nature through community parkruns, where women of different ages and abilities can enjoy their own embodiment within a collectively oriented experience.

Together these observations are suggestive for re-thinking women's continued and inequitable access to third places. Issues such as the continued sexualisation of women through various media, including social media, create the context for the objectification of women. Changes need to occur in relation to how women are portrayed through these media, with regulation and legislation required to change stereotypical representations and online harassment. There have been recent changes in Britain with the Advertising Standards Authority introducing new regulatory standards to reduce gender stereotyping in advertisements; no longer will women be subjected to offensive commercial images that reverberate across multiple third places (such as the 'are you beach body ready?' adverts on billboards, television, social media). Similarly legislation needs to address what occurs when women are harassed or threatened with violence, and how women are dealt with when they report these issues. With the rise of violence against women, it is important that policies that have a role in prevention (urban planning, media regulation, community provision) are informed by feminist research that addresses the issues that have led to its increase. While 'reclaim the night marches' provide a forum for women to protest and raise awareness, creating cities as safer places for women through planning and infrastructure are important considerations. Poor lighting, ill-considered plantings, lack of security in and around transport contribute to gendered risk for women (see Holden, Chapter 6 this volume). This in turn can affect how women participate in the night-time economy through third places such as bars and nightclubs, interact with their surroundings and where they experience shame and humiliation when harassed. Recognising the gendered impact of austerity measures on the provision of leisure places for the facilitation of social relations and cross-cultural interaction is a challenge for policy makers at different levels to address in relation to further marginalisation and isolation that is occurring in many communities. Despite Oldenberg's contention that third places are inherently 'good' much work is still needed to create places in contemporary life that allow different women to exercise their right to the city.

REFERENCES

Adamson, L. and G. Parker (2006), '"There's more to life than just walking": older women's ways of staying healthy and happy', *Journal of Aging and Physical Activity*, 14, 380–391.

Aitchison, C. (1999), 'New cultural geographies: the spatiality of leisure, gender and sexuality', *Leisure Studies*, 18(1), 19–39.

Bird, S. and L. Sokolofski (2005), 'Gendered socio-spatial practices in public eating and drinking establishments in the Midwest United States', *Gender, Place and Culture*, 12 (2), 213–230.

Boyer, K. (2012), 'Affect, corporeality and limits of belonging: breastfeeding in public in the contemporary UK', *Health and Place*, 18, 552–560.

Boyer, K. and J. Spinney (2016), 'Motherhood, mobility and materiality: material entanglements, journey-making and the process of "becoming a mother"', *Environment and Planning D: Society and Space*, 34 (6), 1113–1131.

Brooks, O. (2014), 'Interpreting young women's accounts of drink spiking: the need for a gendered understanding of the fear and reality of sexual violence', *Sociology*, 48 (2), 300–316.

Brown, P., Brown, W., Miller, Y. and V. Hansen (2001), 'Perceived constraints and social support for active leisure among mothers with young children', *Leisure Sciences*, 23, 131–144.

Burden, J. (2000), 'Community building, volunteering and action research', *Loisir et Societe/Society and Leisure*, 23, 353–370.

Butler, J. (1990), *Gender Trouble: Feminism and the Subversion of Identity*. New York: Routledge.

Caddock, E. (2017), 'Caring about and for the cuts: a case study of the gendered dimension of austerity and anti-austerity activism', *Gender, Work and Organization*, 24 (1), 69–82.

Cheang, M. (2002), 'Older adults' frequent visits to a fast-food restaurant: nonobligatory social interaction and the significance of play in the "third space"', *Journal of Aging Studies*, 16, 303–321.

Cho, S., Crenshaw, K.W. and L. McCall (2013), 'Toward a field of intersectionality studies: theory, applications, and praxis', *Signs: Journal of Women in Culture and Society*, 38 (4), 785–810.

Deem, R. (1986), *All Work and no Play? The Sociology of Women and Leisure*. Milton Keynes: Open University Press.

Dixey, R. and M. Talbot (1982), *Women, Leisure and Bingo*. Leeds: Trinity and All Saints' College.

Evans, A., Riley, S. and A. Shankar (2010), 'Technologies of sexiness: theorizing women's engagement in the sexualization of culture', *Feminism and Psychology*, 20 (1), 114–131.

Fairchild, K. and L. Rudman (2008), 'Everyday stranger harassment and women's objectification', *Social Justice Research*, 21, 338–357.

Fenster, T. (2005), 'The right to the gendered city: different formations of belonging in everyday life', *Journal of Gender Studies*, 14 (3), 217–231.

Fileborn, B. (2012), 'Sex and the city: exploring young women's perception and experiences of unwanted sexual attention in licensed venues', *Current Issues in Criminal Justice*, 24 (2), 241–260.

Fincher, R. and K. Iveson (2008), *Planning and Diversity in the City: Redistribution, Recognition and Encounter*. New York: Palgrave Macmillan.

Flanagan, M. and M. Valiulis (2011), 'Introduction: gender and the city: the awful being of invisibility', *Frontiers*, 32 (1), xiii–xx.

Fullagar, S. (2012), 'Gendered cultures of slow travel: women's cycle touring as an alternative hedonism', in S. Fullagar, K. Markwell and E. Wilson (eds), *Slow Tourism: Experiences and Mobilities*. Bristol: Channel View, pp. 99–112.

Fullagar, S. and A. Pavlidis (2012), '"It's all about the journey": women and cycling events', *International Journal of Event and Festival Management*, 3(2), 149–170.

Gill, R. (2009), 'Beyond the "sexualization of culture" thesis: an intersectional analysis of "Sixpacks", "Midriffs" and "Hot Lesbians" in advertising', *Sexualities*, 12 (2), 137–160.

Gilmore, A. (2017), 'The park and the commons: vernacular spaces for everyday participation and cultural value', *Cultural Trends*, 24 (1), 34–46.

Glover, T.D. and D.C. Parry (2009), 'A third place in the everyday lives of people living with cancer: functions of Gilda's Club of Greater Toronto', *Health and Place*, 15, 97–106.

Glover, T.D., Parry, D.C. and C.M. Mulcahy (2012), 'At once liberating and exclusionary? A Lefebvrean analysis of Gilda's Club of Toronto', *Leisure Studies*, 32 (5), 1–20.

Iso-Ahola, S.E. and C.J. Park (1996), 'Leisure-related social support and self-determination as buffers of stress-illness relationship', *Journal of Leisure Research*, 28(3), 169–187.

Jensen, T. and I. Tyler (2012), 'Austerity parenting', *Studies in the Maternal*, 4 (2). http://doi.org/10.16995/sim.34.

Johnson, A.J. (2013), '"It's more than a shopping trip": leisure and consumption in a farmers' market', *Annals of Leisure Research*, 16 (4), 1–17.

Johnson, A.J. and T.D. Glover (2013), 'Understanding urban public space in a leisure context', *Leisure Sciences*, 35 (2), 190–197.

Johnson, C.W. and D.M. Samdahl (2005), '"The night they took over": misogyny in a country-western gay bar', *Leisure Sciences*, 27 (4), 331–348.

Kelly, J-F., Breadon, P., Davis, C., Hunter, A., Mares, P., Mullerworth, D. and B. Weidmann (2012), *Social Cities*. Melbourne: Gratton Institute.

Kern, L. (2010), 'Selling the "scary city": gendering freedom, fear and condominium development in the neoliberal city', *Social and Cultural Geography*, 11 (3), 209–230.

Krenichyn, K. (2006), '"The only place to go and be in the city": women talk about exercise, being outdoors, and the meanings of a large urban park', *Health and Place*, 12, 631–643.

Lahad, K. and V. May (2017), 'Just one? Solo dining, gender and temporal belonging in public spaces', *Sociological Research Online*, 22 (2), 1–11.

Lloyd, K., Fullagar, S. and S. Reid (2016), 'Where is the "social" in constructions of "liveability"? Exploring community, social interaction and social cohesion in changing urban environments'. *Urban Policy and Research*, doi: 10.1080/08111146.2015.1118374.

Lugosi, P. (2012), 'Women, children and hospitable spaces', *The Hospitality Review*, 12 (1), 31–38.

Mair, H. (2009), 'Club life: third place and shared leisure in rural Canada', *Leisure Sciences*, 31 (5), 450–465.

Massey, D. (1994), *Space, Place and Gender*. Cambridge: Polity Press.

Massey, D. (2005), *For Space*. London: Sage.

Minahan, S. and J.W. Cox (2007), 'Stitch'nBitch', *Journal of Material Culture*, 12 (1), 5–21.

Neal, S., Bennett, K., Jones, H., Cochrane, A. and G. Mohan (2015), 'Multiculture and public parks: researching super-diversity and attachment in public green space', *Population, Space and Place*, 21(5), 463–475.

Oldenburg, R. (1999), *Great Good Place: Cafes, Coffee Shops, Bookstores, Bars, Hair Salons and Other Hangouts at the Heart of Community*. New York; Marlow & Company.

Oldenburg, R. and D. Brissett (1982), 'The third place', *Qualitative Sociology*, 5(4), 265–284.

Ortiz Escalante, S. and E. Sweet (2013), 'Migrant women's safety: framing, policies and practice', in C. Whitzman, C. Legacy, C. Andrew, F. Klodawsky, M. Shaw and K. Viswanath (eds), *Building Inclusive Cities: Women's Safety and the Right to the City*. London; New York: Routledge, pp. 53–72.

Orton-Johnson, K. (2014), 'Knit, purl and upload: new technologies, digital mediations and the experience of leisure', *Leisure Studies*, 33 (3), 305–321.

Pain, R. (2001), 'Gender, race, age and fear in the city', *Urban Studies*, 38 (5-6), 899–913.

Pavlidis, A. and S. Fullagar (2014), *Sport, Gender and Power: The Rise of Roller Derby*. Farnham: Ashgate Publishing.

Peattie, L. (1998), 'Convivial cities', in M. Douglass and J. Friedmann (eds), *Cities for Citizens*. Chichester: John Wiley & Sons, pp. 247–253.

Pink, S. (2011), 'From embodiment to emplacement: re-thinking competing bodies, senses and spatialities,' *Sport, Education and Society*, 16 (3), 343–355.

Ringrose, J. and E. Renold (2012), 'Slut-shaming, girl power and "sexualisation":

thinking through the politics of the international SlutWalks with teen girls', *Gender and Education*, 24 (3), 333–343.

Rosewarne, L. (2005), 'The men's gallery: outdoor advertising and public space: gender, fear, and feminism', *Women's Studies International Forum*, 28, 67–87.

Sheard, L. (2011), '"Anything could have happened": women, the night-time economy, alcohol and drink-spiking', *Sociology*, 45 (4), 619–633.

Silverstone, R. (ed.) (1997), *Visions of Suburbia*. London: Routledge.

Skeggs, B. (1999), 'Matter out of place: visibility and sexualities in leisure spaces', *Leisure Studies*, 18 (3), 213–232.

Son, J., Yarnel, C. and D. Kerstetter (2010), 'Engendering social capital through a leisure club for middle-aged and older women: implications for individual and community health and well-being', *Leisure Studies*, 29 (1), 67–83.

Staeheli, L.A. and P.M. Martin (2000), 'Spaces for feminism in geography', *The Annals of the American Academy of Political and Social Science*, 571 (1), 135–150.

Styhre, A. and U. Eriksson-Zetterquist (2008), 'Thinking the multiple in gender and diversity studies: examining the concept of intersectionality', *Gender in Management: An International Journal*, 23 (8), 567–582.

Sweet, E.L. and S. Ortiz Escalante (2015), 'Bringing bodies into planning: visceral methods, fear and gender violence', *Urban Studies*, 52 (10), 1826–1845.

Valentine, G. (1989), 'The geography of women's fear', *Area*, 21, 385–390.

Waitt, G. (2014). 'Bodies that sweat: the affective responses of young women in Wollongong, New South Wales, Australia', *Gender, Place and Culture*, 21 (6), 666–682.

Waitt, G., Jessop, L. and A. Gorman-Murray (2011), '"The guys in there just expect to be laid": embodied and gendered socio-spatial practices of a "night out" in Wollongong, Australia', *Gender Place and Culture*, 18 (2), 255–275.

Watson, B. and A. Ratna (2011), 'Bollywood in the park: thinking intersectionally about public leisure space', *Leisure/Loisir*, 35 (1), 71–86.

Wearing, B. (1995), *Leisure and Feminist Theory*. London: Sage.

Wekerle, G. (1980), 'Women in the urban environment', *Signs*, 5 (3), S188–S214.

Williams, P. and B. Pocock (2010), 'Building "community" for different stages of life: physical and social infrastructure in master planned communities', *Community, Work and Family*, 13 (1), 71–87.

Yuen, F. and A.A.J. Johnson (2017), 'Leisure spaces, community, and third places', *Leisure Sciences*, 39 (3), 295–303.

Zukin, S. (1995), *The Culture of Cities*. Oxford: Sage.

3. Planning for healthy ageing: how the use of third places contributes to the social health of older populations*

Sara Alidoust and Caryl Bosman

INTRODUCTION

Today over half of the world's population resides in urban areas, although the level of urbanisation varies in different countries (United Nations, Department of Economic and Social Affairs 2014). Throughout history, urbanisation has been associated with economic and social transformation, which has produced changes in the urban demography. An example of this demographic change in cities is population ageing (United Nations, Department of Economic and Social Affairs 2014). A low fertility rate, along with longer life expectancy, has resulted in a change to the population pyramids of many countries, creating an increasingly older age population. (United Nations, Department of Economic and Social Affairs, Population Division 2015). Australia is one of the most urbanised countries with over 85 per cent of the population living in cities (ABS 2014). At the same time, the ageing population constitutes a significant proportion of the city dwellers in Australia (ABS 2013).

The ageing of the population poses challenges for the planning of inclusive cities, where the needs of all people, including the older age cohort, are equally accommodated (ALGA 2006). An ageing population has significant implications for urban transport systems, since older people's travel behaviour and mobility is considerably different from that of younger age cohorts (Golob and Hensher 2007). In this context, it is important to note that while mobility refers to 'the movement of people

* This chapter is an edited version of Alidoust, S., Bosman, C. and Holden, G. (2018). Planning for healthy ageing: How the use of third places contributes to the social health of older populations. *Ageing and Society*, 1–26 © Cambridge University Press 2018 and is reproduced here with permission.

or goods' (Litman 2003, p. 29), accessibility refers to 'the ability to reach desired goods, services, activities and destinations' (Victoria Transport Policy Institute 2014). As people age, they are more likely to have limitations in walking and driving their own car and thus they are more reliant on public transport (see for example Collia et al. 2003, Schmöcker et al. 2008, and Schwanen et al. 2001). The retirement lifestyle also means that the everyday activity patterns of older people are different from and potentially limited compared to those of the average, generally younger and employed cohorts. In order for these older cohorts to maintain/ strengthen and develop their social engagement networks, a suite of planning policies is required that address the changing travel behaviour and mobility of people as they age (Davey 2007; Marottoli et al. 2000; Oxley and Fildes 2000; WHO 2007). The policies need to focus on the places that older people go to and the ways through which they travel to socialise with others. The implementation of such planning policies would potentially minimise the chances of social isolation at older age which, in turn, promotes overall health and well-being of this age cohort (Brown 2003; Cornwell and Waite 2009).

This chapter investigates the role of third places (popular public places where many people go to socialise) and accessibility in the social lives of older people. Research is focused on different built-form patterns, including: Master Planned Community (MPC) developments and conventional suburbs. The main question underpinning this research is 'How do third places, and their perceived level of accessibility affect the social lives of older people living in MPC developments and conventional suburban neighbourhoods?' A qualitative methodology was used to investigate how strong, weak and absent ties (Granovetter 1973), as three types of social ties, are formed and maintained for older people living in different neighbourhood built-form patterns. The impact of the built neighbourhood on the social lives of older people is an important area of study. Built on existing literature, the findings of this research have the potential to inform future research and planning policies aimed at promoting the social lives, and thus the social health, of the older age cohort.

The first part of this chapter reviews some of the literature on the importance of third places and accessibility to the social lives of older people. The case study areas are then introduced and the research methodology is outlined. The last part of the chapter focuses on the research findings, highlighting some of the main characteristics of the third places frequented by older people, and the importance of accessibility in allowing older people the opportunities to engage in these places. The findings highlight opportunities for interventions, in particular in relation to planning for third places and accessible spaces that will potentially contribute to the social lives or sociability of older people, and therefore promote their overall health and well-being.

SOCIAL HEALTH, THIRD PLACES AND OLDER PEOPLE

Social life or sociability is a main component of social health (Greenblatt 1976; Keyes 1998; Larson 1993; Renne 1974; Yu et al. 2016) which, in turn, can contribute to people's overall health and well-being (Cornwell and Waite 2009; García et al. 2005; WHO 1948). Strong, weak, and absent ties are three different types of social ties which can be used to measure the level of social life or sociability of individuals. Strong ties or friendships are the most intense types of social ties, concentrated within clusters of friends. Weak ties are not as strong as strong ties. These refer to the relationships with acquaintances. Weak ties are bridges between different clusters of strong ties (friends). Absent ties, on the other hand, are the frailest type of social ties between people. They imply a lack of any significant relation between people and refer to the acknowledgement type of relationship, for example the nodding relationship between people who live in the same neighbourhood and who are not acquainted (Granovetter 1973).

Much of the literature in social networks has focused on the importance of strong ties, and there has been little attention to the role of weaker types of ties between people (Henning and Lieberg 1996). Granovetter (1973, 1983) stressed the significance of weak ties as bridging ties between different (strong) networks which enable people to access resources that otherwise they would be deprived of. In Henning and Lieberg's (1996) research participants stated that weak ties meant a 'feeling of home', 'security' and 'practical as well as social support'. Their research demonstrated the importance of the neighbourhood as a suitable area for weak ties, as proximity and continuity, which are the main factors in the development of these kind of social ties, are encouraged to be established in the local vicinity (Henning and Lieberg 1996). Kavanaugh et al.'s (2005) research also confirmed the importance of weak ties and demonstrated that people with weak (bridging) ties across groups tend to have higher levels of community involvement, civic interest, and collective efficacy than those without bridging ties.

To ensure that older people have opportunities to remain socially active, meaning that they have the ability to establish new, and to maintain existing, strong, weak and absent ties, there is a need for a deeper understanding of the challenges affecting their travel behaviour and mobility. One way to address this concern is to investigate the characteristics of third places where older people socialise, and to understand the challenges that older people face in accessing different third places in different sub/urban neighbourhoods. According to Oldenburg (1989), a third place is not the first place (home) nor is it the second place (work/school). It is a place where people have opportunities to socialise with others and expand their social networks. Third places include a wide range of places from indoor areas (e.g. cafés, restaurants) to public open spaces (e.g. children's playgrounds, urban squares). They provide an accessible, socially-level neutral ground to facilitate social interactions between regulars (Oldenburg 1989). Oldenburg (1997) sees the third place serving functions in response to individualisation, which contribute to the social well-being and psychological health of people.

A growing number of studies have focused on the social dimension of third places and demonstrated the significant role that third places play in creating opportunities for social interaction between people of all ages (Alidoust et al. 2014, 2015; Hickman 2013; Lawson 2004; Matthews et al. 2000; Rosenbaum et al. 2007). A limited number of studies also focused on the particular role of third places in the social life of older people. Some examples are Cheang's (2002) and Rosenbaum's (2006) research which highlighted the role of restaurants as third places which facilitate social interaction between regular older age clients.

Third places are advocated as being important social spaces for older people, as they provide them with opportunities to keep in touch with others (Oldenburg 1997). Accessibility, perceived or otherwise, is essential if these places are to be utilised as places for social engagement (WHO 2007). The importance of accessible neighbourhood amenities and the positive impacts this has on the social lives of older people is supported in the literature (see for example Alidoust and Bosman 2015, 2016; Judd et al. 2010; Levasseur et al. 2011; Richard et al. 2009). Access to public transport and/or the ability to drive is an important indicator of accessibility, and enhances opportunities for older adults' social engagement and community participation (Banister and Bowling 2004; Phillips et al. 2005). A review of the literature suggests a high level of car reliance among older people (Alsnih and Hensher 2003; Banister and Bowling 2004; Schmöcker et al. 2008). For many older people, to some degree, driving contributes to their level of independence and affords them opportunities to engage in social life. Limitations in driving capability can restrict the social lives of older adults (Davey 2007; Oxley and Fildes 2000). This is particularly the case in the sprawling car-dependant suburbs, which are the dominant urban pattern in Australian cities (Hugo 2003). One alternative to private transport for retired drivers is public transport. An effective public transport service can play an influential role in the social lives of older people and can contribute to their social health. Policies are required to ensure the provision of accessible, affordable and reliable public transport services which accommodate the varying needs of the ageing population (WHO 2007).

METHODOLOGY

Qualitative methodology was employed to acquire in-depth information about the role and accessibility of third places for the social lives of older people living in different neighbourhood built-form patterns: (1) conventional suburban neighbourhoods, and (2) Master Planned Community (MPC) developments. Conventional suburban neighbourhoods are comprised largely of detached, and in recent years (post-2000) semi-detached, and attached housing. All types of street patterns (e.g. cul-de-sacs and grid patterns) are included in this grouping. MPC developments, on the other hand, refer to a wide range of housing developments which are designed in line with a specific comprehensive master plan, and they generally have distinct physical boundaries and a uniform design aesthetic (Cheshire et al. 2010). MPCs include a wide range of developments from age-segregated to mixed-age, and from gated to non-gated. High-rise buildings, both age-segregated and mixed-age, are also included in this category.

Study Areas

This research was based in the city of the Gold Coast, Queensland, Australia. The Gold Coast is located on the eastern coast of Australia, and has been known as an overgrown resort town which has now become the sixth largest city of the nation (Dedekorkut-Howes and Bosman 2015). The population of the Gold Coast is ageing and 15 per cent of its population was recorded as being aged 65 years or over in 2013 (ABS 2013). The proportion of older people is similarly high in all three case study areas: Southport, Hope Island and Mermaid Waters-Clear Island Waters. In spite of this similarity, as illustrated in Table 3.1, the three case study areas vary significantly in terms of the population density and some main physical features, such as the land-use mixture, built-form pattern and public transport service. Southport is a mixed-use area with a high level of public transport provision, including bus and light rail, compared to much of the Gold Coast. Southport is a relatively densely populated area by Gold Coast standards, with 18.11 persons per hectare (ABS 2011).

Table 3.1   *The main characteristics of the case study areas selected for*
             this research

Case study	Southport	Mermaid Waters-Clear Island Waters	Hope Island
Population Density (persons per hectare)	18.11	13.61	5.93
Land Use	Residential, commercial	Residential	Residential
Dominant Street Network Pattern	Grid	Cul-de-sac	Cul-de-sac
Dominant Neighbourhood Built-form Pattern	Conventional	Conventional	MPC
Other Neighbourhood Built-form Patterns	MPC	MPC	–

The built-form pattern in Southport is mainly conventional suburban neighbourhood in grid street patterns.

Hope Island is a residential suburb with a relatively low population density of 5.93 persons per hectare (ABS 2011). Given the pattern of gated MPC development and cul-de-sac streets in Hope Island, public transport is generally limited and is not easily accessed by people residing in this suburb. Mermaid Waters-Clear Island Waters is similarly a residential suburb. It has a population density of 13.61 persons per hectare (ABS 2011). It is mainly comprised of conventional suburban neighbourhoods with cul-de-sac street network patterns. Public transport is limited to buses with frequent services to the main roads. Bus services are not easily accessed by many residents, particularly those living in cul-de-sacs, as they are located a considerable distance from the main bus routes in this case study suburb.

Data for this research was collected by conducting observations of older people participating in third places, as well as semi-structured interviews with 54 older people (aged 65 and over). The participants included 19 people from Southport, 15 people from Hope Island and 20 people from Mermaid Waters-Clear Island Waters. The median and mean age of the participants were 75 and 76.37, respectively. Participants included 21 men and 33 women. All participants were retired; 30 were doing some sort of voluntary work. Twenty-four participants were living in some type of conventional suburban neighbourhoods while 40 were living in MPC developments. Participants remained anonymous and were given pseudonyms to ensure confidentiality and to acknowledge them as people with individual life experiences. Interview questions about participants' perceived health status and walking ability revealed that all but one had the ability to walk out of their home. Three other participants also had some degrees of limitation in walking ability, meaning that they were not able to walk long distances (more than 15 minutes) because of health issues, and in some cases, they had to rely on walking aids such as canes and walkers.

Using NVivo 10 data management software, the interview data and observation notes were analysed applying both inductive and deductive approaches (Berg and Lune 2004). Initial coding developed various themes which were informed by the primary research question: 'How can planning respond to the changing mobility of older people in order to support their social lives? and two related sub-questions: (1) What is the role of third places in the formation and maintenance of the three different social ties (strong, weak and absent) of older people? (2) To what degree is neighbourhood accessibility important in the social lives of older people? The themes were then clustered around four categories: third places; accessibility; different neighbourhood built-form patterns; and the three types of social ties (strong, weak and absent).

The Importance of Third Places in the Social Lives of Older People

This research corroborates the important role of third places in the social lives of older people. The majority of research participants stated that when not at home, they spent much of their time in third places, specifically so that they could interact with other people. This research adds to the existing literature by revealing some of the main characteristics of the third places which play important roles in the social lives of older people living in different neighbourhood built-form patterns.

Mixed-use places, as referred to by participants, generally comprised shopping areas, civic places like banks and post offices, and also cafés and restaurants. Participants from both neighbourhood built-form patterns described these places as being important social spaces which were convenient and which offered efficiency, as they afforded them opportunities to undertake multiple activities in one place and minimised their need to travel. Minimisation of travel was seen as a significant advantage, in particular by those with mobility restrictions. Ruth (age: 69) indicated: 'We go to Southport Park [the local shopping centre]. We usually combine going shopping [and meeting each other], I take friends who don't have cars ... so we'll go out and do the shopping and maybe have a cup of coffee together just as a little social bit in the middle of the shopping.' For participants, the mixed-use third places tended not to produce new strong

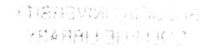

ties, instead, participants were more likely to meet people with whom they already had strong ties, produced through other activities and other places. However, research suggested that the visitation frequency of these third places could lead to the formation of new weak and absent ties. For example, participants who regularly frequented the same local shopping centre were likely to form absent and or weak ties with sales assistants and other regular shoppers.

This research showed the significance of local third places in the social lives of the participants from both types of neighbourhood built-form patterns. Here the local third places refer to the public social spaces which were located outside the MPCs and were open to all people. Most of the participants, particularly those who still drove their own cars, did not tend to restrict themselves to the local cafés and restaurants. However, in the case of other third places, the majority tended to go to the local ones, especially third places such as churches, shopping centres, public libraries and clubs, which were shown to play an important role in forming and maintaining all three types of social ties. Particularly, the participants who have been living in their neighbourhood for longer, tended to attend the local third places more regularly and had more social ties established through these local places. Bella (age: 67) highlighted the importance of the local church to her social life:

> . . .We come together at church and that's where I would meet others . . ..
> I guess that's the thing about church. We don't just go into church and go home. We come to church. We're there for the worship service and then afterwards we are talking to each other, having a drink of coffee and having friendship time after church. So that is why at church activities we do talk to each other, and it's more than just seeing somebody over the room and maybe saying hi and that's all.

Again, visitation frequency was considered to be a significant factor, contributing to forming new social ties for participants. A number of single men and women participants who regularly attended the same local restaurant, bar or café, said they had a strong sense of belonging to that particular place, and that they had established many strong, weak and absent ties with other patrons. This is illustrated by Tony (age: 67), a single older man from Southport:

> We have all drunk there [the local pub] for years and years and years . . . When they revamped the pub they demolished most of it and revamped it, I even worked on that . . . They're friends. As I said I've known most of them, some of them for 50, 60 years, some of them for 10, 15, 20 years. A lot of them I used to work with and they're now retired . . .

The research also revealed the importance of club membership in the social lives of the participants, particularly single older men and women. Most participants who frequented these third places resided in conventional suburban neighbourhoods and they engaged in these activities as a means of interacting with new people and establishing new absent, weak and eventually in a few cases strong ties. For instance, Lyn indicated (age: 74): '. . . I belong to quite a few clubs because I don't have close family you see, so those clubs and those people are my family really.' As the research revealed, the majority of the clubs favoured by the research participants were age-segregated, including the Returned and Services League, the University of the Third Age, singing clubs and bowls clubs. The participants who frequented these third places regularly had a high number of social ties, particularly absent and weak ties with other club members. These ties were acknowledged as being important social relations in the participants' daily lives. In response to a question about the significance of weak and absent ties established in clubs, Shirley (age: 74) pointed out:

> They are [important], it is lovely to talk to them [people with whom you have weak and absent ties] while you are there [in the club] . . .. That's why I go bowling . . .. They are all important to me. Definitely I love people . . .. It's nice to talk to them, here I am on my own, I've got to keep myself busy so that the time goes by, which I do.

The length of residence was also found to contribute to some older people's attachment to clubs as places for social interaction and communication. The participants who have been living in their current place for longer, tended to have favourite local clubs where they attended regularly and through which they established social ties, mainly weak and absent ones.

Other third places favoured by participants were the third places located within the boundaries of the MPC developments which were exclusive to the residents of the MPC. All MPC developments had common areas and leisure centres, where the social interaction between residents was encouraged through various organised social activities and events which all residents were invited to participate in. The availability of some other communal facilities such as gym, swimming pool, and green space, however varied in different MPC developments, depending on their size and socio-economic status. Claire (age: 86), a resident of an age-segregated MPC said:

> . . . well I play cards here with a group one day a week, we have bingo in the hall one day a week, and every second Saturday we have games in the hall, I go to that, any function, I might attend all the functions. It's a nice atmosphere here, you can go, there will be a group sitting down, you can go and sit in the group

and you are part of the group and it's not always the same group you sit with. You try to get around. Well I try to get around and talk to . . .

In a similar vein, Maggie (age: 85) stated that:

There is so much going on at the village, believe me. You can do something, if you want to, every day. Almost every day . . . I love it. But you're only as busy as you want to be. You don't have to do anything. But it's always available if you want to . . .

These communal places created opportunities for MPC residents to meet new people and establish absent, weak and potentially strong ties. The level of social interaction (both number and strength of social ties) was of a higher degree among age-segregated MPC residents than that of mixed age development residents, as there seemed to be more social programmes and events available in the age-segregated developments. A few participants from age-segregated MPCs even reported that they had weak or absent ties with all people living in the development. Paul (age: 70) indicated:

. . . With 227 houses [in the age-segregated MPC], there are always people that you see. So you can have a few chats with people from time to time. If you lived in a suburb, when we lived in Melbourne . . . in the same street there was probably two couples, or two houses with people that I would call friends . . .

Perhaps not unexpectedly, the research revealed that MPC participants, especially those living in age-segregated developments, when not at home generally spend most of their time in the physical environment of their development. For many of these people, the main reason for leaving the MPC development was to shop and access civic services such as post offices and banks, which are not available within the development. Otherwise, participants residing in MPCs agreed unanimously that there were sufficient opportunities within the developments to fulfil all of their social needs. Joan (age: 75) lived in an age-segregated high rise building and pointed out: '. . . This building is my neighbourhood . . . this [building] is where I live, this is where I predominantly function, I go out to do some-thing but I keep pretty much here.' Nevertheless, not all MPC residents choose to mix solely with others living within their neighbourhood, nor do all participate in the organised social activities on offer. This lack of social engagement by some residents was seen by some participants as being anti-social and contrary. Ruth (age: 69) related:

There are still a lot of people here I don't know, because they don't come out of their houses. They truly don't. They don't socialise. They don't attend meetings, they just live in their little houses. Makes me wonder why they didn't just buy an ordinary little house outside, because they're paying a levy and then they're not using any of the facilities . . .

The level of engagement in MPC social activities was higher amongst those who had moved to the developments from another city or neighbourhood and had left behind their social networks. Participants who had moved to the MPC from a nearby area or had lived on the Gold Coast for a long time were found to still have strong ties with their old social networks and so did not always participate in the social activities on offer in the MPC.

This research demonstrates that older people's degree of accessibility to third places is fundamental to their continued participation in these places. Many participants from both neighbourhood patterns preferred to visit local third places, for example, shopping centres, and this illustrates a strong relationship between travel distance and use of these third places. Similarly, the popularity of communal places in MPCs is largely on account of their location and proximity.

The research revealed that, in addition to the travel distance, the mode of travel plays a very important role in participants' perception of the accessibility of third places, which, in turn, impacts their use of third places. Although the majority of participants from all three case study areas perceived their area as being either 'very accessible' or 'accessible', notably most of them acknowledged that their perception of the level of accessibility of the environment was strongly associated with the use of their car as the main mode of transport. Leaving aside the common areas and leisure centres in MPCs, an accessible third place in the context of our case study areas was defined by the majority of participants as a place with easy access by car. Interestingly, driving participants' perception of the accessibility of their environment was similar across all three case study areas in spite of differences in their physical characteristics and population density. For a few other participants who did not drive (13 per cent), accessibility to a third place was defined as the availability of public transport to access it. Among the retired drivers, those who were living in Southport with more public transport and higher population density perceived the environment more accessible. Whereas, the residents of Hope Island, and Mermaid Waters-Clear Island Waters particularly those who were living away from the main public transport routes perceived the area less accessible. Bob (age: 72) from Hope Island pointed out: 'It [Hope Island] is somewhat inaccessible really, if you have not got a car . . . so . . . without having a car it is probably somehow inaccessible. . . .. With car it is very accessible, everywhere is accessible, you can go anywhere.'

The ability to drive was found to contribute to the level of social interaction and community engagement among participants. Almost all respondents reported that ceasing to drive their own car would negatively affect their social life. Many participants feared that when they stopped driving, they would face challenges in attending the majority of third places in the case study areas. Frank (age: 81) from Mermaid Waters-Clear Island Waters said:

> To be honest I haven't thought beyond owning a car. . ... [Without a car] it would be difficult to get to some of our social events. My Probus [a social club for retired or semi-retired professionals] is held at the Turf Club for instance. I would have difficulty getting there without using the likes of a taxi. Mandy [his wife] has two or three organisations to which she goes which public transport would be inadequate.

The challenges that retired drivers face in frequenting different third places were heightened or mitigated by the availability of alternative modes of travel within the case study area. The challenges were found to be particularly difficult in Hope Island, which is a low density urban area without accessible and reliable public transport access to civic facilities and amenities. In Mermaid Waters-Clear Island Waters, the participants who were living on or in proximity to the main roads found the thought of not driving less challenging than those who were residing in cul-de-sacs, as more access to public transport was available on the main roads. Although participants from Southport found driving cessation challenging, most of them indicated that they would be able to use public transport as an alternative means of transport, which helps them to stay socially active. Sara (age: 69), from Southport, indicated:

> . . . it's more convenient for me to hop in my car and just go straight to a certain place and get there . . ... [However] I realise that in the future, that may change, I may have no choice, but that's why I choose to live where I am because the bus is just at the end of the street, so if I need to take a bus then that's available to me.

There are, however, some significant barriers to older people's use of public transport. These barriers were emphasised the most by participants from Hope Island and the least by those from Southport. The current timetabled public transport system, with its limited routes in the sprawled urban context of the case study areas, is not appropriate for many older people. Most participants refrained from using public transport because they perceived it to be inconvenient, indicating their dissatisfaction with the availability, the accessibility and also the inconvenience of services.

The travel distance from the point of departure/arrival to the public transport stop influenced the likelihood of older people using the service. Also, for some participants, the bus service was not reliable, nor did it run frequently enough. The need for the provision of affordable transportation services, buses, taxies, and so on, and improving the awareness of older adults of such services was a significant finding from the data collected for this research.

DISCUSSION AND CONCLUSION

Among scholars in different fields of study, there has been a growing focus on planning for older people as a result of the ageing of the population. Accordingly, the aim of this chapter was to understand the role and accessibility of third places in relation to older people living in different neighbourhood built-form patterns, and how these factors impact on their social lives. A qualitative methodology was used to explore three different types of social ties, strong, weak and absent ties, which are formed and maintained as a result of older adults' engagement in different kinds of third places.

The findings demonstrated that a third place is more than a physical space. It goes beyond physical to social dimensions and creates a place for social interactions. Consistent with the literature (Cheang 2002; Hickman 2013; Lawson 2004; Matthews et al. 2000; Rosenbaum 2006; Rosenbaum et al. 2007), third places researched here, were found to play a significant role in the social lives of older people. A great deal of the social lives of older people was found to happen in different types of third places which were perceived to be accessible. In line with Oldenburg's (1999) definition of the third place, our research showed that different third places hosted the regular, voluntary social interactions of older people beyond their family and work. Third places were found to provide older people with opportunities to meet new people and establish absent, weak and in a few cases strong ties.

Third places provided older people with what Oldenburg termed as 'spiritual tonic' (Oldenburg 1999 p. 55). Our participants enjoyed the third places, and made them feel better about themselves and their social lives. Although the majority of the social ties formed in third places were found to be of absent and weak ties, they were perceived as important to older people and as Oldenburg (1999 p. 20) explained included dynamics that were older people's 'own remedy for stress, loneliness, and alienation'. As a result, third places can be seen as supportive of social health and well-being which is a main component of overall health and well-being (WHO

1948). The findings contribute to geographical gerontology through revealing the associations between spatial planning and social health at older age and highlighting the important role that spatial design and planning can play in enhancing the social health and thus improving the overall health and well-being of the ageing population.

In general, two characteristics of third places were found to be of importance for older people and their social lives, no matter what type of neighbourhood they reside in: (1) presenting multiple services at one place, and (2) being located in close proximity to the housing. The research also revealed that much of the social lives of conventional suburban neigh-bourhood participants happened in different clubs, particularly the local ones and those which were exclusive to older age cohorts. Different clubs were found to contribute to the formation of new absent, weak and in a few cases strong ties among regulars. The importance of clubs exclusive to older people has also been highlighted in Stevens' (2001) and Jerrome's (1983) research as a means of battling loneliness.

On the other hand, the social lives of MPC participants were revealed as taking place mainly within the physical boundaries of the developments and particularly in the common areas and the leisure centres of the MPCs. The MPC participants, especially those living in age-segregated develop-ments, were found to have a high number of social ties, in particular absent and weak ties, with other residents in the development. The major-ity of these social ties were formed in different social events and activities that were exclusive to the age-segregated MPC development residents and held in the common areas and leisure centres within the development.

The research demonstrated that the characteristics of the larger urban context including street network pattern, land-use mixture and public transport infrastructure, are important factors in increasing the level of accessibility of the urban environment and encouraging the constant engagement of older people at different third places outside the MPC developments. Comparing data from the three case study areas, Southport appeared to be the most successful in assuring access to third places outside the MPCs for retired drivers. Factors such as having a relatively dense, mixed-use urban pattern, with grid-street network and frequent public transport services, were found to ease older peoples' access to different third places spread throughout Southport. Not surprisingly, Mermaid Waters-Clear Island Waters and Hope Island ranked second and third in the provision of accessible urban environments for older people. The dominant cul-de-sac street network patterns in these case studies restrict public transport accessibility. In addition, the gated development pattern in Hope Island restricts access and discourages MPC residents from attending different third places outside the developments. The findings suggest developing MPCs in high density, mixed-use urban environments with adequate public transport services to the urban amenities and services. This would assure the constant social engagement of older people in the third places located outside the developments.

The research also highlighted the need to develop alternative transport provisions for retiring drivers. This is particularly the case for those living in cul-de-sac streets without adequate access to the main public transport routes. It was revealed that seniors are seeking flexible modes of public transport and the current, timetabled public transport system with low frequency and limited routes does not suit the majority of older people living in Australia's sprawled urban patterns. New transport interventions are required to be supported by programmes which increase older people's awareness of the alternative modes of travel available to them. In this way older people will be able to access third spaces and more actively engage in society.

REFERENCES

ABS (Australian Bureau of Statistics). 2011. 2011 Census Quickstats. ABS, Canberra.

ABS (Australian Bureau of Statistics). 2013. Population by Age and Sex, Regions of Australia, 2013. ABS cat. no. 3235.0. ABS, Canberra.

ABS (Australian Bureau of Statistics). 2014. Australian Historical Population Statistics, 2014. ABS cat. no. 3105.0.65.001. ABS, Canberra.

ALGA (Australian Local Government Association). 2006. Age-friendly Built Environments: Opportunities for Local Government. ALGA, Deakin.

Alidoust, S. and Bosman, C. 2015. Planning for an ageing population: Links between social health, neighbourhood environment and the elderly. *Australian Planner*, 52, 3, 177–186.

Alidoust, S. and Bosman, C. 2016. Boomer planning: The production of age-friendly cities. *Built Environment*, 42, 1, 107–119.

Alidoust, S., Bosman, C. and Holden, G. 2015. Socially healthy ageing: The importance of third places, soft edges and walkable neighbourhoods. Paper presented at the State of Australian Cities Conference Gold Coast, Australia.

Alidoust, S., Holden, G. and Bosman, C. 2014. Urban environment and social health of the elderly: A critical discussion on physical, social and policy environments. *Athens Journal of Health*, 1, 3, no page numbers.

Alsnih, R. and Hensher, D.A. 2003. The mobility and accessibility expectations of seniors in an aging population. *Transportation Research Part A: Policy and Practice*, 37, 10, 903–916.

Banister, D. and Bowling, A. 2004. Quality of life for the elderly: The transport dimension. *Transport Policy*, 11, 2, 105–115.

Berg, B.L. and Lune, H. 2004. *Qualitative Research Methods for the Social Sciences*. Pearson, Boston.

Brown, W. 2003. Promoting Healthy Ageing in Australia. Department of Education, Science and Training, Canberra.

Cheang, M. 2002. Older adults' frequent visits to a fast-food restaurant: Nonobligatory social interaction and the significance of play in a 'third place'. *Journal of Aging Studies*, 16, 3, 303–321.

Cheshire, L., Walters, P. and Wickes, R. 2010. Privatisation, security and community: How master planned estates are changing suburban Australia. *Urban Policy and Research*, 28, 4, 359–373.

Collia, D.V., Sharp, J. and Giesbrecht, L. 2003. The 2001 national household travel survey: A look into the travel patterns of older Americans. *Journal of Safety Research*, 34, 4, 461–470.

Cornwell, E.Y. and Waite, L.J. 2009. Social disconnectedness, perceived isolation, and health among older adults. *Journal of Health and Social Behavior*, 50, 1, 31–48.

Davey, J.A. 2007. Older people and transport: Coping without a car. *Ageing and Society*, 27, 1, 49–65.

Dedekorkut-Howes, A. and Bosman, C. 2015. The Gold Coast: Australia's playground? *Cities*, 42, 70–84.

García, E.L., Banegas, J., Perez-Regadera, A.G., Cabrera, R.H. and Rodriguez-Artalejo, F. 2005. Social network and health-related quality of life in older adults: A population-based study in Spain. *Quality of Life Research*, 14, 2, 511–520.

Golob, T.F. and Hensher, D.A. 2007. The trip chaining activity of Sydney residents: A cross-section assessment by age group with a focus on seniors. *Journal of Transport Geography*, 15, 4, 298–312.

Granovetter, M. 1973. The strength of weak ties. *American Journal of Sociology*, 78, 6, 1360–1380.

Granovetter, M. 1983. The strength of weak ties: A network theory revisited. *Sociological Theory*, 1, 201–233.

Greenblatt, H.N. 1976. *Measurement of Social Well-Being in a General Population Survey*. California State Department of Health, Berkeley.

Henning, C. and Lieberg, M. 1996. Strong ties or weak ties? Neighbourhood networks in a new perspective. *Scandinavian Housing and Planning Research*, 13, 1, 3–26.

Hickman, P. 2013. 'Third places' and social interaction in deprived neighbourhoods in Great Britain. *Journal of Housing and the Built Environment*, 28, 2, 221–236.

Hugo, G. 2003. Australia's ageing population: Some challenges for planners. *Australian Planner*, 40, 2, 109–118.

Jerrome, D. 1983. Lonely women in a friendship club. *British Journal of Guidance and Counseling*, 11, 1, 11–21.

Judd, B., Olsberg, D., Quinn, J., Groenhart, L. and Demirbilek, O. 2010. *Dwelling, Land and Neighbourhood Use by Older Home Owners*. Australian Housing and Urban Research Institute, Melbourne.

Kavanaugh, A.L., Reese, D.D., Carroll, J.M. and Rosson, M.B. 2005. Weak ties in networked communities. *The Information Society*, 21, 2, 119–131.

Keyes, C.L.M. 1998. Social well-being. *Social Psychology Quarterly*, 61, 2, 121–140.

Larson, J.S. 1993. The measurement of social well-being. *Social Indicators Research*, 28, 3, 285–296.

Lawson, K. 2004. Libraries in the USA as traditional and virtual 'third places'. *New Library World*, 105, 3/4, 125–130.

Levasseur, M., Gauvin, L., Richard, L., Kestens, Y., Daniel, M. and Payette, H. 2011. Associations between perceived proximity to neighborhood resources, disability, and social participation among community-dwelling older adults: Results from the VoisiNuAge study. *Archives of Physical Medicine and Rehabilitation*, 92, 12, 1979–1986.

Litman, T. 2003. Measuring transportation: Traffic, mobility, and accessibility. *ITE Journal*, 73, 10, 28–32.

Marottoli, R.A., De Leon, C.F.M., Glass, T.A., Williams, C.S., Cooney, L.M. and Berkman, L.F. 2000. Consequences of driving cessation decreased out-of-home activity levels. *The Journals of Gerontology Series B: Psychological Sciences and Social Sciences*, 55, 6, S334–S340.

Matthews, H., Limb, M. and Taylor, M. 2000. The street as a third space. In Holloway, S.L. and Valentine, G. (eds), *Children's Geographies: Playing, Living, Learning*. Routledge, London, pp. 54–68.

Oldenburg, R. 1989. *The Great Good Place: Cafés, Coffee Shops, Community Centers, Beauty Parlors, General Stores, Bars, Hangouts, and How They Get You Through the Day*. Paragon House, New York.

Oldenburg, R. 1997. Our vanishing 'third places'. *Planning Commissioners*, 25, 6–10.

Oxley, J. and Fildes, B. 2000. Retiring from driving: the process of reduction and cessation of driving and the role of a handbook to assist in this process. Proceedings of the Older Road User Safety Symposium, 26 November 2000, Centre for Accident Research and Road Safety – Queensland (CARRS-Q), Brisbane, Australia.

Phillips, D.R., Siu, O., Yeh, A.G. and Cheng, K.H.C. 2005. Ageing and the urban environment. In Andrews, G.J. and Phillips, D.R. (eds), *Ageing and Place: Perspectives, Policy, Practice*. Routledge, London, pp. 147–163.

Renne, K.S. 1974. Measurement of social health in a general population survey. *Social Science Research*, 3, 1, 25–44.

Richard, L., Gauvin, L., Gosselin, C. and Laforest, S. 2009. Staying connected: neighbourhood correlates of social participation among older adults living in an urban environment in Montreal, Quebec. *Health Promotion International*, 24, 1, 46–57.

Rosenbaum, M.S. 2006. Exploring the social supportive role of third places in consumers' lives. *Journal of Service Research*, 9, 1, 59–72.

Rosenbaum, S., Ward, J., Walker, B.A. and Ostrom, A.L. 2007. A cup of coffee with a dash of love: An investigation of commercial social support and third-place attachment. *Journal of Service Research*, 10, 1, 43–59.

Schmöcker, J., Quddus, M.A., Noland, R.B. and Bell, M.G. 2008. Mode choice of older and disabled people: a case study of shopping trips in London. *Journal of Transport Geography*, 16, 4, 257–267.

Schwanen, T., Dijst, M. and Dieleman, F.M. 2001. Leisure trips of senior citizens: Determinants of modal choice. *Tijdschrift Voor Economische en Sociale Geografie*, 92, 3, 347–360.

Stevens, N.L. 2001. Combating loneliness: A friendship enrichment programme for older women. *Ageing and Society*, 21, 2, 183–202.

United Nations, Department of Economic and Social Affairs 2014. *World Urbanization Prospects: The 2014 Revision*. United Nations, New York.

United Nations, Department of Economic and Social Affairs, Population Division 2015. *World Population Ageing*. United Nations, New York.

Victoria Transport Policy Institute. 2014. Online TDM Encyclopedia. Available online at http://www.vtpi.org/tdm/tdm84.htm (accessed 12 July 2014).

WHO (World Health Organization). 1948. Preamble to the Constitution of the

WHO as Adopted by the International Health Conference, New York, 19–22 June 1946. WHO, Geneva.

WHO (World Health Organization). 2007. *Global Age-Friendly Cities: A Guide*. WHO, Geneva.

Yu, R.P., Mccammon, R.J., Ellison, N.B. and Langa, K.M. 2016. The relationships that matter: Social network site use and social wellbeing among older adults in the United States of America. *Ageing and Society*, 36, 1826–1852.

4. Child-friendly third places

Geoff Woolcock

INTRODUCTION

The child-friendly cities movement, framed in the rise of attention given to children's human rights through the 1980s, has some important antecedents, most notably the lively North American and European literature which emerged during the 1960s, which attempted to give more explicit thought to the links between urban development and children's welfare. Colin Ward's (1978) *The Child in the City* best distilled this clash with industrial modernism and proposed an urbanism that was much more conscious of children's diverse needs, including their abiding preference for secure homes over broad cityscapes. The growing critical focus on children amongst urban commentators was stimulated by the establishment of a ten-year programme in 1968, called *Growing Up in Cities*, co-ordinated by the United Nations Educational, Scientific and Cultural Organization (UNESCO), the forerunner to the UNICEF Child-Friendly Cities project. Much of this discussion focused on highly particular questions, such as how aspects of child psychology were influenced by environmental conditions or narrow concerns with the physical design of child play areas. While these programmes brought much needed attention to children's needs, their ambition was not so much to re-centre children socially as to urge greater institutional awareness of children's unique and sensitive qualities.

During the 1980s, research into children's issues mostly continued with the themes established during the 1970s. That is, it focused on how the physical environment impacted on the social and mental development of children. Some attempts were made to understand the environment from a child's perspective and incorporate these ideas into policy, but by and large the emphasis remained on children's development and how that is shaped by the physical environment. The key vacuum that persisted throughout this period was the lack of any key policy and research links between the physical environment's effects on children's well-being and the multiple other critical facets of children's development. Simultaneously, national and international debates on children and cities had quietened by the 1990s, despite the growing tide of global population movement into cities, and particularly in Australia, a long-standing highly urbanised nation.

Recent years have witnessed renewed interest in public and professional discussion of urban children's issues in English-speaking countries. A small portion of this revival has been stimulated by global initiatives such as UNICEF's Child-Friendly Cities but there are clearly far more influential triggers. Specifically, children's physical health has emerged as an area of sharp concern with the recognition that levels of physical fitness among urban children have been declining, most notably in Western countries. Scholarly research and popular interest in children's health has continued into the twenty-first century, focusing particularly on the incidence of childhood obesity and the associated decrease in children's physical activity. Responding to concern about childhood obesity, a growing range of studies has examined the links between children's physical activity patterns and built environment form (American Academy of Paediatrics 2009; Kemple et al. 2016) and the beneficial impacts of risky outdoor play for children (Brussoni et al. 2015). Other investigations have pointed to an alarming rise in mental health disorders among children in countries such as the United States, the United Kingdom and Australia. Yet, it has taken considerable time for urban scholarship to have seriously contributed to these population health concerns.

URBAN 'LIVEABILITY' – CHILD-FRIENDLY?

Casually working my way through a weekend paper's travel section recently, I was struck by a quote from one pampered reviewer who claimed that Abu-Dhabi 'must be' one of the world's most child-friendly cities. Reluctantly delving further into her 48-hour stay observations, she waxed lyrical about how many children's entertainment options there were to enjoy amongst the vast and opulent shopping plazas that characterise the United Arab Emirates' capital city. Apart from the mild shock that one could perceive giant plasma TVs screening Disney's latest as characteristic of a child-friendly city, it was also a reminder about how much investment is now put towards measuring the quality of life or 'liveability' of cities.

The 'liveability' of cities is often ranked on surveys which privilege adult understanding of place. It seems virtually every week that another liveability survey's results fills our print media and airwaves, absorbing a public hungry to see whether their home postcode, town or city ranks higher or lower than the list that came out the week before. While this generates bubbles of intense local interest, the superficiality and elements of absurdity in these scorecards is revealing. No more so than when in early 2008 the *Sydney Morning Herald* trumpeted the fact that the most notable of these global city surveys had Sydney above Melbourne in the top five world rankings, only to turn the page and see a damning photo of nightmarish traffic logjams crawling into the Sydney CBD.

Rarely do any of these surveys acknowledge that they report the views exclusively of the adult population, and invariably a limited one at that. Just what do our children and young people think of the towns and cities they live in? Where they have been asked, it indicates a very different set of results, as discussed below (see NSW CCYP 2007). The same global survey, geared as it is to the wealthy tourist market, puts a heavy weighting in its scoring on a city's capacity to serve good coffee after 2:00 am. A few new sleep-deprived parents might rate such a trait highly as they pace the hallways, but a liveable city or community would surely hope its children are getting necessary rest in the wee hours so as to enjoy the delights of their surrounding physical environment from the break of dawn.

Ranking and scoring is not of course consigned to cities and towns. Children's well-being has long had a raft of measures compiled, primarily using health indicators, most prominently in Australia through the release of two Report Cards (2008 2012) on the Wellbeing of Young Australians by the Australian Research Alliance for Children and Youth (ARACY). While the report cards draw useful public attention to the areas where Australian children are least healthy relative to other countries, they contain very little that tells how our kids actually perceive their well-being in relation to their surrounding built and natural environment. There is some irony in this, given that such scorecards gain their prominence primarily on their capacity to compare between different geographical places.

This is puzzling, given that our leading child health experts, most notably Professor Fiona Stanley, have long trumpeted the importance of the built and natural environments in determining children's well-being, an issue magnified by the rampant children's obesity epidemic that shows little sign of easing. Indeed, her popular *Children of the Lucky Country?* (Stanley et al. 2005) goes to considerable lengths exploring how the qualities of built environments help to determine the life chances of children. Arguably the most pivotal ongoing measure of children's well-being in Australia comes through the massive sample size that constitutes the Australian Early Development Census (AEDC, originally the Australian Early Development Index), a teacher-conducted comprehensive assessment of children's development in their first year of schooling. Perhaps what's most intriguing about the AEDC in results compiled from the three waves conducted thus far (2009, 2012, 2015) is the small but significant number of communities with low vulnerability scores in socio-economic disadvantaged areas and vice versa. The more in-depth research that is being conducted in these communities (Goldfeld et al. 2015; Christian et al. 2017) throws some much-needed light on what is going on behind the often crude aggregate numbers that can only describe so much. In fact, the study is already revealing the nuances that inevitably accompany a more thorough analysis, producing findings such as how much all kids prize parent-free open space play areas – third places – as those of us promoting child-friendly communities are reminded of frequently at community meetings.

Increasing barriers to accessing parks in an increasingly urbanised world has seen the Centers for Disease Control and Prevention (CDCP 2014) estimate that less than half of US children have a playground within walking distance of their homes. Certainly, we know that hearing directly from children and young people about what they value in the built and natural environment is increasingly driving influential community-wide movements such as *Child in the City*, *Play for Life*, *Playborhood*, *Nature Play*, *Play Australia* and *Project Wild Thing*.

What then might a revised set of measures of child-friendly cities and communities look like if we started asking children and young people about this? Work undertaken by the New South Wales (NSW) Commission for Children and Young People on the basic premise of *Ask the Children* (NSW CCYP 2007) has led to a range of activity throughout NSW local government areas about child-friendly indicators focused on practical outcomes that meet kids' real physical needs (Woolcock and Steele 2008). Research conducted in conjunction with a *Child-Friendly by Design* project in the Illawarra region (Langridge and Woolcock, 2010) has prioritised children and parent's perceptions of what makes a physical environment tick by using photos of local outdoor areas and asking them to rank these in order of their child-friendliness. Very similar approaches have been used by Professor Karen Malone (2007) working with a number of Australian communities seeking recognition as a UNICEF child-friendly city, a long-standing project emphasising the following characteristics:

- A place with a sustainable future;
- A place where children participate in making decisions and expressing their views;
- A place where special attention is given to disadvantaged children;
- A place where children are not discriminated against;
- A place where children have access to services;
- A place where local authorities act in best interests of the children;
- A place with safe environments that nurture children; and

- A place where children are able to engage in recreation, learning, social interaction, psychological development and cultural expression.

It is revealing that most of these characteristics are echoed directly by children themselves, not only in the *Ask the Children* exercise but in scores of other activities undertaken on the same theme, both in Australia and overseas, most commonly articulated at the annual European Child in the City conferences.

URBAN SCHOLARSHIP AND CHILD-FRIENDLY THIRD PLACES

Urban analysis is essential to improved scientific understanding of children's contemporary problems and needs. Urban environments are where the vast majority of people in Western countries reside and are the principal context within which we must provide flourishing conditions for children. But they are more than mere context: cities and suburbs are dynamic, even fluid, social places where constant transformation acts independently to shape the communities that inhabit them. This recognition is seeping through to the non-urban professions – in health, community development, education, recreation, criminology – who look increasingly to urban analysis for enhanced understanding of how complex environments influence the well-being of children. However, this renewed focus on children's well-being and the relationship to the built environment is not well served by a developed urban understanding (see Gleeson and Sipe 2006). A key example of this underdeveloped understanding is the lack of historical analysis of cities in the UNICEF Child-Friendly Cities initiative that persists in projecting a globally homogenous picture of a city's dynamics.

There is, nonetheless, reason to be optimistic that increasing instances of assessing places through a child's lens will be the catalyst for more child-centred urban planning and sensitivity to the importance of child-friendly third places. Certainly, very successful examples of adult participation in helping design effective places, as highlighted by *Project for Public Spaces*,[1] could easily be replicated with children, based on the basic principle of active listening. This has visibly materialised in the small northern Italian village of Coriandoline (not surprisingly, very close to the pioneering early childhood development practice and movement of Reggio Emilia) where

---

[1]   See pps.org.

hundreds of children in kindergartens and primary schools have been actively involved in the design and construction of the town's built and natural environments for more than a decade. Closer to home, there are plentiful examples of how children and young people's almost universally positive responses to climate change through, for example, community and school gardens (see Dolley, Chapter 8 this volume and Pascoe and Wyatt-Smith 2013) and eco-friendly housing design are shaping urban and suburban landscapes for the better. A largely European-led movement to conduct most primary education in natural settings (often shorthanded as 'Forest Schools') presents forest and nature schools as idealised venues to investigate and understand the necessary balance of risk-taking and safety in child development (Harper 2017).

CHILDREN AND THE PUBLIC DOMAIN: SOUTH BANK PARKLANDS AS A THIRD-SPACE CASE STUDY

The public domain of the city is its 'common ground'. It comprises every part of the physical environment that we as citizens have access to and which provide the essential setting for cultural, social and commercial exchange. The public domain frames and conditions our private choices and it is therefore central to the political and social life of a city. It is democratic in essence because in it, we as citizens have rights defined only by laws. In any civilised society, access to high-quality public space should be a fundamental human right for all. Public places define a city's unique character and display its generosity of spirit. Neglect of the public domain on the other hand, erodes the very fabric of society.

From its spectacular origins as the host site for the 1988 World Exposition, South Bank Parklands in Brisbane, Australia has been conceived, planned and redeveloped as an inner-city precinct that is highly attractive to families and children. As a major international event credited with giving global exposure to the capital city of Queensland on a scale previously not experienced, it is the social legacy of Expo '88 that 22 years on, continues to resonate with the citizens. South Bank Parklands today is Brisbane's pre-eminent public domain, supporting a rich array of civic and community events, activities and visitor experiences. In an increasing variety of ways, South Bank Parklands has evolved from its Expo origins to become a cluster of highly effective third places. Unlike its private theme park rivals with their contrived and commercialised play environments, South Bank Parklands' success – with more than 11 million visitors annually – stems from its deliberative efforts in creating and managing a network of high-quality public places and facilities that are not only free but highly adaptive in the play, leisure and learning experiences they provide. South Bank Parklands' popularity has been attributed to many factors; the key success factors are its accessibility, both physically and socially, and its acknowledged qualities as a welcoming and safe place. It has also enjoyed significant patronage from the neighbouring Queensland Performing Arts Centre (QPAC) precinct where close to 1.5 million people annually attend QPAC events.

Contrary to popular depictions of a vast, unpopulated continent, Australia is one of the world's most urbanised countries with nine in ten Australians living in the cities. Our cities, however, have been developed in a very inefficient form and we are paying the price. With rampant problems such as congestion and a lack of community services in the new suburban fringe communities, virtually all our capital cities are now faced with the challenge of consolidating their sprawling urban footprints due to sustained growth pressures fuelled by a strong national economy and an ambitious immigration programme. Increasingly more Australians, or at least those who can afford to, are joining an escalating socio-demographic shift and being encouraged to reimagine the great Australian Dream of a suburban detached dwelling with a large back yard and move into an inner-city apartment with a small balcony or a suburban detached dwelling with no back yard (Hall 2010). As a direct consequence, access to public places such as parks for active leisure and contact with nature, particularly by children, are becoming more critical to the redevelopment of parts of our cities. Australian city planners still look to Old World cities with their denser urban patterns to understand and appropriate those aspects of public space planning, design and use that they see as being relevant in finding solutions to the challenges they now face. In many cities, existing public places and parks have to be redesigned to accommodate not only much higher levels of usage but also new roles as multi-purpose places.

As a contemporary, master-planned precinct South Bank Parklands has been able to anticipate this shift in both demand and use and created a public environment which not only welcomes children but invites their exploration of the structured and unstructured play experiences on offer. The enduring place-making principles that have guided the precinct's development and public domain management have, since 1997, been consistently applied and the benefits of this tenacity are today clearly evident. Recent market research confirms this with more than eight out of ten of Brisbane's 2.5 million residents alone having visited South Bank Parklands in the previous six months.

SOUTH BANK PARKLANDS' CHILD-FRIENDLY THIRD PLACES

Good public place attributes of social inclusiveness, egalitarianism, freedom of exchange, sensory stimulation and flexibility of use are aligned with the third place characteristics (as mentioned in many chapters of this book); that is, levellers, neutral ground, playful mood, access and accommodation and conversation. A key test of the presence and application of these qualities is how children, who too commonly are regarded as a minority interest group, are attracted to and engage with the facilities offered. South Bank Parklands' enduring appeal to children and caregivers is achieved primarily through the variety of innovative play and learning environments it has created and sustains through its place management practices. These practices emphasise the value of activating informal third places that invite children to engage with diverse landscapes and playspaces.

South Bank Parklands provides clear evidence that an effective public domain replete with third places is inherently child-friendly, including the following traits:

- *Character*: A place with its own identity with the objective to promote character in townscape and landscape by responding to and reinforcing locally distinctive patterns of development, landscape and culture.
- *Continuity and enclosure*: A place where public and private places are clearly distinguished with the objective to promote the continuity of street frontages and the enclosure of space by development which clearly defines private and public areas.
- *Quality of the public realm*: A place with attractive and successful outdoor areas with the objective to promote public places and routes that are attractive, safe, uncluttered and work effectively for all in society, including disabled and elderly people.
- *Ease of movement*: A place that is easy to get to and move through with the objective to promote accessibility and local permeability by making places that connect with each other and are easy to move through, putting people before traffic and integrating land uses and transport.
- *Legibility*: A place that has a clear image and is easy to understand with the objective to promote legibility through development that provides recognisable routes, intersections and landmarks to help people find their way around.
- *Adaptability*: A place that can change easily with the objective to promote adaptability through development that can respond to changing social, technological and economic conditions.

- *Diversity*: A place with variety and choice with the objective to promote diversity and choice through a mix of compatible developments and uses that work together to create viable places that respond to local needs.[2]

A meandering bush stream, a rainforest, an interactive water playground incorporating sound and light, and a working maritime museum are just some of the settings children find highly attractive within the Parklands. These are complemented by a busy calendar of events, many of which have a strong active leisure and sports focus in recognition of the need to support public policy on reducing childhood obesity levels. The precinct is unusual in that unlike the other Australian capitals, virtually all Brisbane's major cultural institutions are co-located within it. Without exception, these arts bodies fund and co-ordinate comprehensive children's programmes that feature creative learning and educational themes that are integrated with the school curricula. The early and active involvement of other government and community-based agencies has in turn attracted strong philanthropic and private-sector sponsorship.

South Bank Parklands' many positive place attributes when considered in the broader national urban context are, however, somewhat of an anomaly. There is, regrettably, still evidence of a clear disconnect between the planning and design of Australian cities and their third places in providing environments that not only welcome children but also establish social and psychological connections that stimulate learning and ultimately, active civic participation. Too easily, the public environment of many Australian cities, but particularly their inner areas falls short in considering the child's experience of public space and the potential that experience offers to shape an understanding of how children exercise their democratic rights and in turn, accept their responsibilities as future citizens. The reasons for this condition are interrelated but stem primarily from a lack of concern for the interests of children at the formative stage of determining what role a city's public domain should necessarily support and what audiences it should engage. Public place designers, managers and their clients still commonly approach the task without any meaningful attempt being made to consider the full breadth of user needs, and as a result they create or modify environments that unthinkingly have the effect of excluding children, or worse, placing them at increased risk of harm. This failing is slowly being recognised and its significance understood at a practitioner level, but

2   From *By Design Urban Design in the Planning System* (2000) Commission for Architecture and the Built Environment, Department of Transport, Local Government and Regions, London, UK, p. 4.

the clear onus remains on public authorities whose responsibility it is to address the needs of all citizens, to rethink current policies and practices.

SECURITY AND RISK: COUNTERPOINT TO CHILD-FRIENDLY DISCOURSE

A key reason for the success of children's connection with South Bank Parklands is the facility's provision of security mechanisms and technology that ensure safety for children and families. Popularly seen as a critical inhibitor of children's rights to play and participate, security and risk management procedures at South Bank Parklands have in fact become crucial enablers for participation across the age spectrum and through to after-dark hours.

Juvenile crime rates and the incidence of anti-social behaviour in public places across all Australian cities remain high. The nexus between these negative trends and the design and management of the public domain demands greater attention from different levels of government and from different professions. Urban planners and designers can, however, be much stronger champions of children's rights and needs in how they shape and then manage the urban landscape (see Holden, Chapter 6 this volume). Focusing exclusively on crime reduction in the public domain, however, runs the risk of masking other important dimensions of children's experience and use of third places.

CHILDREN'S HEALTH AND WELL-BEING, URBAN BUILT AND NATURAL ENVIRONMENTS AND THIRD PLACES

Traditionally, community interventions to address perceived problems for children and young people have been targeted through schools, recreational settings, or families and individuals considered most at risk. However, it is only recently that the built environment has been recognised as an alternative intervention point for improving health and well-being. For children and young people, outdoor environments such as South Bank Parklands are not just the typical places to play, but also provide a place to socialise, be physically active, explore, have fun, 'hang out', be in contact with nature, escape from indoors, or just be free from the encumbrances of an increasingly adult world. Outdoor environments are also increasingly important places in the face of a diminishing public space and disappearing Australian backyards (Hall 2010).

Scholarly research and popular interest in children's health has continued into the twenty-first century, focusing particularly on the incidence of childhood obesity and the associated decrease in children's physical activity (see Gill 2007 and Louv 2008 for two of the most popular examples of these concerns). Responding to concern about childhood obesity, a growing range of studies has examined the links between children's physical activity patterns and built environment form (e.g. Richardson and Prior 2005; Davison and Lawson 2006; Cutumisu and Spence 2008; American Academy of Pediatrics 2009). Few of these studies, however, focus on informal physical activity in third places such as South Bank Parklands.

And while there have been important tributary streams of interest in children in urban scholarship – including, for example, the work of Tranter and Sharpe (2007) on children's rights, Malone (2007) on residential living and Walsh (2006) on play environments – this renewed focus on children's well-being and the relationship to the built environment is not well served by a developed urban understanding (see Gleeson and Sipe 2006). Most contemporary developed Western cities are hybridised landscapes containing surviving (frequently gentrified) historical accretions from industrialism, significant suburban swathes bequeathed by twentieth-century planned growth and new and emergent compact urban forms (including both brownfield redevelopment and compact suburbia). These contemporary landscapes are also marked by socio-spatial polarisation, revealed in the contrast between localised concentrations of poverty/exclusion and new places of affluence and selective inclusion, such as gated communities. Whatever the context, it is also unfortunately true that the vast majority of both the creation and adaptation of built environments occurs with a complete absence of children and young people's voice (Nordstrom 2010).

How then do we link the importance of children's relationships with built and natural environments to significant third places like South Bank Parklands? Talen and Coffindaffer's (1999) important children and environments research in the US tells us much about the importance of third places in child development, concluding that children experience their environments differently to adults, and that their experience is highly personal. It is about 'texture and variety', rather than function. Children also prefer places that are diverse and accessible, with opportunity for social interaction, as opposed to homogeneous and isolated; it is about shared places. The same authors also note that gender differences are important to consider in children's use of third places and that their usage is not exclusively 'fun and play', often showing a level of civic mindedness. Other Canadian contributions have been highlighted by McAllister (2008) who argues that a community's design and land-use decisions have a significant impact on their physical, social and mental health. The four main issues discussed in her paper – safety, greenspace, access and integration – she believes 'should be at the top of every planner's list in order to create healthy, child friendly cities' (McAllister 2008 p. 56).

In the case of South Bank Parklands, as already discussed, it covers nearly 20 hectares of a riverfront site within the central city and features a sub-tropical landscape which supports a rich bio-diversity of flora and fauna some of which are protected native species. While children's interaction with the Parkland's plants and animals is discreetly managed, South Bank Parklands powerfully demonstrates that children can experience and establish genuine connection with the natural environment and the ecology of the city, a connection that does not necessarily need to be limited to botanical or zoological gardens and other highly regulated public places.

CHILD-FRIENDLY URBAN PLAY PLACES AS THIRD PLACES

South Bank Parklands' popularity underscores the growing importance of safe and supportive environments able to nurture children of all ages with opportunities for recreation, learning, social interaction, and cultural expression, thereby promoting the highest quality of life for its young citizens. Building such third places demands embracing child friendly design principles.

Play England (2008) has outlined in its *Design For Play* resource what they consider makes a successful play space, including each of the following traits that South Bank Parklands lays claim to:

- A space that offers movement and physical activity – with space and features that allow a range of energetic and strength-building play experiences;
- A space that stimulates the five senses – maybe providing music and sound, and different smells made by plants and leaves;
- A space that provides good places for social interactions – allowing children to choose whether and when to play alone or with others, to negotiate, cooperate, complete and resolve conflicts;
- A space that allows children to manipulate natural and fabricated materials, use tools, and have access to bits and pieces of all kinds; and
- Places that offer children challenge and activities that test the limits of their capabilities, including rough and tumble, sports and games, and opportunities to climb.

Most importantly, Play England (2008 p.15) states that making a successful child-friendly place involves adhering to the golden rule: 'a successful
play space is a place in its own right, specially designed for its location, in
such a way as to provide as much play value as possible'.

Third places – distinctly different to our own backyards (first place)
or school playgrounds (second place) – are, in principle, accessible to
everyone, regardless of where they live. Research shows that the interactions that take place in third places provide a rich education for children
in terms of the world around them, and the people who live in it. Places
where children play are important social places, not just for children and
young people, but also for parents, carers and the wider community.
South Bank Parklands is an obvious demonstration of what Play England
(2008, p. 8) argues they should be places 'where children and young people
can enjoy spending time, be physically active, interact with their natural
surroundings, experience change and continuity, take risks in an environment where they feel safe and, of course, play – alone or with others – in a
wide variety of ways'. However, the contemporary constraints of the vast
majority of urban public places sees children's play mostly occurring in
much less prominent public places, indeed the third places of local pocket
parks and shared backyards.

The importance of play is becoming increasingly recognised as an abso-
lutely fundamental element of children's well-being. Little and Wyver's
(2008) comprehensive paper examines the current status of outdoor
play in urbanised Western societies such as Australia, and provides a
critical analysis of the literature to present a persuasive argument for the
inclusion of positive risk-taking experiences in children's outdoor play.
Again, South Bank Parklands is challenged in this regard by sustaining
the delicate balance between its provision of a range of play experiences
whilst maintaining a sense of safety and well-being. There are certainly a
diversity of play places within the South Bank Parklands complex but the
Parklands layout – with an arts precinct at its eastern end and recreational
play areas towards the western end – presents a significant ongoing challenge to ensure that children and young people's experience of third places
is integrated and accessible to all.

CHILDREN'S THIRD PLACES AS CRITICAL
CONTRIBUTORS TO 'COLLECTIVE IMPACT'

Fiona Stanley's Australian of the Year tenure in 2003 brought attention to
an issue that ought to strike fear into the heart of any civilisation, namely
that all indications are showing we are raising the first generation in this

nation's history whose average life expectancy will be less than their parents, data confirmed in the regular series of national child well-being data from UNICEF's Innocenti Research Centre. Dubbing it 'Modernity's Paradox' – where increasing wealth and opportunity has also resulted in increased social differences and more problems for children and youth, including increases in asthma, obesity, diabetes, child abuse, binge-drinking, drug abuse and mental health problems – there are disturbingly increasing signs that the shock value of this paradox is losing traction. Not only is this obvious in the despair that still largely pervades efforts to improve Indigenous Australian children's well-being but it is apparent too in the widespread downplaying of growing inequalities in children's access to quality experiences in the built and natural environments.

How, for example, can we collectively overcome the multitude of driving forces that have resulted in the average six-year-old spending up to seven hours per day in front of some form of screen and less than five minutes per day engaging in informal play (US National Wildlife Federation 2010)? Transport advocates will push for more walk to school options, environmentalists more access to nature and parks, physical education for more opportunity to participate in sport, and so on but perhaps a more confronting contributing factor is Australia's long-standing leadership of the highest average working hours per week across all OECD countries. More obvious factors behind the decline of outdoor urban play are captured in popular commentaries such as Hall's (2010) *The Life and Death of the Australian Backyard*. The popularity of children and young peoples' grassroots sports in the suburbs (e.g. football, netball, cricket) should not be overlooked as an important third place and contributor to physical activity.

Furthermore, the highly laudable movement to de-sensationalise the actual versus perceived risk to children engaging with the outdoors (see Gill 2007; Skenazy 2010) nonetheless must still confront the genuine concerns many parents have about their kids' exposure to 'stranger danger' and other potential harm. And how significant children's increasing uptake of new information technologies (ICTs) is in impacting on their relationship to place still remains largely unexamined (see Williams and Kim Chapter 9 this volume). Australian data on young people's use of ICTs is patchy with very little that directly examines their ICT activity alongside physical and spatial patterns of activity, although there is a growing body of research that highlights the role of social media in facilitating children's engagement and social connectedness (Allen et al. 2014).

These challenges and more lie behind another Fiona Stanley-inspired creation, the Australian Research Alliance for Children and Youth (ARACY) and in particular its action plan, *The Nest* which aims to align efforts to improve the well-being of Australia's 0–24-year-olds. *The Nest* is about collectively identifying what it is we should be aiming to achieve for children and young people, the most effective prevention focused and evidence-informed ways to achieve this change, and how we can best align our collective effort to achieve it. It is fundamentally based on the under-standing that governments alone cannot meet all the needs of children and young people – and the significant issues facing young Australians cannot be improved by one 'magic' programme, one policy, or one organisation working in isolation.

In its contemporary form, many place-based initiatives focused on children's well-being are understandably drawn to the notion of Collective Impact, a largely North American driven approach which actively seeks to concentrate the energies of its collaborators to achieve real, long-term, measurable and sustainable outcomes. Much of this work in Australia is now operating under the auspices of the Foundation and its ten years of considerable funding and support for twenty communities committed to Australia's most vulnerable children and young people. These noble aims to achieve large-scale and long-term change at scale ultimately requires much courage, including a collective willingness to invest in prevention science, sometimes at the expense of secondary and tertiary care. A crucial component in any efforts focusing on children at the top (rather than the bottom) of the metaphorical cliff will invariably need more critical engage-ment with the sustainable provision of child-friendly third places.

CONCLUSION

As each day seemingly heralds more stresses and pressures on our cities, it is hoped that the needs of our children in planning progressive built and natural environments do not recede into the background. Perennially shrill debates about housing affordability pressures, for example, that will increasingly impact younger people through the necessity for denser living arrangements, still barely seem to mention children, let alone focus on their welfare. As several sage opinion leaders have noted, the most effective policy and community responses cannot be just directed at enhancing young people's resiliency and adaptability – it also requires re-shaping social structures to suit *their* needs. Enhancing the options for more third places could immediately be progressed by recognising where the bulk of children's outdoor activity takes place. For example, in the now-commonplace writers festival session on the future of cities, panellists inevitably thump the familiar drum of the desperate need for more public amenity and interaction in our inner cities, seemingly oblivious to the thriving social world fuelled by grassroots sports throughout our suburbs on any given weekend. A more rounded and informed understanding of children's contemporary physical activity and engagement with the outdoors would be a good start in meeting children's physical and psychological development needs, including their pervasive engagement with third places.

REFERENCES

Allen, K.A., Ryan, T., Gray, D.L. and Waters, L. (2014) 'Social media use and social connectedness in adolescents: the positives and the potential pitfalls', *Australian Journal of Educational and Developmental Psychology*, 31 (1), 1–14.

American Academy of Pediatrics (2009) 'The built environment: designing communities to promote physical activity in children', *Pediatrics*, 123 (6), 1591–1598.

Brussoni, M., Gibbons, R., Gray, C., Ishikawa, T., Sandseter, E.B.H., Bienenstock, A., Chabot, G., Fuselli, P., Herrington, S., Janssen, I., Pickett, W., Power, M., Stanger, N., Sampson, M. and Trembla, M.S. (2015) 'What is the relationship between risky outdoor play and health in children? A systematic review', *International Journal of Environmental Research & Public Health*, 12, 6423–6454.

Centers for Disease Control and Prevention (CDCP) (2014) *State Indicator Report on Physical Activity*, Atlanta, GA: U.S. Department of Health and Human Services.

Christian, H., Ball, S.J., Zubrick, S.R., Brinkman, S., Turrell, G., Boruff, B. and Foster, S. (2017) 'Relationship between the neighbourhood built environment and early child development', *Health & Place*, 48, 1–12.

Cutumisu, N. and Spence, J.C. (2008) 'Exploring associations between urban environments and children's physical activity: making the case for space syntax', *Journal of Science & Medicine in Sport*, doi:10.1016/j.jsams.2008.09.002.

Davison, K.K. and Lawson, C.T. (2006) 'Do attributes in the physical environment influence children's physical activity? A review of the literature', *International Journal of Behavioral Nutrition and Physical Activity*, 3, 19–35.

Gill, T. (2007) *No Fear: Growing Up in a Risk-Free Society*. London: Calouste Gulbenkian Foundation.

Gleeson, B. and Sipe, N. (eds) (2006) *Creating Child Friendly Cities: Reinstating Kids in the City*. London: Routledge.

Goldfeld, S., Woolcock, G., Katz, I., Tanton, R., Brinkman, S., O'Connor, E., Mathews, T. and Giles-Corti, B. (2015) 'Neighbourhood effects influencing early childhood development: conceptual model and trial indicator measurement methodologies from the Kids in Communities Study', *Social Indicators Research*, 120 (1), 197–212.

Hall, T. (2010) *The Life and Death of the Australian Backyard*. Sydney: CSIRO Publications.

Harper, N.J. (2017) 'Outdoor risky play and healthy child development in the shadow of the "risk society": a forest and nature school perspective', *Child & Youth Services*, doi: 10.1080/0145935X.2017.1412825.

Kemple, K.M., Oh, J., Kenney, E. and Smith-Bonahue, T. (2016) 'The power of outdoor play and play in natural environments', *Childhood Education*, 92 (6), 446–454.

Langridge, D. and Woolcock, G. (2010) 'Bringing child friendly by design to the heart of liveable cities – the Illawarra experience', *Healthy Cities National Conference*, Brisbane, July.

Little, H. and Wyver, S. (2008) 'Outdoor play: does avoiding the risks reduce the benefits?' *Australian Journal of Early Childhood*, 33 (2), online http://www.early childhoodaustralia.org.au.

Louv, R. (2008) *Last Child in the Woods: Saving our Children from Nature Deficit Disorder*. Chapel Hill, NC: Algonquin Books.

Malone, K. (2007) 'The bubble-wrap generation: children growing up in walled gardens', *Environmental Education Research*, 13 (4), 513–527.

McAllister, C. (2008) 'Child friendly cities and land use planning: implications for children's health', *Environments*, 35 (3), 45–61.

Nordstrom, M. (2010) 'Children's views on child-friendly environments in different geographical, cultural and social neighbourhoods', *Urban Studies*, 47 (3), 514–528.

NSW Commission for Children and Young People (CCYP) (2007) *Ask the Children*. Surry Hills, NSW: NSW CCYP.

Pascoe, J. and Wyatt-Smith, C. (2013) 'Curriculum literacies and the school garden', *Literacy Learning: The Middle Years*, 21 (1), 34–47.

Richardson, S. and Prior, M. (eds) (2005) *No Time to Lose: The Wellbeing of Australia's Children*. Melbourne: Melbourne University Press.

Shackell, A., Butler, N., Doyle, P. and Ball, D. (2008) *Design For Play: A Guide to Creating Successful Play Places*, Play England: Department for Children, Schools & Families, http://www.playengland.org.uk/media/70684/design-for-play.pdf (accessed 30 December 2018).

Skenazy, L. (2010) *Free-Range Kids: How to Raise Safe, Self-Reliant Children*. New York: Jossey-Bass.

Stanley, F., Richardson, S. and Prior, M. (2005) *Children of the Lucky Country? How Australian Society Turned its Back on Children and Why Children Matter*. Melbourne: Pan Macmillan.

Talen, E. and Coffindaffer, M. (1999) 'The utopianism of children: an empirical study of children's neighbourhood design preferences', *Journal of Planning Education and Research*, 18, 321–331.

Tranter, P. and Sharpe, S. (2007) 'Children and peak oil: an opportunity in crisis', *International Journal of Children's Rights*, 15, 181–197.

US National Wildlife Federation (2010) *Whole Child: Developing Mind, Body and Spirit Through Outdoor Play*. Reston, VA: NWF.

Walsh, P. (2006) 'Creating child-friendly play places: a practitioner's perspective'. In: Gleeson, B. and Sipe, N. (eds), *Creating Child Friendly Cities: Reinstating Kids in the City*. London: Routledge, pp. 136–150.

Ward, C. (1978) *The Child in the City*. London: The Architectural Press.

Woolcock, G. and Steele, W. (2008) *Towards the Development of an Indicators Framework for a Child-friendly Community – Literature Review*. Report Commissioned by the NSW Commission for Children & Young People, NSW, Australia.

5. Planning for third places through evidence-based urban development

Elizelle Juaneé Cilliers

PUBLIC SPACE FOR PUBLIC USE

Planning as a profession has evolved from a designing art to a multi-disciplinary science. It encompasses many different disciplines under a single umbrella, with the aim of changing spaces into liveable, functional places. Normative theories of spatial planning dealt with the question of how to create the ideal urban place (Lynch 1960), defined in terms of the values and benefits it offers to communities and surrounding environments (Stein 2003 p. 4). Today, planning is seen as the management of change, a political process by which a balance is sought between all interests involved, public and private, to resolve conflicting demands on space. Planning's multi-disciplinary approach therefore aims to view the urban environment holistically, identifying and acknowledging all impacting elements, forces and functions that co-exist in this complex continuum in order to create a sustainable, liveable, future environment.

The continuous process of anticipating and preparing for foreseeable future changes (Wyporek 2000 p. 7) lies at the core of the planning profession. The complexity of spatial planning processes has recently become even more complex because modern, highly-developed societies are becoming increasingly dynamic with regard to social, sustainability and economic issues (people, planet, profit), and societies want their urban environments to be a reflection of their needs, demands and preferences. Paradoxically, urban environments are traditionally slow changing environments, hosting societies that are increasingly becoming more dynamic (see Figure 5.1), in line with constantly changing community needs (Barendse et al. 2007 p. 3). Planning therefore facilitates changes in society, and it concerns the most important aspects of life, namely people.

However, with current population growth and increasing urbanisation pressures, our public spaces suggest a loss of quality and function, especially in city centres where such spaces are often competing against other, more pressing, land uses for commercial and development purposes. Our societies and cities now call for an approach to reclaim public space for public use, to revisit the concept of third places, to provide opportunities for people to meet and interact and to develop a sense of belonging to a place. Third places, manifesting as a component of good public spaces, are argued to be a vital ingredient of successful cities, enhancing civic identity, cultural identity, quality of life, social capital, economic development and community revitalisation (PPS 2012 p. 1; Beck 2009 p. 240; Liu et al. 2007 p. 1; Kazmierczak et al. 2010; Woolley et al. 2003). Third places, as defined by Oldenburg (1999 p. 41), are a general designation for various different public places that host regular, informal and voluntary meetings or gatherings of individuals and communities outside the work and home realm. As such, third places are set to create the framework for public life, and if planned correctly, these spaces not only provide aesthetically pleasing escapes, but also enhance the emotional well-being of the city's residents, as well as advancing the interests of social justice and inclusion. Although there is a broad theoretical base for understanding the importance of such public spaces in modern societies, there are relatively few studies demonstrating models for planning and facilitating third places. This chapter employs theory-based sampling as part of a qualitative enquiry into three core public place planning approaches, namely place-making, green planning and lively planning, as points of departure for rethinking the planning of third places.

Theoretical sampling emerged with the foundation of grounded theory, implying a pragmatic purpose of generating a theory (Glaser and Strauss 1967). Theory-based sampling was employed as part of this research to conduct a qualitative enquiry into three core planning approaches aiming to enhance the planning of public places. For the purposes of this research, the approaches of: (1) place-making, (2) green planning, and (3) lively planning were considered and captured accordingly.

PLACE-MAKING APPROACHES

The core of the practice of place-making is the advocacy of a return of public space to people (Silberberg et al. 2013). Place-making is the process by which people transform the locations they inhabit into the places they live (PPS 2007). The academic literature on place and the related idea of place-making is growing swiftly across a spectrum of multiple professions (Friedmann 2010 p. 152), as place-making capitalises on a local community's assets, inspiration and potential, ultimately creating good public spaces that promote people's health, happiness, and well-being.

Place-making aims to create places to socialise and interact, building upon the belief that when cities and neighbourhoods have thriving public spaces, residents have a strong sense of community. Human congress, in this sense, is the genius of the place, its reason for being, and its marginal edge (Whyte 1980 p. 341). The objective of place-making is to create such spaces, based on the premise that successful public spaces function for the people who use them (PPS 2009 p. 10). Third places, our public spaces, have long been studied and celebrated by urban theorists, emphasising the important role public spaces play in creating necessary 'social friction', the interaction between different groups of people who would otherwise not meet (Silberberg et al. 2013). From a strong social perspective, place-making approaches are built upon design considerations of access, comfort and image, uses and activities, and sociability (PPS 2009). These considerations are described in Table 5.1, together with the design elements of each, as well as evaluation criteria.

GREEN PLANNING APPROACHES

Green planning refers to the strategic planning of green spaces, green infrastructure and green networks as part of spatial planning approaches. Green planning is gaining importance as the relationship between urban liveability and green spaces is incorporated in overall urban green structures, and it has recently become the focus of international studies (Casepersen et al. 2006 p. 7). The direct and indirect benefits of such green spaces within the urban environment are well documented and are motivations for sustaining the green and natural environment. The value of green spaces, especially in terms of public space usage, is emphasised by social benefits (Thaiutsa et al. 2008; Cilliers and Timmermans 2013; Luttik 2000), environmental benefits (Bolund and Hunhammer 1999; Stiles 2006; Yang et al. 2005) and economic benefits (Stiles 2006; Cilliers et al. 2011; Rodenberg et al. 2001). As such, many new green planning approaches have been introduced in the last couple of years in an attempt to strengthen the green identity and green values within cities and neighbourhoods (Cilliers et al. 2011; Cilliers and Timmermans 2013; Cilliers et al. 2013). From a strong environmental perspective, green planning approaches are primarily built upon design considerations of green infrastructure and the strategies for building urban resilience, namely through multi-functionality, redundancy, diversity, multi-scale networks and adaptive planning. These elements are captured in Table 5.2, along with the design elements and evaluation criteria.

Table 5.1   Design considerations of place-making approaches

Design considerations	Design elements	Evaluation criteria
Access	Physical entrance and exit to and from the space Visibility and perception of safety Proximity to other functions and spaces Internal and external connectedness of the space Walkable spaces Linkages to other networks	Movement patterns Movement data
Comfort and image	Perceptions about safety and cleanliness Overall character of the space Availability of public furniture and facilities Convenient spaces Attractive, with aesthetic values Enhancing cultural elements Pedestrian scale	Environmental statistics Site analysis
Uses and activities	The basic building blocks of the place Unique characteristics Unique selling point Active spaces Function connected to space Transitions	Land-use patterns Property values Market analysis
Sociability	The synergy that injects a public space with life Sense of place that fosters social activities Diverse uses Interactive, welcoming spaces Draws on a diverse community and population	Street life patterns Social analysis Sense of place

Source: PPS (2009); Lanham (2007); Silberberg et al. (2013); City of Tempe (2015).

LIVELY PLANNING APPROACHES

Lively planning is a controversial planning approach, focusing on including lively elements, functions and linkages to enhance the usage of urban spaces. The lively planning approach recognises the need for an integrated approach, incorporating the city-scale, neighbourhood-scale, site-scale, and regional cross-boundary scale, together with key attributes and elements. From a strong integrated perspective, lively planning approaches are primarily built upon design considerations, including planning

Table 5.2   Design considerations of green planning approaches

Design considerations	Design elements	Evaluation criteria
Multi-functionality	Multiple eco-system services	Site analysis
	Combined services	Ecological data
Redundancy	Availability of alternative sources	Network analysis
	Infrastructure is decentralised	
	Resilient to disturbances	
Diversity	Biodiversity	Bio-physical analysis
	Social and functional diversity	
Multi-scale networks	Connectivity	Land-use patterns
	Interconnected systems	Zonings
	Integration between blue-green networks	
Adaptive planning	Flexibility	Potential analysis
	Innovation and experimental design	

Source: Ahern (2007, 2011); Carmin et al. (2012); Harrison et al. (2014); Pauleit et al. (2011); Cilliers and Cilliers (2016).

elements linked to the virtual dimension, the marketing dimension and the functional dimension, the environmental dimension, the social dimension and the psychological dimension, the visual dimension and the movement dimension, as captured in Table 5.3.

THE INTERFACE BETWEEN PLACE-MAKING, LIVELY PLANNING AND GREEN PLANNING APPROACHES

A comparative analysis of the three core approaches included in this research enabled the identification of overlapping and correlating thematic issues. Table 5.4 captures the interface between place-making, lively planning and green planning approaches, based on the design considerations of each approach. It captures a synthesis of the interface between the three approaches, re-coded into an integrative approach to be used in the empirical section of this research.

While these approaches of place-making, green planning and lively planning have been much theorised, there is limited research on the interface between them, as well as how such interface could guide planning practice. There are relatively few studies which demonstrate models for planning and facilitating third places as part of broader spatial planning

Table 5.3   Design considerations of lively planning approaches

Design considerations	Design elements	Evaluation criteria
Virtual dimension	Informative spaces Connected spaces Driven by the digital world and 'virtual spaces'	Virtual reality of space Social media analysis
Marketing dimension	Vitality of the space Quality of life Unique selling point	Land-use values Market analysis
Functional dimension	Flexible uses for various users Quantity and quality of functions	Land-use analysis
Environmental dimension	Sustainable development approaches Green initiatives and potential	Site analysis
Social dimension	Social cohesion Opportunities for interaction Sense of community	Stakeholder analysis
Psychological dimension	Range of experiences Sense of place	Stakeholder analysis
Sound dimension	Atmosphere Noise	Soundscaping
Visual dimension	Colour and texture Diversity of scale	Site analysis
Movement dimension	Providing mixed-use spaces Pedestrian friendly and walkable Design driven by linkages and movements	Movement analysis Stakeholder analysis

Source: Cilliers et al. (2015); Kaymaz (2013); Catalyst Architecture (2009 p. 27); Berger-Schmitt (2000).

approaches. This chapter aims to consider evidence-based research to identify best practices based on the above-mentioned integrative approaches (re-coded elements), to guide the planning of third places, in an attempt to reclaim public space for public use.

EVIDENCE-BASED RESEARCH

Evidence-based practice has emerged as one means of helping to bridge the gap between traditional practice and formal research (Krizek et al. 2009 p. 460). Most commonly, it is proposed as a way of making professional

Table 5.4   Synthesis of planning approaches along with re-coded design elements

Place-making	Green planning	Lively planning	Re-coded (integrative approach)
Sociability[1]	Social	Diverse users[1]	[1] Social spaces
Synergy[1]	diversity[1]	Social cohesion[1]	Sociability level
Sense of place[1]	Multi-scale	Interaction[1]	Sense of place
Social activities[1]	networks[2]	Sense of community[1]	Quantity social activities
Diverse uses[1]	Connectivity[2]	Psychological[1]	Quality social activities
Interactive[1]	Interconnected	Experiences[1]	Diverse uses
Welcoming	systems[2]	Sense of place[1]	Diverse users
spaces[1]	Integration[2]	Perception of space[1]	Convenience level
Diverse	Alternative	Perceived safety[1]	Level of social cohesion
community[1]	sources[2]	Accessibility[1]	Safety perceptions
Uses[1]	Multi-	Sound dimension[1]	Sound ranking
Activities[1]	functional[3]	Atmosphere[1]	Context-driven
Building blocks[2]	Eco-system	Marketing[2]	(cultural)
Uniqueness[2]	services[3]	Vitality[2]	
Selling point[2]	Combined	Quality of life[2]	[2] Economic spaces
Active spaces[1]	services[3]	Unique selling point[2]	Unique selling point
Function of space[2]	Infrastructure	Sustainable	Marketability
Transitions[2]	decentralised[3]	development[3]	Diverse functions
Comfort and	Resilience[3]	Green initiatives[3]	Proximity
image[3]	Biodiversity[3]	Green potential[3]	Alternative sources
Safety	Adaptive	Green networks[3]	Vitality ranking
perceptions[1]	planning[4]	Virtual dimension[4]	Quality of life
Cleanliness[3]	Flexibility[4]	Informative spaces[4]	
Overall character[3]	Innovation[4]	Connected spaces[4]	[3] Environmental spaces
Public furniture[4]	Experimental	Digital spaces[4]	Image of space
Public facilities[4]	design[4]	Functional[4]	Character ranking
Convenient	Functional	Flexible uses[1]	Aesthetic values
spaces[1]	diversity[4]	Quantity functions[4]	Biodiversity ranking
Attractive spaces[3]		Quality functions[4]	Green initiatives
Aesthetic values[3]		Visual dimension[3]	Green networks
Cultural elements[1]		Colour[3]	
Pedestrian scale[1]		Texture[3]	[4] Physical spaces
Access[4]		Creative combinations[4]	Quantity public facilities
Physical entrance[4]		Diversity of scale[4]	Quality public facilities
Visibility[4]		Movement[4]	Accessibility to space
Proximity[4]		Mixed-use spaces[2]	Movement in space
Connectedness[4]		Pedestrian friendly[1]	Visibility
External linkages[4]		Walkable[1]	Virtual dimension
Walkable spaces[1]		Design driven[4]	Design driven
		Linkages[4]	Diversity of scale

Note: Theory-based sampling recoded to 1: Social spaces, 2: Economic spaces, 3: Environmental spaces, 4: Physical spaces.

decision making more scientifically rational, and it draws on a wide variety of research methods linked to collaborative and participatory approaches that place a greater emphasis on jointly defining problems and consensus-based solutions (Healey 2003). It can enrich the field of planning by linking research to practice (Krizek et al. 2009 p. 460). As such, case studies (evidence-based practice) were considered in this research, and best practices relating to the theory-based sampling and re-coded design elements of the integrative three planning approaches were identified and are included. As a result, evidence-based research identified best practices relating to these design elements, which in turn, informs the planning of third places. Five case studies were included in the evidence-based research. These case studies include three spaces in Belgium, namely the public space Jardin de la Maison in Namur, public space Louvain-La-Neuve and a public parking lot, Place du Cardinal Mercier in Wavre, as well as a residential neighbourhood in Eindhoven, the Netherlands, and a child-friendly space in Ikageng, South Africa.

These cases were purposefully selected to identify best practices relating to the re-coded design elements in Table 5.4. The research does not elaborate on all elements but does elaborate on elements considered best practices within the specific case in order to draw conclusions, and to inform the further planning of third places.

Public Space Jardin de la Maison, Namur, Belgium

Jardin de la Maison is a green open space in the city of Namur, located adjacent to the river that runs through the city's centre. Originally this urban green space was not very visible to residents, lacking adequate signage, safety and maintenance. It was not frequently used and was identified as a neglected urban space in need of transformation. A redesign transformed the space into a more user-friendly and qualitative space, where social life and green public spaces were emphasised. Landscape elements (an urban garden), aesthetic aspects (an enhanced view of the river, the use of colour and urban furniture) and activities (attractions and an inviting design) were introduced, along with adequate public furniture to attract users and create a sense of place. The transformation process of the public open place Jardin de la Maison in Namur is shown in Figure 5.1, illustrating the space in relation to surrounding buildings prior to transformation, during transformation and after transformation, capturing the social function and use connected to the space as a direct result of the design.

Based on theory-based sampling and re-coded design elements, the best practices that were evident in the redesign of the Jardin de la Maison public space were identified. These practices are captured in Table 5.5.

Source: The author and CI in conjunction with the LICI research team 2014.

Figure 5.1   Public place Jardin de la Maison in Namur before, during and after redesign

Table 5.5   Best practice evaluation of re-coded design elements in Jardin de la Maison

Re-coded (Integrative approach)	Best practices from case study	
[1] Social spaces	Sociability level	Transformation to relaxation space
	Sense of place	Transformation of reclaimed public space for public use
	Convenience level	Provision of public furniture
	Safety perceptions	Nature-based solutions to enhance safety of space
	Sound ranking	Enclosed from bypassing city traffic
[2] Economic spaces	Proximity	Central location in city
	Quality of life	Transformation to social, recreational space
[3] Environmental spaces	Image of space	Integration of natural textures and green networks
	Aesthetic values	Natural space, view of river and integration of colours
	Biodiversity ranking	Transformation and inclusion of green infrastructure
[4] Physical spaces	Accessibility to space	Central location with accessibility from various points
	Design driven	Nature-based design approach
	Diversity of scale	Considering human scale in design

Note: Theory-based sampling recoded to 1: Social spaces, 2: Economic spaces, 3: Environmental spaces, 4: Physical spaces.

Public Space Louvain-La-Neuve (Belgium)

Place des Wallons in Louvain-La-Neuve (Belgium) is a public space within the University City. This space was recently transformed from a walkthrough area to a public space with a social function. The redesign focused on increasing movement patterns during both daytime and night-time. To enable increased movement, diverse functions and facilities were incorporated to enhance accessibility and visibility, such as the snake-shaped placement of the seating, which interrupted movement patterns. The redesign entailed a strong green planning focus, introducing green initiatives such as the city tree initiative that strengthened sense of place, as well as green graffiti and green roofs which enhanced the identity of the area and strengthened the green network. The space was transformed to a functional space with mixed uses, stimulating socialisation and social cohesion within the area. The transformation process of the public Louvain-La-Neuve is illustrated in Figure 5.2, capturing the space in relation to surrounding buildings prior to transformation, during trans-formation and after transformation, capturing the spatial interventions (furniture and green initiatives).

Source: The author and CI in conjunction with the LICI research team 2012.

Figure 5.2   Public space Louvain-La-Neuve before, during and after redesign

Based on theory-based sampling and re-coded design elements, the best practices that were evident in the redesign of the public space Louvain-La-Neuve were identified. These practices are captured in Table 5.6.

Public Parking Lot Place du Cardinal Mercier in Wavre (Belgium)

Place du Cardinal Mercier is a public parking area (open space), located in the city centre of Wavre, thus in close proximity to commercial, cultural and entertaining spaces. Apart from its core function of providing park-ing space, it was occasionally utilised for public markets. However, the central location of this space called for a better use of space. A redesign

Table 5.6   Best practice evaluation of re-coded design elements in Louvain-La-Neuve

Re-coded (integrative approach)	Best practices from case study	
[1] Social spaces	Sense of place	Transformed from mono-functional to multi-functional
	Diverse users	Accommodating a diverse community
	Convenience level	Adequate creative public furniture provided
	Sound ranking	Natural elements to enhance sound elements
	Context-driven (cultural)	Focused on university students transiting
[2] Economic spaces	Proximity	Walking distance to university and commercial facilities
	Alternative sources	Incorporating green roofs and green infrastructure
[3] Environmental spaces	Image of space	Enhanced by CityTree initiative
	Character ranking	Creative redesign with colourful public furniture
	Aesthetic values	Focus on visible design criteria
	Biodiversity ranking	Inclusion of green CityTrees and green graffiti
	Green initiatives	CityTrees with adequate natural support features
[4] Physical spaces	Quantity public facilities	Functional space with mixed uses
	Movement in space	Enhance movement patterns
	Design driven	Green element orientated design

Note: Theory-based sampling recoded to 1: Social spaces, 2: Economic spaces, 3: Environmental spaces, 4: Physical spaces.

transformed the space into a temporary, qualitative, usable public open space and urban garden named 'Jardin Urbain'. The transformation process included the hard space being transformed into a soft, green open space, covering it with grass for a limited time period. The transformation included public furniture, and pictures, bright colours and the creation of a play area for children. Figure 5.3 captures the transformation process that was applied in Place du Cardinal Mercier in Wavre, as perceived prior to the transformation, and after completion of the transformation.

Source: The author and CI in conjunction with the LICI research team 2014.

Figure 5.3   Place du Cardinal Mercier in Wavre before and after redesign

Based on the theory-based sampling and re-coded design elements, the best practices that were evident in the redesign of the Place du Cardinal Mercier were identified and are captured in Table 5.7.

Residential Neighbourhood in Eindhoven (Netherlands)

Doornakkers, a residential neighbourhood in Eindhoven (the Netherlands), was characterised by the 'normal' urban complexities of degeneration and shortage of qualitative social and public spaces. This neighbourhood was redesigned to include a qualitative green environment and a network of green spaces, providing adequate qualitative public spaces and redeveloping the 'new heart' of Doornakkers. An initiative for intervention was proposed as part of the redesign and planning process of the neighbourhood space, with the aim of increasing the use of spaces in this area, focusing on movement patterns and accessibility to and from public spaces. The green identity formed a core part of the redesign as it emphasised connectivity and linkages (through green walking routes) with other green networks (green zones) within and around the area. A variety of functions was

Source: The author and CI in conjunction with the LICI research team 2012.

*Figure 5.4   Public spaces in the Doornakkers neighbourhood during and
                after redesign*

*Table 5.7   Best practice evaluation of re-coded design elements in Place du
Cardinal Mercier*

Re-coded (integrative approach)	Best practices from case study	
[1] Social spaces	Sociability level	Transformed from mono-functional to multi-functional
	Sense of place	Creation of inviting public space in city centre
	Quantity social activities	Variety activities from play and recreation to relaxation
	Quality social activities	Qualitative green approach with public furniture
	Diverse users	Accommodate whole community
	Context-driven (cultural)	User-need transformation of space
[2] Economic spaces	Unique selling point	Social space in commercial hub
	Proximity	Located within city centre
[3] Environmental spaces	Image of space	Green design as focus point of public space
	Aesthetic values	Nature-based transformation
	Green initiatives	Temporary transformation to raise green awareness
[4] Physical spaces	Accessibility to space	Proximity to commercial hub
	Virtual dimension	Wi-Fi provision in the space

Note: Theory-based sampling recoded to 1: Social spaces, 2: Economic spaces,
3: Environmental spaces, 4: Physical spaces.

included to accommodate a diverse user group. The transformation process of the area is illustrated in Figure 5.4, capturing the space in relation
to surrounding networks during transformation and after transformation,
illustrating the green networks and green initiatives introduced.

Based on the theory-based sampling and re-coded design elements,
the best practices that were evident in the redesign of the public spaces in
Doornakkers were identified and are captured in Table 5.8.

Child-friendly Space in Ikageng (South Africa)

The King's Kids Nursery School is a primary school situated in Ikageng, a
rural suburb of the town of Potchefstroom, South Africa. The school houses

Table 5.8   Best practice evaluation of re-coded design elements in Doornakkers

Re-coded (integrative approach)	Best practices from case study	
1 Social spaces	Quantity social activities	Range of social and public spaces within neighbourhood
	Diverse users	Accommodate neighbourhood population
	Safety perceptions	Green corridors enhance movement patterns
2 Economic spaces	Marketability	Neighbourhood value increase
	Diverse functions	Social, recreational, relaxation functions provided
	Quality of life	Neighbourhood level design approaches
3 Environmental spaces	Character ranking	Overall neighbourhood character transformed
	Aesthetic values	Nature-based solutions introduced
	Biodiversity ranking	Green corridors created
	Green initiatives	Green walking routes, green zones
	Green networks	Neighbourhood design a green network
4 Physical spaces	Quantity public facilities	Variety of facilities planned holistically
	Movement in space	Supported by green corridors
	Diversity of scale	Walkability and pedestrian-level orientated

Note: Theory-based sampling recoded to 1: Social spaces, 2: Economic spaces, 3: Environmental spaces, 4: Physical spaces.

approximately 90 toddlers who are cared for in the poorest of circumstances. The Equilibria School of Life participated in the transformation of this functionless space and transformed it into a child-friendly space with diverse functions and activities for children. Intervention included ways to enhance activities within the space, the introduction of colour and function and providing a safe play space for the children. The transformation process of the area is illustrated in Figure 5.5, capturing the space in relation to surrounding networks prior to transformation and after transformation, illustrating the change of use, green initiatives and activities.

Based on theory-based sampling and re-coded design elements, the best practices that were evident in the redesign of the public space in Ikageng were identified, as captured in Table 5.9.

Source: The author 2015.

Figure 5.5   Public space in Ikageng before, during and after redesign

Table 5.9   Best practice evaluation of re-coded design elements in Ikageng

Re-coded (integrative approach)	Best practices from case study	
[1] Social spaces	Sense of place	Created sense of belonging for children
	Quality social activities	Age-related child infrastructure provided
	Safety perceptions	Primary concern for children stakeholder group
	Context-driven (cultural)	Rural community focus
[2] Economic spaces	Unique selling point	Play space in rural community
	Vitality ranking	Educational and recreational benefits for children
[3] Environmental spaces	Aesthetic values	Colourful and energetic space
	Green initiatives	Natural play space created
[4] Physical spaces	Movement in space	Enhanced free mobility for children stakeholder group
	Diversity of scale	Focused on child-level planning

Note: Theory-based sampling recoded to 1: Social spaces, 2: Economic spaces, 3: Environmental spaces, 4: Physical spaces.

INGREDIENTS FOR PLANNING THIRD PLACES

A synthesis of the five case studies and evaluations of each in terms of the re-coded design elements led to the identification of best practices based on the frequency of use of each element. Table 5.10 captures the combined best practices identified in the case studies, in relation to the frequency of usage within the five case studies, as well as the re-coded design elements that were considered.

Table 5.10   Synthesis of best practice identification in five case studies

Re-coded (integrative approach)	Re-coded design elements	Frequent usage	Best practices
[1] Social spaces	Sociability level	2	From mono-functional to multi-functional
	Sense of place	4	Reclaimed public space for public use
	Quantity social activities	2	Variety of activities to be introduced in single space
	Quality social activities	3	Nature-based solutions seem adequate
	Diverse uses	0	Linked to activities provided
	Diverse users	3	Accommodating a diverse community
	Convenience level	2	Adequate creative public furniture provided
	Level of social cohesion	0	Indirect result of planning and transformation
	Safety perceptions	3	Nature-based solutions to enhance safety of space
	Sound ranking	2	Enclosed and natural elements enhance sound element
	Context-driven (cultural)	3	User needs (specific) transformation of space
[2] Economic spaces	Unique selling point	2	Contradicting spaces (social-commercial)
	Marketability	1	Neighbourhood value to be emphasised
	Diverse functions	1	Social, recreational, relaxation functions provided
	Proximity	3	Centrality is core
	Alternative sources	1	Incorporating green roofs and green infrastructure
	Vitality ranking	1	Educational and recreational benefits inclusion
	Quality of life	2	Integrative design considerations
[3] Environmental spaces	Image of space	3	Integration of natural textures and green networks
	Character ranking	2	Creative redesign with colourful public furniture
	Aesthetic values	5	Nature-based solutions primary consideration

Table 5.10   (continued)

Re-coded (integrative approach)	Re-coded design elements	Frequent usage	Best practices
	Biodiversity ranking	3	Transformation and inclusion of green infrastructure
	Green initiatives	4	Raise green awareness through creative ideas
	Green networks	1	Holistic planning considerations
[4] Physical spaces	Quantity public facilities	2	Functional space with mixed uses
	Quality public facilities	0	Needs to be defined according to context
	Accessibility to space	2	Proximity to commercial hub and networks
	Movement in space	3	Enhanced free mobility for all stakeholders
	Visibility	0	Good design would attract users
	Virtual dimension	1	Wi-Fi provision in the space
	Design driven	2	Nature-based design approach found beneficial
	Diversity of scale	3	Considering human scale in design

From this synthesis various conclusions were drawn, informed by the theoretical and empirical investigations. The research agrees that third places form part of the constructed environment that contributes to the conditions of living (Jeffers et al. 2009 p. 334). However, as third places (or related public places) are not enforced by policy or legislation (and are sometimes even restricted by zoning controls), their successful planning and implementation is often constrained.

It is time to rethink the planning of third places. The social component should be emphasised not only as part of needs analysis, but as part of design. From the case study synthesis, the core design elements to consider when planning third places (based on frequency of usage in the selected case studies) include aesthetic values, sense of place, green initiatives, quality social activities and diverse users, as captured in Table 5.11.

Based on four themes, the conclusions of this research into the planning of third places include that:

1. A sense of community is enforced by a sense of place.
2. The quality of the space is perceived in terms of aesthetics values (image of the space, strongly supported by green initiatives), diversity of scale (acknowledging human-scale planning) and the safety of the space as perceived from the diverse users of the space.
3. The function of the space should be directly linked to the context-driven cultural design. Contrary to literature, this research did not find visibility to be an important design consideration in the planning of third places.
4. Usage aims to include diverse users and not necessarily diverse uses. It is about the quality of social activities, not about the quality of public facilities. The opportunities for social activity are ranked far above and beyond the physical equipment provided.

Ultimately it was concluded that as a result of the current interdisciplinary environment, there is an increasing need for integrated planning approaches

Table 5.11   Design elements to consider when planning third places

Aesthetic values	In all five cases this was evident, in line with the findings of Thaiutsa et al. (2008) and Soholt (2004 p. 28) stating the importance of aesthetics when considering the success of a public place.
Sense of place	In four cases, the importance of creating sense of place was emphasised. According to Loudier and Dubois (2001), appearance and function connected to the space is central in this regard. Sense of place manifests as attractive designs seeking interest (Cilliers et al. 2015).
Green initiatives	In four cases, green initiatives were strongly emphasised. Such initiatives bring many important environmental benefits to urban areas (Future of Places 2015; Stiles 2006; Bolund and Hunhammer 1999), emphasising why environmental considerations have become an integral part of developmental thinking and decision making (Weiland et al. 2005).
Quality social activities	The cases illustrated the importance of providing quality social activities, supporting the findings of Loudier and Dubois (2001 p. 6) who stated the importance of providing socialisation opportunities within public open spaces.
Diverse users	The research confirmed that the challenge is to create open spaces for people whose needs are constantly changing, and for a society which is becoming more dynamic (Barendse et al. 2007 p. 3). Differing strengths of spaces that will attract skills, knowledge and creativity should be explored (Choe and Roberts 2011 p. 2).

(Sutanta et al. 2009 p. 1). Finding interfaces between concepts of place-making, green planning and lively planning can inform the planning of third places. The creation of third places, as a vital component of urban life, should be a cross-cutting theme present within all planning scales, driven by the various benefits which such spaces provide to communities and their hosting cities. To change life, we must first change spaces into third places.

ACKNOWLEDGEMENTS

This research (or parts thereof) was made possible by the financial contribution of the NRF (National Research Foundation), South Africa. Any opinion, findings and conclusions or recommendations expressed in this material are those of the author(s) and therefore the NRF does not accept any liability in regard thereto.

REFERENCES

Ahern J. 2007. Green infrastructure for cities: The spatial dimension. In Novotny, V. and Brown, P. (eds) *Cities of the Future Towards Integrated Sustainable Water and Landscape Management*. IWA Publishing, London, UK, pp. 267–283.

Ahern J. 2011. From fail-safe to safe-to-fail: Sustainability and resilience in the new urban world. *Landscape and Urban Planning*, 100(4): 341–343.

Barendse, P., Duerink, S. and Govaart, Y. 2007. A multi stakeholder collaborative urban planning model. ENHR 2007 International Conference 'Sustainable Urban Areas', Workshop 21: Tools to facilitate housing and urban processes. Rotterdam.

Beck, H. 2009. Linking the quality of public spaces to quality of life. *Journal of Place Management and Development*, 2(3): 240–248.

Berger-Schmitt, R. 2000. Social cohesion as an aspect of the quality of societies: Concept and measurement. EuReporting Working Paper No. 14. Centre for Survey Research and Methodology (ZUMA), Mannheim.

Bolund, P. and Hunhammar, S. 1999. Ecosystem services in urban areas. *Ecological Economics*, 29(2): 293–301.

Carmin, J., Anguelovski, I. and Roberts, D. 2012. Urban climate adaptation in the global south: Planning in an emerging policy domain. *Journal of Planning Education and Research* 32(1): 18–32.

Casepersen, O.H., Konijnendijk, C.C. and Olafsson, A.S. 2006. Green-space planning and land use: An assessment of urban regional and green structure planning in Greater Copenhagen. *Geografisk Tidsskrift, Danish Journal of Geography*, 106(2): 7–20.

Catalyst Architecture. 2009. Eco-logical placemaking. http://catalystarchitecture.com/presentations.html (accessed 10 December 2016).

Choe, K. and Roberts, B. 2011. Competitive cities in the 21st century: Cluster-based local economic development. Asian Development Bank, Mandaluyong City, Philippines.

Cilliers, E.J. and Cilliers, S.S. 2016. Planning for green infrastructure: Options for South African cities. South African Cities Network, August 2016, Johannesburg.

Cilliers, E.J. and Timmermans, W. 2013. Approaching value added planning in the green environment. *Journal of Place Management and Development*, 6(2): 144–154.

Cilliers, S.S., Cilliers, E.J., Lubbe, C.E. and Siebert, S.J. 2013. Ecosystem services of urban green spaces in African countries: Perspectives and challenges. *Urban Ecosystems*, 16(4): 681–702.

Cilliers, E.J., Diemont, E., Stobbelaar, D.J. and Timmermans, W. 2011. Enhancing sustainable development by means of the Workbench Method. *Environment and Planning B: Planning and Design*, 38(4): 579–584.

Cilliers, E.J., Timmermans, W., Vandden Goorbergh, F. and Slijkhuis, J.S.A. 2015. Green place-making in practice: From temporary spaces to permanent places. *Journal of Urban Design*, 20(3): 349–366.

City of Tempe. 2015. Placemaking design principles and guidelines. Alameda, City of Tempe, Arizona. https://www.tempe.gov/home/showdocument?id=36132 (accessed 3 June 2017).

Friedmann, J. 2010. Place and place-making in cities: A global perspective. *Planning Theory and Practice*, 11(2): 149–165.

Future of Places. 2015. Benefits of public space. http://futureofplaces.com/wp-content/uploads/2015/04/FoP_Benefits-of-Public-Space.pdf (accessed 10 September 2015).

Glaser, B. and Strauss, A. 1967. *The Discovery of Grounded Theory: Strategies for Qualitative Research*. Aldine Transactions, Aldine Publishing: Chicago.

Harrison, P., Bobbins, K., Culwick, C., Humby, T., La Mantia, C., Todes, A. and Weakley, D. 2014. *Resilience Thinking for Municipalities*. University of the Witwatersrand, Gauteng City-Region Observatory.

Healey, P. 2003. Collaborative planning in perspective. *Planning Theory*, 2(2): 101–123.

Jansen, R. and Ruifrok, R.J. 2012. Green solutions for public spaces: For city managers and placemakers. Thesis Management Exterior, University of Applied Sciences, Van Hall Larensteun. ABTRepro, Arnhem, pp. 80.

Jeffers, L.W., Bracken, C.C., Jian, G. and Casey, M.F. 2009. The impact of third places on community quality of life. *Applied Research in Quality of Life*, 4(4): 333–345.

Kaymaz, I. 2013. Urban landscapes and identity. In Ozyavuz, M. (ed.) *Advances in Landscape Architecture*. IntechOpen, Chapter 29, pp. 739–760.

Kazmierczak, A.E., Armitage, R.P. and James, P. 2010. Urban green spaces: Natural and accessible? The case of Greater Manchester, UK. In Muller, N., Werner, P. and Kelcey, J.G. (eds) *Urban Biodiversity and Design*. Conservation Science and Practice Series, Wiley-Blackwell: Oxford, pp. 383–405.

Krizek, K., Forsyth, A. and Slotterback, C.S. (2009). Is there a role for evidence-based practice in urban planning and policy? *Planning Theory and Practice*, 10: 459–478.

Lanham, K.F. 2007. Planning as placemaking: Tensions of scale, culture and identity. Major Paper Submitted to Virginia Polytechnic Institute and State University, School of Public and International Affairs, College of Architecture and Urban Studies. April 2007.

LICI. 2014. Lively Cities Project. Reclaim public space for public use. http://www.lively-cities.eu/urban-lifestyle-point-ulp-rubrique-15-2.htm (accessed 30 December 2018).

Liu, Z., Mao, F., Zhou, W., Li, Q., Haung, J. and Zhu, X. 2007. Accessibility assessment of urban green space: A quantitative perspective. Conference: IEEE International Geoscience and Remote Sensing Symposium, IGARSS 2008, 8–11 July 2008, Boston, MA, Proceedings.

Loudier, C. and Dubois, J.L. 2001. Public spaces: Between insecurity and hospitality. Les Cahiers de l'Institut d'aménagement et d'urbanisme de la région d'Île-de-France, pp. 20–25.

Luttik, J. 2000. The value of trees, water and open spaces as reflected by house prices in the Netherlands. *Landscape and Urban Planning*, 48: 161–167.

Lynch, K. 1960. *The Image of the City*. MIT Press, Cambridge, MA.

Oldenburg, R. 1999. *The Great Good Place: Cafes, Coffee Shops, Bookstores, Bars, Hair Salons, and Other Hangouts at the Heart of a Community* (3rd edn). Da Capo Press, Cambridge, MA.

Pauleit, S., Liu, L., Ahern, J. and Kazmierczak, A. 2011. Multifunctional green infrastructure to promote ecological services in the city. In Niemela, J. (ed.) *Urban Ecology: Patterns, Processes and Applications*. Oxford University Press, New York, pp. 272–285.

PPS (Project for public spaces). 2007. Project for Public Spaces, Place-making tools. https://www.pps.org/article/what-is-placemaking (accessed 4 September 2017).

PPS (Project for public spaces). 2009. Project for Public Spaces, Why public spaces fail. https://www.pps.org/article/failedplacefeat (accessed 4 September 2017).

PPS (Project for public spaces). 2012. Project for Public Spaces, Placemaking and the future of cities. https://www.pps.org/article/placemaking-and-the-future-of-cities (accessed 10 December 2017).

Rodenburg, C., Baycan-Levent, T., van Leeuwen, E. and Nijkamp, P. 2001. Urban economic indicators for green development in cities. *Greener Management International*, 36: 105–119.

Silberberg, S., Lorah, K., Disbrow, R. and Meussig, A. 2013. Places in the making: How placemaking builds places and communities. MIT Department of Urban Studies and Planning. Massachusetts Institute of Technology. https://dusp.mit.edu/sites/dusp.mit.edu/files/attachments/project/mit-dusp-places-in-the-making.pdf (accessed 3 June 2017).

Soholt, H. 2004. Life, spaces and buildings – turning the traditional planning process upside down. Walk21-V Cities for People, 5th International Conference on Walking in the 21st Century, 9–11 June 2004, Copenhagen, Denmark.

Stein, N. 2003. Urban design between theory and practise: From conceptualisation to realisation and back again. Paper for the AESOP-ACSP Third Joint Conference, Leuven, Belgium, 8–12 July.

Stiles, R. 2006. Urban spaces – enhancing the attractiveness and quality of the urban environment. WP3 Joint Strategy. University of Technology, Vienna, December 2006.

Sutanta, H., Rajabifard, A. and Bishop, I.D. 2009. An integrated approach for disaster risk reduction using spatial planning and SDI platform. Proceedings of the Surveying & Spatial Sciences Institute Biennial International Conference, Adelaide 2009, Surveying & Spatial Sciences Institute, pp. 341–351.

Thaiutsa, B., Puangchit, L., Kjelgren, R. and Arunpraparut, W. 2008. Urban green space, street tree and heritage large tree assessment in Bangkok, Thailand. *Forestry and Urban Greening*, 7(3): 219–229.

Weiland, U., Richter, M. and Kasperidus, H.D. 2005. Environmental management and planning in urban regions – are there differences between growth and shrinkage? *Sustainable Development and Planning II*, 1: 441–450.

Whyte, W.H. 1980. *The Social Life of Small Urban Spaces.* Project for Public Spaces, New York.

Woolley, H., Swanwick, C. and Dunnet, N. 2003. Nature, role and value of green space in towns and cities: An overview. http://www.atypom-link.com/ALEX/doi/abs/10.2148/benv.29.2.94.54467 (accessed 18 September 2009).

Wyporek, B. 2000. ISoCaRP millennium report findings for the future. The work of the congresses of ISoCaRP 1965–1999. http://isocarp.org/app/uploads/2014/08/millenium_report.pdf (accessed 1 September 2015).

Yang, J., McBride, J., Zhou, J. and Sun, Z. 2005. The urban forest in Beijing and its role in air pollution reduction. *Urban Forestry and Urban Greening*, 3: 65–78.

6. Eyes on the street: the role of 'third places' in improving perceived neighbourhood safety

Gordon Holden

INTRODUCTION

This chapter seeks to unravel the multidimensional and interconnected aspects of perceived and actual safety within the context of third places in neighbourhoods. Equipped with relevant identified aspects, several case study neighbourhoods at the Gold Coast in Queensland are studied to test relationships between third places and safety in actual places. Multidimensional aspects do not only apply to safety. Lang (1994) convincingly outlines the interconnected nature of all aspects of the designed and constructed environment underpinned by the inclusive Maslow's hierarchy of human needs (1943, 1954, 1987). Lang (1994) presents a graphic model which dynamically shows interdependent links between the needs of: physiological provision; safety and security; affiliation; esteem and self-actualization including cognitive and aesthetic needs. He states that 'the interrelationships form a complex web that shows the futility of any simplistic model of the concerns of urban design' (Lang 1994 p.156). Recent researchers confirm Lang's conclusions, that the constructed environment is a complex interconnection of multidimensional aspects (Del Castillo et al. 2016; Howley et al. 2009; McIndoe et al. 2005).

While accepting Lang's complex web, on considering the title of this chapter, leads us to the need for clear understanding of key concepts. First, to explore the concept of 'third places'. Oldenburg (1989) conceptualizes third places as locations where incidental neighbourhood interactions occur. Third places are distinct from first places, the home and second places the work or school places. Third places may include cafés, restaurants, parks, urban squares, religious buildings, social clubs and like places that people regularly access. Attributes of third places identified by Oldenburg: they are neutral in terms of obligation, people may come and go as they please with there being no financial, political or legal implications; they represent a level social status, all participants having equal access; light conversations are the predominant pursuit; third places are easily and comfortably accessible across long opening hours; typically there are regular users of third places and there is welcoming acceptance of newcomers into them, though not everybody knows everybody else closely, they are readily accessible; and, they don't stand out extravagantly, they have a low profile being simple in character and the ambience is generally lighthearted.

This chapter's focus is on the links between third places and perceptions of neighbourhood safety. Within this context important concepts need discussion informed by the literature including: perception; safety; neighbourhood and, eyes on the street. These will be addressed under the following sub-headings after which third places will be further engaged and lead into selected aspects of crime in neighbourhoods.

Perception

People gain understanding of the built environment through their senses, guided by motivations and needs (Lang 1994). Sensing is one aspect of perception, the other being the way in which something is regarded, understood, or interpreted, a belief or opinion held by people based on how things seem (Cambridge University Press 1995). Both meanings have relevance to safety in the constructed environment: senses convey physical aspects while belief or opinions convey psychological and values aspects. Physical aspects are discussed further under the sub-heading 'safety'.

Psychological aspects of perception of the constructed environment mostly relate to fear of victimization. Garofalo (1981) concludes that fear is an emotion expressed as a sense of danger evoked by perceived cues in the situation that may relate to crime for the person, while Delbose and Currie (2012) highlight that fear of crime is often not a reflection of actual risk and may vary across gender, age, ethnicity and socio-economic status. Other potential influences on fear of crime include a person's occupation, frequency of travel, crowds, visible security, neighbourhood physical maintenance, time of day/night, seasons, streetlights, street types (narrow/wide) and whether people are alone or together. To give this scope more immediate dimensions, an audit of crime perception in Blackburn, UK, shows that the main problems sparking fear are litter and rubbish, young people hanging around in groups, drugs, speeding cars and personal safety after dark (Colquhoun 2004). Shepherdson (2014) identifies potential remedy responses to fear of crime including: high physical maintenance of the environment; community cohesion; public behaviour; alcohol-free areas to discourage bad behaviour; and, high visibility of surveillance.

Relatively simple behaviour responses to perception of safety in a potentially hostile place, at the level of the individual, are proposed by Garofalo
(1981): stay away; install locks; move to a safer neighbourhood; change
shopping patterns (go to different shops); go out less; and, carry weapons.

The Victorian Health Indicator Survey: Perceptions of Safety, concludes that the way the constructed environment is designed and maintained impacts greatly on perceptions of safety 'Neighbourhoods which
are perceived as safe, foster community participation, encourage physical
activity, community connectedness and add to health and well-being of
local residents and visitors' (Community Indicators Victoria 2011).

Gabriel and Grieve (2003) in *The Psychological Fear of Crime* propose
that fear tends to relate to individuals, in an immediate sense relating to a
specific situation, where individuals interpret themselves as potential victims. Over time repeated experience of personal fear across many people
may develop into a general community fear. If such experiences occur
frequently for many persons on many occasions this may be perceived as
a wider crime problem reflecting an erosion of community values. Similar
to Delbose and Currie (2012), Austin et al. (2002) conclude from reviewing
the literature that key factors influencing fear of crime and perceptions
of safety include: demographics (gender, age and socio-economic status);
personal experience of crime; and, physical conditions (urban quality).
Women and older people experience higher fear but lower actual victimization of crime. Higher socio-economic status people have lower levels of
fear of crime. In summary Austin et al.'s research shows that 'residents
who were more satisfied with the physical environment in their neighbourhood and the people in their neighbourhood were more likely to express
higher levels of perceived safety' (Austin et al. 2002 p. 9).

Safety

In his all-inclusive hierarchy of needs theory of human motivations,
Maslow considers that basic needs for humans include safety and security
together with physiological needs for air, food, water and shelter (Maslow
1987). It is widely accepted in urban design and planning that people
expect and require safety in the constructed environment (Jacobs 1961;
Lang 1994; Cooper Marcus and Francis 1998; Colquhoun 2004). Lang
links physiological and physical safety needs with psychological needs
for harm avoidance. He adds that having a sense of self-determination
in the environment through understanding and assessing it in space and
time contributes to self-confidence. This in turn contributes to security
which may be further enhanced through belonging to a social network
(Lang 1994). While the expectations of people regarding safety vary across

individuals and their age, harm avoidance is common to all. Harm avoidance in the constructed environment is conveniently considered in two main ways, safety from personal injury accidents and safety from criminal victimization.

Safety from accidents relates to people accessing the constructed environment mainly by walking, wheel-chairing, jogging, cycling, driving and taking public transport. Provision of a safe public environment is largely the responsibility of state and local government through planned infrastructure and facilities. Private citizens also have the potential to initiate particular projects through lobbying local government officers or elected representatives. The scope of such infrastructure and facilities include: roadways and speed limits; street crossings; traffic lights; bus pull-in spaces; parking areas; curb and channeling; bicycle pathways; paved footpaths; steps; handrails at steep pedestrian gradients; street signs for way-finding; shelters; benches; and, street lighting. Street lighting is especially important in maintaining safety from injury at night, while also having a critical role in reducing fear from crime. Continuous paved footpaths are important as they encourage use rather than people choosing to walk on the even surface of adjacent roads, despite the safety risk. Desirably, cycle paths are clearly separated from pedestrian paths.

Well-constructed public environments will safely accommodate people through life cycles, from small children to adolescents to young, middle and senior aged adults. The walking pace capacity of pedestrian movement across ages varies and account of this should be incorporated in fine-tuning elements such as traffic-light controlled crossings. It is reported that over 80 per cent of pedestrian injuries happen when people are crossing roads and those most at risk are the young, the old and the inebriated (Neilsen 2014).

Van Melik et al. (2007) highlight that western cities commonly upgrade public places to create 'secured' space, which increase safety and reduce fear. This is often achieved through the installation of CCTV to influence peoples' behaviour, especially of potential criminals. But it is also acknowledged that CCTV may also influence normal people negatively, increasing fear by highlighting that there may be a high crime environment requiring CCTV.

A safety programme, initiated in the USA, may effectively contribute to safety from injury for the elderly and potentially contribute to better cardiovascular health through encouraging walking. The New York 'Safe Routes for Seniors' programme was influenced by analysis of data which revealed that while 13 per cent of the population are seniors, they account for 33 per cent of pedestrian injuries (Tsay 2010). These programmes identify suitable routes for upgrading practical physical aspects such as pavements, seats, safe pedestrian crossings and way finding through better signage and aesthetic enhancements through improved landscaping. It follows that such improvements will benefit the whole community across life cycles (Thompson and Kent 2011).

Neighbourhood

Despite the common use of the term 'neighbourhood' within the constructed environment lexicon the word remains ambiguous, often used synonymously with the term 'community', especially in social science literature. Lang argues that the two terms have clearly separate meanings, with 'neighbourhood being a physical entity and community being a social one' (Lang 1994 p. 257). This separation is more recently reinforced by others including Burton et al. (2010 p. 31) 'neighbourhood is about place and community is about people'. Notwithstanding the convenience in discussing neighbourhood and community as clearly separate definitions, Lupton (2003) recognizes the complexities imbedded in both concepts including that neighbourhood embraces both physical and social dimensions as linked aspects. Lupton further recognizes the subjective nature wherein sense of neighbourhood is different for different people and may vary for the same person over time.

For convenience in accessing census data, many urban studies of neighbourhoods adopt government definitions such as the 'statistical area level 2' (SA2) in Australia with similar approaches in other countries. These have in common, convenient geographic boundaries, such as streets. These definitions rarely coincide with individual perceptions, which are more an expression of how people actually use their nearby constructed environment, rather than be bound by statistical definition although nodes, paths and edges such as streets and watercourses (after Lynch's 'image' criteria, 1960) may influence perceptions (Alidoust et al. 2017). Use may be influenced by the urban form of the place, the range of social ties that individuals have in 'their' neighbourhood as well as by convenience of access to services, such as shops and to walking or cycling routes for enjoyment, exercise and travel.

Use of the constructed environment is different for groups in different life cycle categories, for different socio-economic categories and is also different for individuals across their life cycle. As well as people-place and different experiences of individuals, senses of neighbourhood are also influenced by external factors including land use, access linkages, natural features such as shore lines, parks and land form (Lupton 2003). Potential problems arise from spatial analysis that underpins policy for the provision of urban facilities, when statistical definition data is used to explain human behaviour in neighbourhoods, rather than also taking account of lived experience.

Further variation of neighbourhood definition derives from different urban forms. Gated communities, low-rise or high rise, as well as intentional communities, such as Currumbin Eco Village, Gold Coast, tend to be self-defined neighbourhoods in terms of real-estate marketing and this is supported by residents' perceptions (Miller and Bentley 2012). Resident perceptions of neighbourhood in conventional suburbs including gridded streets and cul-de-sac streets, tend to be of larger geographic areas than for gated communities, but do not align with statistical boundaries (Alidoust et al. 2017).

Linked to neighbourhood, but more so to community, is the concept of 'neighbouring', an expression of degrees of ties residents of a neighbourhood have with each other. Introduced by Granovetter (1973), the strength of ties is a combination of time, intensity and intimacy that individuals give to the tie. The engagement of ties, both intentionally and incidentally, may be through the use of public transport, private motor vehicles, cycling or through walking and in accessing third places (see Alidoust and Bosman Chapter 3 this volume).

Two recent research topics undertaken at the Gold Coast, Queensland, by Griffith University PhD students supervised by the writer, separately explore both social and spatial dimensions in Gold Coast neighbourhoods (see Del Castillo et al. 2016; Alidoust 2017). Both studies use perception survey techniques, including mental mapping and both accommodate place and people concepts as perceived and engaged by individuals. Alidoust et al. (2017) revealed features perceived by residents that align with Lynch's (1960) 'image' criteria derived from individuals' mental maps – paths, edges, districts, nodes and landmarks. For residents in gated communities, nodes that had social functions prevail, while residents in conventional suburbs tend to identify nodes which had physical functions, such as for shopping (Alidoust et al. 2017). Del Castillo's study scopes widely and categorizes dimensions of perceived neighbourhood across themes of: personal; physical; social; and, political, with social themes dominating.

Given that both PhD studies were based on open-ended questions answered in the respondents' own terms, they reliably reflect the multi-dimensional nature of neighbourhood as perceived by individuals. This chapter acknowledges this conclusion and adopts an individual perception and linked aspects framework across place and people similar to Alidoust and Del Castillo and supported by earlier researchers.

Eyes on the Street

Creation, or at least popularization, of the term 'eyes on the street' is credited to Jane Jacobs in her 1961 book *The Death and Life of Great American Cities*. Based on phenomenological observation, Jacobs established three main characteristics for successful community oriented and safe city neighbourhoods: clear demarcation between public and private space; such spaces cannot ooze into each other as they do typically in suburban settings; the need for 'eyes on the street' eyes belonging to those who are the natural proprietors of the street; and, the sidewalks must have users fairly continuously, adding to the number of effective eyes. Jacobs also added that successful neighbourhoods should have streets to handle strangers that comprise a mixture of people across age levels, socio-economic profiles and ownership and rental housing. They should include a mixture of functions and services including shops, restaurants, hotels and public buildings.

Jacobs' 'eyes on the street' was conceived as one linked aspect in a multidimensional framework that mainly pertains to mid to high density multifunctional urban environments, which she favoured over low density, single function suburban environments. Jacobs' conceptualization does not suit much of the western new-world's urban development, which is predominantly suburban in form. There are contemporary new forms growing in occurrence including 'Master Planned Communities' (such as gated communities), 'Intentional Communities', such as Eco Villages and 'Co-housing' complexes. These contemporary forms may be accommodated in low, medium or high rise buildings, provide for age segregated or open-access residents and may be 'gated' or not. Unlike conventional free access neighbourhoods, gated communities have strictly controlled access, with guards or electronic surveillance, within a closed perimeter wall or fence.

Notwithstanding the origin of Jacobs' 'eyes on the street' being imbedded within the particular urban form that she favoured, the concept has expanded in common usage to embrace all urban forms and is regularly adopted in urban policy, plans and design guidelines at local government level to control existing and planned urban development.

Focused on managing levels of crime, Oscar Newman (1972) built on aspects of Jacobs' 'eyes on the street' concept. Newman studied crime rates in different urban forms and found that rates were lower in places where there was clear demarcation between private, semi-private, semi-public and public territories and where there was little open space under nobody's influence or location for casual overseeing, referred to as natural surveillance. Newman also found that well-maintained buildings and landscapes had lower crime levels than those that were untidy, conveying that well-presented areas were perceived by intruders as under watchful care while messy areas appear to have no guardians. Newman coined the term 'defensible space' to describe the relationship between social and physical aspects wherein the community takes responsibility for overseeing nearby areas which are conducive to being observed because of good design and maintenance. Night lighting is required to improve perception of security. Newman expanded on the importance of social aspects through a later book *Community of Interest* (Newman 1981) wherein he advocated for age and lifestyle groupings of residents who with common interests would likely be more supportive and watchful, adding to mutual security.

Jacobs and Newman have in common with others including Alexander (1964), Sennett (1973), Lang (1994) and Gehl (2010) that cities are multidimensional, embracing of civility, difference and choice with no simple or linear dimension to understand them. This appreciation includes the acceptance if not celebration of people different from us, indeed strangers. However, safety and security imperatives drive many parts of today's urban environments including gated communities and high-rise apartments, both potentially rejecting strangers. This needs to be balanced with the constant reminder of wider function and purpose of the city to enjoy vitality, acknowledge responsibility, accept diversity and celebrate communal civic life (Sennett 1973). MacMillan and Stevens (2017) in *The Conservation* article advocate a human-centered framework for equitable, safe, accessible and inclusive neighbourhoods: people as assets; technology as tools; quality of life as an imperative; respect for individual differences; and, collective responsibility.

Beyond Jacobs and Newman's natural surveillance and community building to improve security of residential areas, is the crime prevention programme 'Neighbourhood Watch' run by police services. Being voluntary, at its most effective level as well as potentially reducing crime, Neighbourhood Watch strengthens community spirit and bonds by developing a common focus on mutual safety and household security (Queensland Police Service 2017). A more formal if not coercive form of emerging Neighbourhood Watch that has had some success is '3rd party policing' which seeks to involve managers and landlords of places such as shopping centres, large buildings and business owners to take responsibility for control of criminal and disorderly behaviour in their immediate place. Police seek to establish crime control guardians (3rd parties) in locations where there were none previously (Mazerolle and Ransley 2004).

Watching and being watched is the common thread across Jacobs and Newman's theories and is central to Neighbourhood Watch and 3rd party policing. For criminals, being watched is a deterrent as it generally instills fear in an individual contemplating crime of higher risk of being caught. However, for some criminals the risk factor is not intimidating but the opposite, it is the source of thrill, possibly a form of addiction (Burt and Simons 2013). Offenders act strategically to avoid being caught (Geason and Wilson 1989). The main emotion that constrains potential criminals is fear linked to sanctions. Legal sanction is paramount, such as fear of punishment, also informal sanctions such as CCTV which allows individual identification and alarms that alert others may reduce criminal activity. Criminals may also be constrained through potential victim responses such as the victim screaming out or having a guard dog and resistance defence or counter attack by the victim, through the use of a weapon (Cusson 1993).

Loewen et al. (1993) tested aspects of Appleton's (1975) 'prospect–refuge theory', which focuses on the ability to see (prospect) but not be seen (refuge), in terms of potential relationships between prospect and refuge with perceived safety from crime. They found that there were three physical features of the environment most important to perceived safety: light, open space; and, access to real refuge. Loewen concludes that a 'combination of all three is safest, followed by a combination of light and open space, then light and access, and finally light alone. Perception of safety may be increased by having some buildings open, with non-dangerous people present 24hr a day' (Loewen et al. 1993 p.330), such buildings could be third places. Loewen proposes that an increase in night lighting should lead to places being actually safer from crime and also being perceived as safe.

Surveillance concepts expressed by Jacobs and Newman together with those of Jeffrey (1971) underpin Crime Prevention through Environmental Design (CPTED) which has been incorporated by police services and local governments in many countries to address crime before it happens. CPTED is based on the belief that criminals make strategic choices and consequently may not proceed with a crime if the situation appears to be difficult or dangerous. The premise is that through physical design of buildings and landscapes that trigger 'eyes on the street', the criminal may decide to not proceed because of being watched. Some CPTED principles may be applied retrospectively to establish constructed environments while all principles may be incorporated into new environments (Heal and Laycock 1986; Queensland Government 2007).

THIRD PLACES

Having explained Oldenburg's original characteristics of third places in the chapter introduction, other dimensions are now explored. Recognizing that society has changed since Oldenburg's conceptualization, Memarovic et al. (2014) revisit the characteristics within the context of contemporary communication technology. Memarovic found that Oldenburg's neutral social status still prevails, however third places without complimentary Internet availability or individuals without communication devices contribute to socio-economically unlevel environments, unlike the level circumstance originally conceived. Light conversation still has a place but is now compromised, being interrupted by people interacting online through technology. Regular users and welcoming accessibility remain relevant, although, as with level circumstances, this is now modified through Internet access. Today's third places that provide Internet access generally advertise this facility, making the place stand out more so than in the original notion. In summary, Memarovic et al. do not consider that modern technology has significantly modified Oldenberg's original thesis.

Given the wide range of what is now seen as potential third places (Jeffres et al. 2009) in the context of this chapter, types of third places need to be categorized into degrees of internalization or externalization. For example, coffee shops could be entirely internal environments, or a combination of internal and external, or they could be completely external. For patrons to have the capacity to provide 'eyes on the street' they need to be located in positions to see out into the surrounding space. Certain potential third places, such as churches, are internalized during services but may be externalized afterward, while parks are almost entirely externalized. Third places themselves that may contribute to 'eyes on the street' need to have externalization characteristics. Further aspects that embrace both internalized and externalized third places is that people need to get to the place. Typically, as pedestrians, either from their homes or from where they were let off from a form of transport. In the period when individuals are moving towards the third place, by whatever means, they will contribute to eyes on the street.

CRIME: URBAN FORM, FUNCTION, DENSITY AND SOCIO-ECONOMIC STATUS

Many countries report crime across several categories under key headings with numerous sub-headings. In Queensland the main headings are: Homicide; Assault; Sexual Offences; Robbery; Offences Against the Person; Unlawful Entry; Arson; Other Property Damage; Other Thief; Fraud; Handling Stolen Goods; Offences Against Property; Drug Offences; Prostitution Offences; Liquor Offences; Gaming Offences; Breaching Domestic Violence Offences; Trespass and Vagrancy; Weapons

Offences; Good Order Offences; Stock Related Offences; Traffic and Related Offences (Queensland Police Service 2015).

Beavon et al. (1994 p. 21) highlight that 'criminal offenders behave non-criminally most of the time', making it difficult for ordinary neighbourhood residents to anticipate criminal activity. Successful control of crime measures in particular places displaces or pushes crime to other less secure areas. Such displacement is said to be more prominent with gated communities pushing crime to adjacent areas (Blakely and Snyder 1998; Addington and Rennison 2013; Anderson 2013). Beavon et al. also found that crime opportunities have a greater likelihood of being exploited if they are at relatively accessible and frequently travelled streets. Property crimes are more likely to occur on streets which are highly accessible within road networks, with higher levels of traffic, or people, flow and include attractive targets such as apartments, bars or motels. This is because criminals can easily blend into the ordinary pace of street life. Crime is lower in less accessible areas. However, a journal article based on research by Papachristos et al. (2011) with the catchy title of 'More Coffee Less Crime?' found that crime rates measured over 14 years in Chicago by the growth in numbers and geographic spread of coffee shops show a clear decline in crime. Beavon et al. conclude that accessibility potentially masks criminal behaviour but may be contained by having more 'eyes on the street'. Beavon et al. (1994) and notwithstanding differences in urban forms studied, Shu (2000) found that streets with active edges, such as shops, cafés and other services, had lower crime levels than streets with no edge activation. The ongoing presence of cars and people on streets and sidewalks and their connectivity adds to lower crime levels, due to the higher 'natural surveillance'.

Research into crime and land use functions include that by Wo (2016) who found differences in neighbourhood crime levels where there are different types of local institutions that provide residents with a host of services and activities. Third places institutions such as coffee shops and cafés help to reduce actual crime while bars, liquor stores and banks have an adverse effect on violent crime levels. Third places also reduce the perception of crime. Others have concluded that the presence of institutions such as libraries, recreation centres and religious buildings (of any denomination) also help to control crime (Peterson et al. 2000; Beyerlein and Hipp 2005).

CASE STUDIES GOLD COAST, AUSTRALIA

It is beyond the scope of this chapter to attempt to unpick all the relationships between all of the multi-dimensions that have been identified in the literature, so a selective approach to the dimensions is adopted. The case studies focus is on eyes on the street, accessibility, well-constructed and maintained pedestrian environments, lighting and activity level. The following case studies explore the presence or absence of third places within the context of recorded crime in those places and how their eyes on the street contribute to safety. The cases range across constructed environments that represent different urban form types, different densities and different socio-economic profiles and ages, thereby providing the opportunity to expose broad issues and for robust analysis and conclusions that may be generalizable. The cases are all in Gold Coast City, Queensland, a sun-belt tourism centre of about 600,000 population and the fastest growth city in Australia (Dedekorkut-Howes and Bosman 2014). Gold Coast is a linear city along a shoreline, about 60 km long and 15 km wide bound by a mountainous hinterland.

There are very few previous studies of neighbourhood crime at the Gold Coast to benchmark against, prominent among them being the research by Minnery and Lim (2005) which sought to test CPTED criteria (design of the constructed environment) in terms of reduction in crime and resident perceptions of safety from crime. The survey areas of the Minnery and Lim study range across socio-economic levels but similar to the case studies in this chapter they focus on detached dwellings and low-rise multiple dwellings. Crime in terms of resident perceptions relate mainly to property, such as burglary and break-ins and to a lesser extent to personal victimization, such as assault. Minnery and Lim found that fear of crime (perception) was not strongly linked to the level of CPTED elements present in the neighbourhood but actual levels of crime are clearly linked, demonstrating that CPTED is effective (Minnery and Lim 2005 p. 338).

The case studies in this chapter do not attempt to engage specifically with testing the effectiveness of specific CPTED measures. However, it is recognized that the key matters of relevance revealed through the literature substantially (not surprisingly) overlap CPTED criteria. Key elements have been initially evaluated by the author based on observations, while recognizing the need for more rigorous evaluation criteria in future research. Each case study area is assessed for performance on a scale from 1 (very low) to 5 (very high). The cases are also assessed for the presence of different types of third places and the level of crime offences per 100 persons per annum during the day and night. All of the above matters are shown in Table 6.1 for ease of summary and for comparative analysis.

The data for a particular study area may be interrogated and compared with other areas to underpin conclusions. Taking account of the key matters pertaining to this chapter's focus: urban form; socio-economic profile; the presence of third places; the presence of elements conducive to safety

Table 6.1   Gold Coast case studies showing third places, key constructed environment matters and crime offences per 100 people per annum

Case study group		Hope Island		Chirn Park		Mermaid Waters		Currumbin	
URBAN FORM		Gated Community HALCYON	Regular Suburb COVA	Regular Suburb	Shopping Street and Suburb	Regular Suburb	Shopping Street and Suburb	Intentional community ECO VILLAGE	Rural Residential
DENSITY (Scale: Low, Medium, Medium+, Medium-High, High)		Medium+	Medium+	Medium	Medium+	Medium	Medium+	Low	Low
SOCIO-ECONOMIC STATUS (Scale: Gold Coast Median)		Median	Median	Below Median	Below Median	Above Median	Median	Above Median	Above Median
Third Places (number)	Parks	0	1	1	1	0	2	1	0
	Coffee Café	0	1	0	Multiple	0	Multiple	1	0
	Retail	0	1	0	Multiple	0	Multiple	0	0
	Social Club	1	1	0	0	0	0	1	0
	Church	0	0	0	0	0	0	0	0
	Alcohol outlet	0	0	0	1	0	2	0	0
Element helpful to safety (5=high) (1=low)	Eyes on the Street	4	3	3	4	3	4	2	1
	Accessibility	4	4	4	4	4	4	4	2
	Well-Constructed & Maintained Pedestrian Environment	5	4	3	3	4	3	4	2
	Lighting	4	4	4	4	4	4	3	2
	Activity Level	3	3	4	4	3	4	3	2
Offence per 100 persons per annum (Qld 2014/15 = 13.8 per 100)	Day	0.2 (50%)	1.07 (50%)	4.82 (57%)	3.60 (57%)	2.28 (56%)	2.88 (52%)	0.64 (50%)	1.67 (65%)
	Night	0.2 (50%)	1.07 (50%)	3.63 (43%)	2.73 (43%)	1.79 (44%)	2.66 (48%)	0.64 (50%)	0.90 (35%)
	Total	0.4	2.5	8.45	6.33	4.07	5.54	1.28	2.57

(eyes on the street, accessibility, well-constructed and maintained pedestrian environment, good lighting, high activity level); and, the level of actual crime. The categories of crime occurrences across the combination of the case study areas fall mainly (about 65 per cent) under the category of property crime including: unlawful entry; other property damage; and, other theft. Traffic-related offences accounted for about 20 per cent. The range of other crimes (15 per cent) in smaller percentages include: fraud; drugs; vehicle-related; and, assault. It should be noted that while the actual number of offences were low, the Hope Island and Currumbin Valley cases had higher incidents of property crime at about 75 per cent, than the average across all case studies. Eight cases are discussed in four groups with each group having two contrasting adjacent study areas (refer to Figure 6.1 for the location of case study sites):

- Hope Island, a 2000s canal-based medium-high socio-economic profile suburban area at the north end of the Gold Coast. One study area is a gated community (Halcyon) while the other is a nearby free access conventional modern residential suburb (Cova).
- Chirn Park, a long established medium-low socio-economic profile, conventional residential suburb, adjacent to Southport, one of the first European settlements on the Gold Coast, dating from the late 1880s. One study area is residential only while the other is an adjacent residential area but including a shopping street.
- Mermaid Waters, a 1960s canal-based medium socio-economic profile conventional suburb about half way along the city's long north–south geography. One study area is residential only while the other is an adjacent residential area but including a shopping street.
- Currumbin Valley, toward the South end of the city, a medium-high socio-economic profile semi-rural area established in the 1990s. One study area is an intentional community (Currumbin Eco-Village) while the other is an adjacent rural residential low density suburb.

For each case study the Queensland Crime Map (Queensland Crime Map 2017) was accessed. The Crime Map is an open Internet access data bank of all crimes recorded in Queensland, typically over a 10–15 year period. Crimes are categorized under Queensland Police recording classifications, summarized annually. The map covers the whole of Queensland and the Internet access provides the capacity to zoom-adjust at different scales by centring onto any place in the State. Selected parts of the study areas were centred, providing a 400 m diameter circle about the centre point selected. This process provides crime data within the 400 m diameter study area. For this study it was convenient to zoom at

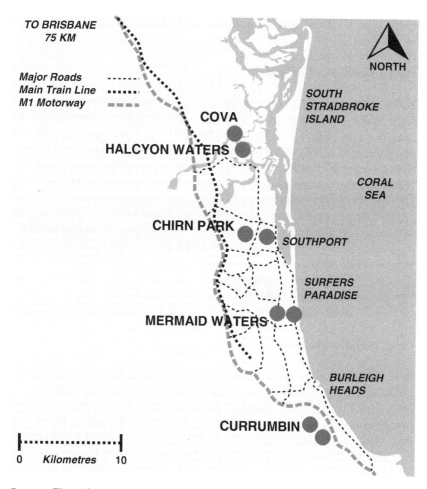

TO BRISBANE
75 KM

Major Roads
Main Train Line
M1 Motorway

COVA

HALCYON WATERS

CHIRN PARK

MERMAID WATERS

CURRUMBIN

NORTH

SOUTH
STRADBROKE
ISLAND

CORAL
SEA

SOUTHPORT

SURFERS
PARADISE

BURLEIGH
HEADS

0   Kilometres   10

Source: The author.

Figure 6.1   Gold Coast city map showing locations of case studies

a scale that allows the identification of the outline of individual houses and house-sites and to print on to an A3 size sheet. At this size a suitable amount of detailed information may be identified and marked-up on the print-out including: the layout of roads and public space; land use, such as location of commercial and residential functions, including 'third places'; and, the number of households which when multiplied by average occupancy data obtained from Bureau of Census, allows for reasonably reliable people-density conclusions. Crime site information scopes across crime type, time and date of the crime, and whether the crime was solved or unsolved.

Hope Island Cases Comparison

Halcyon Waters gated community has a very low crime rate, about one-sixth of the level at nearby Cova suburb and about one-twentieth of the level at Chirn Park. Given that both Hope Island cases have quite similar performances across density, socio-economic status and the elements conducive to safety, the outstanding difference is that Halcyon Waters is a controlled gated community. The high level of security provided here may be interpreted as more significant than the third place and eyes on the street in providing actual safety. Alidoust's PhD thesis (2017) reveals that the perception of safety is higher at Halcyon Waters than for regular suburbs, possibly confirming research by Van Melik et al. (2007) and Blakely and Snyder (1998). Cova does not have a particularly high rate of crime, about the same as the rural residential area, but considerably better than the higher density areas at Chirn Park and Mermaid Waters. The third places and surveillance system may contribute to perception of safety at Cova.

Chirn Park Comparisons

Both the Chirn Park regular suburb and the Chirn Park shopping street areas have similar and relatively high rates of actual crime, compared to the Hope Island and Currumbin Valley cases, as well as having a high perception of crime, as identified by Del Castillo et al.'s research at Chirn Park (Del Castillo et al. 2016 p. 8). The regular suburb has the highest rate of crime of all cases studied and other than a linear park bound by streets (a marginal third place), it has the lowest number of third places of all cases studied. However, without further research it would be difficult to confidently conclude that the absence of third places alone has caused the higher crime rate. The regular suburb performs similarly to the Chirn Park shopping street area in terms of density, socio-economic status and the elements conducive to safety. Chirn Park shopping street includes numerous third places, in the form of cafés and restaurants as well as retail outlets, yet the area has the second highest crime rate of all cases studied. The shopping street area has a lower crime rate than the regular suburb, possibly attributed to the presence of third places. In terms of potential influence on crime rates, both of the Chirn Park study areas fall within the lowest socio-economic profile of all cases studied, potentially confirming Austin et al.'s (2002) research relating to perception and Webster and Kingston's (2014) research relating to actual crime being linked to socio-economic status.

Mermaid Waters Comparisons

Both of the Mermaid Waters cases have higher crime rates than the Hope Island and Currumbin Valley cases, but lower than the Chirn Park cases. Both cases perform similarly to the Chirn Park cases and to Cova in performances across the elements conducive to safety, so these are not seen as influencing differences in the crime rates. The regular suburb area, which has above median socio-economic status, has a lower rate of crime than the shopping street area, which has a median socio-economic status. The regular suburb has no third places, while the shopping street area has numerous third places, in the form of cafés and restaurants as well as retail outlets. The tavern and alcohol outlet have attracted a higher number of crimes to their proximity than for adjacent residential areas, possibly confirming Wo's research (2016). The regular suburb performs similarly to the Chirn Park case studies as well as to Cova in terms of the elements conducive to safety, so these are not seen as influencing the different crime rates. The regular suburb has a higher crime rate than the Cova case study, possibly due to the street network having higher accessibility with there being several alternative connecting streets to places outside of the area, potentially confirming Beavon et al.'s (1994) research.

Currumbin Valley Comparisons

Currumbin Eco Village has a very low crime rate despite being a freely accessed development. The crime level is second only to Halcyon gated community across the cases studied. There are three third places at the Eco Village and none at the adjacent rural residential area. The Eco Village out-performs the rural residential area on all of the elements conducive to safety, possibly confirming Newman's proposition (1981) and research by Battin and Crowl (2017). Being an intentional community, the values to which individuals subscribe, provides for a caring and supportive community spirit which is likely to contribute to actual and perceived safety. This is despite the density of housing development being relatively low thereby providing fewer eyes on the street. The rural residential area is also low density, but without a binding social network. It has about double the crime rate of the Eco Village.

CONCLUSIONS

It may be deduced from the research literature that more eyes on the street provided by third places do contribute to improving perception of safety from victimization as well as improving actual safety from crime in neighbourhoods. However there is a significant qualification to this conclusion, being that circumstances at a particular place will vary influenced by one or a combination of numerous factors: the function of the third place; its location in relation to the street; its use of communications technology; its accessibility; the level of lighting provided; the quality and maintenance of the adjacent constructed environment; the functional uses of land and buildings; and, the level of pedestrian and vehicular activity nearby.

The case studies confirm that third places add to 'more eyes on the street' and contribute to but are not solely responsible for actual and perceived safety in gated and intentional communities. Other significant contributing factors to safety in the case of the gated community studied are gate control for all entrants and surrounding fence barriers, both of which restrict access to residents and unauthorized visitors, thereby keeping strangers out. While such security provides a low crime environment, this is a social and economic privilege for the residents within the gates but may come at the cost of their engagement with open communities and subscription to a broader social contract (Blakely and Snyder 1998). In the case of the open access Eco Village intentional community, collective commitment to a sustainable lifestyle, which strengthens community spirit and social support networks, also contributes to safety through generating stronger neighbouring where individuals, despite their low numbers, more keenly provide 'eyes on the street' to look out for each other. Third places, such as the community centre and coffee shop, help build community social support.

In the conventional neighbourhoods studied including at Cova, Chirn Park and Mermaid Waters, the elements conducive to safety are about the same relatively high level. 'Eyes on the street' alone while possibly contributing to perception of safety do not seem to have much effect on actual safety. The two shopping streets studied (Chirn Park and Mermaid Waters) contained the highest number of third places, yet they were amongst the worst areas for crime. Modifying factors include: the type and location of third places; activity level; accessibility of urban form; land use; density; and, socio-economic level. Across all of the cases studied recorded crimes occurred almost equally across day and night, possibly confirming the important role of night lighting in moderating crime.

On balance, the literature and case studies indicate that having more eyes on the street, including in the broader sense of having more defensible spaces, appears to be more significant in supporting perception of safety as well as actual safety, than the role of third places alone. More eyes on the street are engaged through conducive pedestrian environments that are well maintained and lit.

It is concluded that third places are clearly a piece of the complex puzzle surrounding improving safety in neighbourhoods, albeit a significant positive piece. Each place must be studied for context and the presence of other influences on perception and actual safety before proceeding to introduce third places as a potential remedy to improve safety. A blanket policy approach for the establishment of third places to neighbourhoods to improve safety would not suffice.

REFERENCES

Addington, L. and Rennison, C. (2013), Keeping the Barbarians Outside the Gate? Comparing Burglary Victimization in Gated and Non-Gated Communities. *Justice Quarterly*, 32, 168–192.

Alexander, C. (1964), A City is Not a Tree. *Architectural Forum*, 122, 58–61.

Alidoust, S. (2017), Planning for Socially Healthy Ageing – A Study of Neighbourhood Environments and their Impacts on the Social Lives of Older People. PhD, Griffith University.

Alidoust, S., Bosman, C., Holden, G. (2017), The Spatial Dimensions of Neighbourhood: How Older People Define It. *Journal of Urban Design*, Published Online, 12 June 2017, 1–21.

Anderson, R. (2013), *Gated Communities – A Systematic Review of the Research Literature*. University of Glasgow, Sheffield Hallam University.

Austin, D., Furr, A. and Spine, M. (2002), The Effects of Neighbourhood Conditions on Perception of Safety. *Journal of Criminal Justice*, 30 (5), 417–427.

Battin, J. and Crowl, J. (2017), Urban Sprawl, Population Density, and Crime: An Examination of Contemporary Migration Trends and Crime in Suburban and Rural Neighborhoods. *Crime Prevention and Community Safety*, 19 (2), 136–150.

Beavon, D., Brantingham, P.L. and Brantingham, P.J. (1994), The Influence of Street Networks on the Patterning of Property Offenses. *Crime Prevention Studies*, 2, 115–148.

Beyerlein, X. and Hipp, Z. (2005), Social Capital, Too Much of a Good Thing? American Religious Traditions and Community Crime. *Social Forces*, 84, 995–1013.

Blakely, E. and Snyder, M. (1998), Separate Paces – Crime and Security in Gated Communities, in Felson, M. and Preiser, R. (eds), *Reducing Crime through Real Estate Development and Management*. Washington, DC: Urban Land Institute, pp. 53–70.

Burt, C. and Simons, R. (2013), Self-control, Thrill Seeking and Crime. *Criminal Justice Behavior*, 40 (11), 1326–1348.

Burton, H., Grant, M., Guise, R. (2010), *Shaping Neighbourhoods for Local Health and Global Sustainabilty* (2nd edn). London: Routledge.

Cambridge University Press (1995), *Cambridge Advanced Learners Dictionary*. Cambridge: Cambridge University Press.

Colquhoun, I. (2004), Design out Crime: Creating Safe and Sustainable Communities. London: Architectural Press.

Community Indicators Victoria (2011), Perceptions of Safety, Vic Health.

Cooper Marcus, C. and Francis, C. (1998), *People Places: Design Guidelines for Urban Open Space*. London: John Wiley & Sons.

Cusson, M. (1993), Situational Determinism: Fear During Criminal Events, in Clarke, R. (ed.), *Crime Prevention Studies V1*. New York: Criminal Justice Press, pp. 55–68.

Dedekorkut–Howes, A. and Bosman, C. (2014), Gold Coast: Australia's Playground. *Cities*, 42, 70–78.

Del Castillo, N., Holden, G. and Skates, H. (2016), Liveability in the Gold Coast: Neighbourhood as Social Practice, in Zuo, J. et al. (eds), 50th International Conference of the Architectural Science Association, pp. 1–7.

Delbose, Z. and Currie, G. (2012), Modelling the Causes and Impacts of Personal Safety Perceptions on Public Transport Ridership. *Transport Policy*, 24, 302–309.

Gabriel, U. and Grieve, W. (2003), The Psychological Fear of Crime. *British Journal of Criminology*, 43 (3), 600–614.

Garofalo, J. (1981), The Fear of Crime – Causes and Consequences. *Journal of Criminal Law and Criminology*, 72 (2), 839–856.

Geason, S. and Wilson, P. (1989), *Designing out Crime: Crime Prevention Through Environmental Design*. Canberra: Australian Institute of Criminology.

Gehl, J. (2010), *Cities for People*. London: Island Press.

Granovetter, M. (1973), The Strength of Weak Ties. *American Journal of Sociology*, 78 (6), 1360–1380.

Heal, K. and Laycock, G. (1986), *Situational Crime Prevention – From Theory to Practice*. London: HMSO.

Howley, P., Scott, M. and Redmond, D. (2009), Sustainability Verses Liveability – An Investigation of Neighbourhood Satisfaction. *Journal of Environmental Planning and Management*, 52 (6), 847–864.

Jacobs, J. (1961), *The Death and Life of Great American Cities*. London: Random House.

Jeffres, L., Bracken, C., Jian, G. and Casey, M. (2009) The Impact of Third Places on Community Quality of Life. *Applied Research in the Quality of Life*, 4, 333–345.

Jeffrey, R. (1971), *Crime Prevention through Environmental Design*. Beverley Hills: Sage.

Lang, J. (1994), *Urban Design: The American Experience*. New York: Van Nostrand Reinhold.

Loewen, L., Steel, G. and Suedfeld, P. (1993), Perceived Safety from Crime in the Urban Environment. *Journal of Environmental Psychology*, 13, 323–331.

Lupton, R. (2003), *Neighbourhood Effects: Can We Measure Them and Does It Matter?* London: Centre for Analysis of Social Exclusion, London School of Economics.

Lynch, K. (1960), *The Image of the City*. Cambridge: MIT Press.

MacMillan, C. and Stevens, N. (2017), Contested Spaces: Who Belongs on the Street Where You Live? *The Conversation*, 6 March.

Maslow, A. (1943), A Theory of Human Motivation. *Psychological Review*, 50 (4), 370–396.

Maslow, A. (1954), *Motivation and Personality*. New York, Harper and Row.

Maslow, A. (1987), *Motivation and Personality* (3rd edn). Delhi: Pearson Education.

Mazerolle, L. and Ransley, J. (2004), Third Party Policing: Prospects, Challenges and Implications for Regulators. Queensland: Griffith University Research & Public Policy Series.

McIndoe, G., Chapman, R., McDonald, C., Holden, G., Howden-Chapman, P. and Sharpin, A. (2005), *The Value of Urban Design: The Economic, Environmental and Social Benefits of Urban Design*. New Zealand: Ministry for the Environment.

Memarovic, N., Fels, S., Anacleto, J., Calderon, R., Gobbo, F. and Carroll, J.M. (2014), Rethinking Third Places: Contemporary Design with Technology. *The Journal of Community Informatics*, 10 (3), e-publication.

Miller, E. and Bentley, K. (2012), Leading a Sustainable Lifestyle in a 'Non-Sustainable World': Reflections from Australian Ecovillage and Suburban Residents. *Journal of Education for Sustainable Development*, 6 (1), 137–147.

Minnery, J. and Lim, B. (2005), Measuring Crime Prevention through Environmental Design. *Journal of Architecture and Planning Research*, 22 (4), 330–341.

Newman, O. (1972), *Defensible Space: Crime Prevention Through Urban Design*. New York: Macmillan.

Newman, O. (1981), *Community of Interest*. New York: Anchor Books.

Oldenburg, R. (1989), *The Great Good Place: Cafes, Coffee Shops, Community Centers, Beauty Parlors, General Stores, Bars, Hangouts, and How They Get You Through the Day*. Boston: De Capo Press.

Papachristos, A.V., Smith, C.M., Scherer, M.L. and Fugiero, M.A. (2011), More Coffee, Less Crime? The Relationship Between Gentrification and Neighbourhood Crime Rates in Chicago, 1991 to 2005. *City and Community*, 10, 215–240.

Peterson, R., Krivo, L.J. and Harris, M.A. (2000), Disadvantage and Neighbourhood Violent Crime: Do Local Institutions Matter? *Journal of Research in Crime and Delinquency*, 37, 31–63.

Queensland Crime Map (2017), https//crimemap.info/ (accessed 28 June 2017).

Queensland Government (2007), Crime Prevention through Environmental Design, The State of Queensland.

Queensland Police Service (2015), Annual Statistics Review 2014/15. Queensland Police Service.

Queensland Police Service (2017), Neighbourhood Watch Queensland. Queensland Government.

Sennett, R. (1973), *The Uses of Disorder*. Harmondsworth, Penguin.

Shepherdson, P. (2014), Perceptions of Safety and Fear of Crime Research Report, Auburn City Council and Bankstown, Canterbury and Huntsville Councils.

Shu, S. (2000), Housing Layout and Crime Vunerability. *Urban Design International*, 5, 177–188.

Thompson, S. and Kent, J. (2011), Healthy Built Environments: A Review of the Literature. Sydney: City Futures Research Program, UNSW.

Tsay, Shin-pei (2010), Safe Routes for Seniors – Improving Walkability for Seniors in New York City. Proceedings, Aged Living Research Annual Conference, 9–11 February.

Van Melik, R., Van Aalst, I. and Van Weesep, J. (2007), Fear and Fantasy in the Public Domain: The Development of Secured and Themed Urban Space. *Journal of Urban Design*, 12–1, 25–42.

Webster, C. and Kingston, S. (2014), Anti-Poverty Strategies for the UK Poverty and Crime Review, Applied Social Research (CeASR) Leeds Metropolitan University.

Wo, J. (2016), Community Context of Crime: A Longitudinal Examination of the Effects of Local Institutions on Neighbourhood Crime. *Crime and Delinquency*, 62(10), 1286–1312.

7. Understanding popular music heritage practice through the lens of 'third place'

Lauren Istvandity, Sarah Baker, Jez Collins, Simone Driessen and Catherine Strong

INTRODUCTION

In his writing on third place, Oldenburg refers to sites such as bars, cafés and barbershops as typifying outlets in which people could find respite between home and work. Much of the existing literature which applies or builds on Oldenburg's work seeks to categorise spaces, both physical and online, as third places, for example, cafés (Harris 2007), libraries (Aabø and Audunson 2012; Montgomery and Miller 2011), and online communities (Robinson and Deshano 2011; Soukup 2006). Other research explores the ways in which relationships occur within these places (e.g. Cheang 2002), and the motivations and benefits in attending third places (e.g. Rosenbaum 2006). In contemporary society however, there are a growing variety of liminal spaces to which the concept of third place can be applied. Though these may vary slightly in their alignment with Oldenburg's original characterisations of third places, they are worth closer examination in terms of what could be thought of as extensions of third place.

Cultural heritage and its related places, practices, and relationships, is one such arena that has so far received limited attention regarding its potential conceptualisation as a third place. This chapter narrows its focus to a consideration of popular music heritage and presents four case studies that draw on the empirical work of individual authors. In discussing the ways popular music heritage activities can resemble third places through physical (Baker) and virtual (Collins) community-run popular music archives and museums, music heritage walking tours in Melbourne, Australia (Strong), and reunion tours of 'heritage' music acts (Driessen), these case studies reveal a continuum of tangible and intangible representations of third place as it relates to popular music heritage.

HOW CAN POPULAR MUSIC HERITAGE BE A THIRD PLACE?

As an emerging area, it is necessary to think more broadly about how the idea of heritage places and practices in the arts could be considered conforming to the principles of third place. One of the few research studies to directly consider arts heritage places and Oldenburg's conceptualisation of third place is that by Slater and Koo (2010) who compared visitor experiences in the Tate Modern (an art gallery) and the South Bank Centre (a performance space) in London. Interviews with visitors revealed these venues as third places in all but one aspect: there was an absence of conversation. The authors suggest that perhaps arts spaces such as these are the third places of the twenty-first century, where people seek 'places to escape in their leisure time and face to face conversation is often replaced by electronic communication' (Slater and Koo 2010 p. 109). That third places may have adapted to the digital age is an idea that has been raised by researchers such as Soukup (2006), Steinkuehler and Williams (2006) who indicate that online platforms such as forums and gaming spaces reflect the renewed ways in which we communicate, bond, and relax outside work or home obligations. It is this flexibility of characterisation that precedes our understanding of popular music heritage as a potential third place.

With the identification of virtual sites as third places, the capacity for third places to exist in both tangible and intangible forms can be realised. Music, as an often intangible, aural and bodily experience, entrenched in private and popular memory, extends its grasp to communities, dwelling in both physical, moveable and online places. The heritage of music practices is somewhat nebulous to define (see for example, Bennett 2009; Kong 1999; Schmutz 2005), but essentially exists in between collective (public) memory and history – that which is thought to be worth efforts to be gathered, preserved, protected and remembered. Popular music heritage is also considered more than the contents or subject of preservation, but as Roberts and Cohen note, 'heritage increasingly encompasses a range of practices that are not reducible to "the music itself" but linked to the wider social, cultural and economic processes surrounding the production and consumption of popular music histories and heritage canons' (Roberts and Cohen 2014 p. 242). It is these practices in particular that help to construct music heritage as a third place – the practices of preserving popular music history are frequently joint ventures that engage local and global communities, in physical and virtual places. Here, people are neither 'at work' nor 'at home', though they may indeed be undertaking these practices in either space. The invocation of music heritage practice is often connected to notions of dedication and enthusiasm, which produce aspects of third place communities such as conversation and mutual interest, conducted in typically neutral spaces. The following case studies further detail how contrasting methods of enacting popular music heritage can be characterised as third places. We begin with a consideration of community-run places of popular music preservation both in physical and online forms before moving on to examine mobile heritage experience and place.

COMMUNITY-RUN PLACES OF POPULAR MUSIC PRESERVATION

Community-run archives, museums and halls of fame of popular music are grassroots institutions which adopt a do-it-yourself approach to heritage. Often run entirely by volunteers, community archives are founded by enthusiasts of popular music cultures and serve the culture's community of interest. Sometimes these archives, museums and halls of fame are based geographically in a community, but in other cases serve and represent translocal, geographically dispersed yet affectively connected communities. Existing literature on community archives by scholars such as Flinn (2007), Caswell et al. (2016) and Wakimoto et al. (2013) point to the valuable contribution of grassroots heritage initiatives to the collection and preservation of cultural heritage. Baker's work, which is the focus of this section of the chapter, further suggests that these are also institutions which foster the well-being of volunteers who participate in the work of heritage management. These places are as much about personal and community enrichment by way of orientations towards learning, loving and living as they are about the management of popular music's material past (Baker 2017b). It is this dimension of community archives that make them akin to third places. Drawing on in-depth interviews with 125 grassroots heritage workers and site observations, Baker's research has explored the experiences of volunteers in 23 DIY institutions. From the data we can paint an ethnographically informed picture of community archives as third places based on Oldenburg's (1996–1997) ten indicators of third place.

As third places, community archives create community in a similar vein that Oldenburg emphasised the unifying of neighbourhoods. Interviews with volunteers at the Heart of Texas Country Music Museum (Brady, United States) underscored the role of their institution in bringing people together in a way that makes the museum central to the life of the town. As a collective body, the volunteers aimed to do 'everything that's right for Brady' (interview, 3 April 2014), taking a 'whole community' approach (interview, 4 April 2014). Indeed, many volunteers had little interest in country music and instead highlighted their involvement with the museum to be based on a desire to support and contribute to their town and local communities (interview, 4 April 2014).

Community archives also work to assimilate newcomers into the community through community of practice (Baker 2017b). Newcomers learn to navigate the work of the archive or museum, its processes, policies and practices, from experienced volunteers (Baker 2017a). Assimilation into the institution's community can extend a volunteer's connection to the broader community in which the archive or museum is located. For example, a volunteer at the Heart of Texas Country Music Museum described how as 'a new person in town' her interactions with other museum volunteers assisted her to develop 'a social network' and become a part of wider communities (interview, 4 April 2014).

For Oldenburg (1996–1997 p. 7), a characteristic of third place was the bringing together of youth and adults. In the community archives and museums of Baker's research, intergenerational interaction was often promoted. For the director of Tónlistarsafn Íslands (Kópavogur, Iceland) some of the most rewarding moments at the museum involve visits and enquiries by young people. He recalled how he had received a letter from a teenage boy who had been directed for a school project to explore the museum's online database: 'I'm 16-years-old, my grandmother died 20 years ago so I never met her. But here I met her' (interview, 23 August 2010). The director described this as a 'wow moment', providing much needed 'energy' to continue with the mission of preserving Iceland's music history (interview, 23 August 2010). Like many other community archives, Tónlistarsafn Íslands engages in outreach activities with schools to generate such moments, seeing these as opportunities to bridge generational divides. When young people enter the space of an exhibition and are involved in creating content, such as posters that reflect the theme of the display, the director 'feel[s] that in some ways there is [an opportunity for them to] come back to our grandparents' period, their grandparents' period' (interview, 11 October 2011).

As third places, community archives and museums foster a community of interest. In her interview, the secretary/librarian of the South Australian Jazz Archive (Adelaide, Australia), described an intellectual function served by this community archive. This is a place where like-minded people who share a love of jazz and a deep knowledge of jazz culture can gather productively together. She observed that the archive provides an opportunity for volunteers to engage in an 'intellectual exercise' which provides them with an outlet for the use and display of the extent of their vernacular knowledge (interview, 11 June 2013). This is particularly evident in the archive's book club meetings in which 'extraordinarily knowledgeable' people can 'hold forth' (interview 11 June 2013). Although, as the secretary/librarian observed, book club meetings have gradually morphed into 'seminars' (interview 11 June 2013) they still seem to serve the archive well in providing an opportunity for interested parties to get together socially, in a way that emphasises knowledge exchange, while putting to good use the duplicates in the archive's book collection.

Similarly, community archives and museums are sites of conversation. Indeed, the opportunities they provide to speak with fellow enthusiasts on wide-ranging topics beyond the preservation of music heritage is a motivating factor for volunteering in community archives. Volunteers at the Nederlands Jazz Archief (Amsterdam, the Netherlands) observed how these places offer 'something different from your job before retirement' because at the archive 'you work with people with the same interest' (interview, 5 February 2013). The archive's curator and co-directors emphasised how volunteers at the archive 'chat a lot' while undertaking archival tasks, with their conversations centred on such things as yesterday's events, politics, and bargain holidays in addition to reminiscences about the music they were archiving (interview, 4 February 2013). Oldenburg (1996–1997 p. 9) identifies 'conversation which is variously passionate and light-hearted, serious and witty, informative and silly' as a key characteristic of third place. Although conversing sometimes hampered the timely completion of archival tasks, in community archives conversations between volunteers are central to the success of the cultural mission as socialising between volunteers helps support the completion of desired preservation outcomes (Ohlandt 2013).

In addition to the serious conversations held by volunteers, these are institutions filled with jokes and laughter. The founder-curator of Museum RockArt (Hoek van Holland, the Netherlands), described his institution as a place for volunteers and visitors to have fun: 'that's what we do it for. To make people happy, to share the love of music' (interview, 24 September 2011). At the Australian Jazz Museum (Wantirna, Australia) having fun is a mantra and volunteers proudly emphasised that beyond the mission of preservation, 'we don't take ourselves too seriously here' (interview, 31 May 2011). As Oldenburg observes, 'Third places are entertaining' (1996–1997 p. 9). The emphasis on fun contributes to the feel of community archives, their affective atmospheres (Baker 2015). They are places of serious preservation, but the heritage work is accompanied by the sounds of laughing and light-hearted banter.

Unsurprisingly perhaps, given the above emphasis on conversation, fun and the coming together of like-minded people, community archives and museums nurture friendship. The 'gift of friendship', as Oldenburg calls it, is a vital aspect of third place and involves 'the tonic of friends met in numbers' (Oldenburg 1996–1997 p. 9). Volunteers at the Australian Jazz Museum emphasised how it is a 'friendly operation' run by a 'friendly bunch of people' (interview, 19 July 2011). Bringing together old-timers who have a long history in Melbourne's jazz scene alongside newcomers with little to no background in jazz, the Australian Jazz Museum provides opportunities to make 'good new friends' as well as foster 'old ones' (interview 19 July 2011). The museum provides the 'camaraderie of day to day activity' that retired volunteers would once have received from paid employment (interview, 31 May 2011). This highlights the social function of the community archive. As another put it, 'it's a wonderful place for meeting new people . . . and they're a lovely, wonderful group to work with' (interview, 8 October 2013).

The social function of these heritage organisations resonates with Oldenburg's (1996–1997 p. 8) observation that 'third places help care for the neighbourhood'. The community archives and museums of Baker's (2017b) study were characterised as caring environments. This was particularly evident at the Australian Jazz Museum where the collections manager was highly regarded by volunteers as someone deeply concerned with the well-being of the institution's people, not just its artefacts. In interviews, volunteers spoke of his commitment to getting elderly volunteers back on their feet after suffering bad falls by taking them to hospital appointments and to the physio and how he would draw on his past life as a pharmacist to provide volunteers with advice about their medication (e.g. interview, 26 June 2012). His concern for the health of volunteers' loved ones suffering from illnesses was also noted by volunteers (e.g. interview, 26 June 2012). As Oldenburg (1996–1997 p. 8) confirms, third places tend to be run by people who forge strong connections with their community of interest, contributing to the development of an environment predisposed to offering 'help and support'. Indeed, for the collections manager, community archives have the capacity to provide much needed 'social therapy' to volunteers (interview, 8 October 2013), beyond more general notions of the friendship opportunities that places like this can offer (see also Cantillon and Baker 2018).

Baker (2017b) also observed that community archives enable a productive retirement. Oldenburg (1996–1997 p. 9) understands third places to be 'important for retired people' in that they provide an opportunity to stay connected and to enjoy life beyond work. Volunteers at the Sarasota Music Archive (Sarasota, United States) explained that their work at the archive provided them with a sense of 'accomplishment' (interview, 7 April 2014). Similarly, those at the Nederlands Jazz Archief described the importance of continuing to have a 'job in society' post-retirement, seeing their contributions to the protection of vulnerable jazz artefacts as important work (interview, 5 February 2013). A volunteer at the Australian Jazz Museum described the organisation as providing 'a whole new career' but without the 'stress and strain' of employment (interview, 8 October 2013). The new sense of purpose fostered in this volunteer by the Australian Jazz Museum has given him 'a new interest in life, it's given me an activity, and a great feeling of satisfaction because my work's being recognised' (interview, 8 October 2013).

Ultimately, what all of the above ensure is that, as third places, community archives are places for living. For a number of volunteers, volunteering in the community archive was experienced as transformative: working towards the preservation of popular music's past and being a member of a vibrant community of volunteers provided meaning to their life. Volunteers at the Australian Country Music Hall of Fame (Tamworth, Australia) emphasised how their participation 'keeps the brain going' and the 'mind active' (interview, 3 August 2011). One volunteer noted that without the community archive 'I don't know where I'd be today, I really don't' (interview, 3 August 2011), while another described how the archive became 'like a family outside my family . . . we lift each other up' (interview, 4 August 2011). When describing the importance of third places for retirees, Oldenburg (1996–1997 p. 10) emphasises that the 'elderly' need 'community' and need it 'acutely'. Baker's (2017b) research supports the important place of the community archive and museum in the lives of older volunteers for whom these places can be life-sustaining. As the Hall's curator stated, 'What else am I going to do? Put myself in a house and lock it up and die? I don't think so, baby, I don't think so. Just give me country music and I'll die happy' (interview, 4 August 2011).

THIRD PLACE, VIRTUAL THIRD PLACE OR THIRD SPACE? ONLINE MUSIC ARCHIVES

While Baker's research focused on physical spaces of popular music preservation, author Collins' work examines online music archives. In the later revisions to The Great Good Places Oldenburg turned his attention to the virtual world as source of third place activity. Oldenburg is rather dismissive of the notion, stating new media has 'so atomized citizenry that the term "society" may no longer be appropriate' (Oldenburg 1999 p. 204). Oldenburg continues to state that in this environment it is the 'accumulated associations of a single individual' (Oldenburg 1999 pp. 264–265) that create networks of personal communities. For him this results in a weakening rather than a strengthening of society which is contrary to his idea of the third place as a place of community building. Furthermore,

Oldenburg re-emphasises his belief that third places should be physically located in the neighbourhood that they serve.

Written before the advent of Web 2.0 (O'Reilly 2005) and the growth of social media platforms, subsequent discussions of Oldenburg's third place have challenged this view and suggested that what has emerged is a 'virtual third place' (Soukup 2006) and a 'third space' (Wright 2012). For Soukup virtual third places share three components; localisation, accessibility and presence. These places aren't reliant on sharing physical locations but are constructed through discourse where individuals share a 'common 'symbolic space' which emphasises distinct local community-based commitments, goals and values' Soukup (2006 p. 434).

In his article, Wright critiques Soukup's analysis and suggests the term 'third space' is more appropriate. Third spaces, he suggests, are not to be thought of as virtual equivalents to Oldenburg's third place but should be considered in relation and context to the Internet. Thus, third spaces can be determined by the 'analysis of the discourse and patterns of participation' (Wright 2012 p. 10) within them and so for third spaces, as opposed to third places, location is no longer the key concern but rather the shared links that bring people together to interact in virtual spaces.

Both analyses can be seen in the online music heritage sites Birmingham Music Archive and The Golden Age of British Dance Bands, highlighted below. With a 'doing-it-together' approach (Collins 2015) to the construction of popular music histories and heritage, individuals come together online, forming communities dedicated to creating, populating, sustaining and celebrating alternative popular music histories. In such virtual third places and spaces the sharing and exchanging of memories and artefacts relating to popular music's past is manifest and indeed voluminous.

Birmingham Music Archive

Founded by Jez Collins, The Birmingham Music Archive (BMA) elicits its users to 'Tell us what you know' calling on the collective knowledge and expertise of the community to 'capture the entire history of popular music in and from the city' (Birmingham Music Archive 2008). Seeking memories, photographs and related artefacts of the city of Birmingham, UK, users of the BMA have formed a sizeable community numbering over 2500 people who share materials and engage in conversation. The nature of these exchanges can often appear mundane and scrappy when taken in isolation. However, when taken in context they can reveal themselves as part of a larger narrative in which contributors enter into conversation with one another, sometimes over a period of years, revealing deep connections to place, space and community.

Barbarella's is a fondly remembered disco, soul and then punk club located in Birmingham which opened in 1972 and closed in 1979. Posted in 2013, was this comment 'Hi I remember Barb's very well, I was in the band Model Mania, we played there many times. We were a kind of resident support band . . . our manager was the DJ at Barb's, Wayne Rossington Myers.' Replying to this post, one contributor triggered an ongoing conversation that was to develop over a period of three years: 'I thought you were pretty good! You played a song that had a great bit that went something like, 'Oh bay-ay-aybee you through [sic] shit in my fay-ay-ay-ace!' I still remember that all these years later and still think it is a cracking good sing-a-long chorus.'

A year later Wayne's sister wrote 'Just looking through archives of Rebecca's and Barbarella's and was really surprised and pleased to see my brother Wayne mentioned. As you know he was killed in a car crash in 1984. I would love to hear anything you can remember about him and his time at the clubs.' This was replied to the following year:

> I remember Wayne really well from those days. At my request he played a (just released) single by the band I played with. This took some guts as he'd never heard it but gave it a go anyway. To our relief it sounded great. I am sorry to say I did not know of the accident and am truly sorry to hear about it. Wayne was a good egg as was Christine. Happy memories of both at a brilliant time.

This example serves as an illustration of Oldenburg's third place as site of community participation anchored to a specific geographical location. But it can also be understood as both Soukup's virtual third place and Wright's third space. In these exchanges (which are still evolving three years after the initial post), we find the creation of community, of shared interests, of distinct localness and friendship and the shared histories and memories that bring people together long after individuals shared the same physical space.

The Golden Age of British Dance Bands

The Golden Age of British Dance Bands is a restricted Yahoo Group that was founded in 1999 and describes itself as a 'forum for all who love the Great British Dance Bands of the 1920s, 1930s and 1940s (and relevant bands thereafter) as well as the popular music of that era known as The Golden Age of British Dance Bands' (The Golden Age of British Dance Bands, n.d.). To join the group and its 759 members, prospective members have to apply to administrators. However, its associated Facebook Group is a public group and has 2219 members, a substantial community for what might appear as a niche subject.

The restricted nature of the group, and its lack of a grounded locational anchor would appear to be the antithesis of Oldenburg's ideal of a third place. It also contradicts Soukup's three key factors he suggests are needed when considering virtual third places; localisation, accessibility and presence. Wright's suggestion to shift the emphasis from place and its connotations with specific locations (Oldenburg's physical community centre or Collins' virtual Birmingham Music Archive for example) to space is useful here for groups such as The Golden Age of British Dance Bands who utilise platforms such as Facebook, Yahoo and Twitter to build their communities.

Wright suggests we need to look for particular examples of patterns of talk and participation around subjects rather than place in order to identify third spaces. This can be applied to the case of The Golden Age of British Dance Bands where members exchange information, knowledge and materials pertaining to British dance bands, linked together by a shared interest rather than being bound by notions of place.

As can be witnessed within the Yahoo Group a prodigious community building ethos is manifest in the group. Members seek answers to questions about specific musicians, records or events. They share links to YouTube and other footage found on the Internet relating to the group's interest, enter into discussion and debate about the merits of certain songs, albums, bands and recording quality, list records for sale (and inform members if they've seen records for sale) and arrange informal meet ups and events offline thereby blurring the boundaries between the virtual and physical third place and space. There is an ongoing process of strengthening of community ties that Oldenburg would recognise, far removed from the weakening of community and society that he predicated could happen with the advent of new media.

The Golden Age of British Dance Bands Facebook Group is just one of many groups, estimated to number in the thousands, that utilise Facebook's group function for celebrating and sharing music memories and building community (Collins and Long 2014; Long and Collins 2016). Here members of the community share knowledge and display their affection for British dance bands. Members enter into detailed conversations about the subject and embed YouTube and other sound files for members to listen to the music and they also upload historical photographs that trigger discussion and reminiscence. There is a constant flow of new content to the Group which appears more at-risk of loss when compared to the materials shared on the Yahoo Group. Authors of this chapter have written elsewhere about concerns for the long term sustainability of such communities, the archive materials they hold and the need for this to be addressed (Baker and Collins 2016).

Rather than atomising citizenry as Oldenburg lamented, it is apparent in the actions and coming together of so many people that there exists online thriving and vibrant communities who take it upon themselves to archive popular music's history and heritage and in so doing are creating and populating both 'virtual third places' and 'third spaces' as a means of achieving this.

THIRD PLACES BETWEEN THE PAST AND PRESENT: MUSIC WALKING TOURS

Whereas Baker and Collins have looked at discrete sites of community archiving of popular music on- and offline, Strong has explored the experience of music heritage in the form of walking tours. While there is a growing body of work on how popular music has become part of heritage, and the relationship between music and memory (see Strong 2015 for an overview of this literature), including work on how the physical space of urban environments plays a role in how popular music is remembered (for example, Lashua and Cohen 2010), there appears as yet to be little work on music walking tours. Given the urban nature of most popular music scenes, walking tours make sense as a way of creating experiences of this history for tourists and other interested parties, and indeed have been established in cities across the world. The walking tour avoids some of the problems museum-type displays can encounter that relate to the removal of music from its original (messy, noisy) contexts (Leonard 2010), and allows for an embodied experience that can create collective memories and a sense of place-making (see Wynn 2010). Third places may be a key factor in enabling this to take place, by allowing walkers to experience being part of the music scene they are learning about. This section then examines whether third places can be used to bring music heritage and the ongoing music activities of a city closer together, and how this might work.

The walking tour to be considered here is the Melbourne Music Walk, created by the City of Melbourne (the local council for the area covering the Melbourne CBD). This was launched on the City of Melbourne website in June 2017, as an online brochure that maps out a 3.5 kilometre route through the CBD, with points of interest noted and a guiding narrative that explains the significance of these places (City of Melbourne 2017). In recent years, Melbourne has been working to enhance its position as a 'music city' – a city that has an international reputation for having a strong music culture, particularly in relation to live music (Homan and Newton 2010). A focus on heritage has always been a part of this, and strategies to highlight Melbourne's music heritage, such as the naming of laneways after musicians and the establishment of a permanent music museum (the Music Vault), have increased in number and scale. The Melbourne Music Walk clearly fits into these activities and performs a number of functions. It focuses on current, ongoing music making in the city, but to an equal extent highlights the heritage aspects of Melbourne music. The route taken by the walk incorporates sites that are purely heritage-related (for example, Amphlett Lane, a small service street named after the singer from the band The Divinyls who passed away in 2014); sites that are current working venues that the narrative of the walk does not attempt to connect to the past (for example, venues Boney and Loop Bar); and other sites that sit between these. Venues such as the Cherry Bar, the Forum Theatre and Max Watt's are described both in terms of their ongoing music activities and in terms of their past contributions to Melbourne's musical reputation. Lists of touring bands that have performed at these venues that are included in the walk brochure serve to locate Melbourne as an important music hub nationally, internationally and historically. These venues all (to a greater or lesser extent) can be described as third places, as they are sites where people come together outside home or work to engage in pleasurable activities. Some serve this function precisely in line with Oldenburg's original discussion of third places; bars, a number of which are included in this walk, are one of his archetypal third places. Other venues that only hold ticketed events may not be attended on a regular basis in quite the same way, but are embedded in the same circuit of leisure spaces that bars inhabit. The question in relation to the Melbourne Music Walk was how an outsider, a tourist taking the walk, might encounter these third places. Were the venues best considered as heritage sites, third places to be looked at, or third places that might be encountered as third places in the context of this walk?

The author undertook the walk on two occasions in mid-July 2017; once in the late afternoon on a Tuesday, and once in the evening on a Saturday, in order to see how the experience might differ at these times, especially in relation to how a participant would interact with the venues being highlighted. Undertaking the walk at different times revealed very different possibilities for participants. Participating in the walk during the day, when venues are less likely to be open, significantly reduced the likelihood that walkers could do more than look at the outside of buildings. On the afternoon walk, a participant encounters a city at work, encountering the everyday activities this entails. Other people on the streets are likely to be workers or other tourists, especially at some of the sites highlighted on the walk such as ACDC Lane. The afternoon walk, then, had something in common with a museum visit, in that what was encountered was seen at a distance and appreciated as important through the explanations given about it. Although one was in the place where important events had taken place, and at the site of the third places related to these, there was a limited amount of engagement, and that which was possible was often highly controlled (for example, on guided tours of sites such as the Town Hall).

However, this changed significantly on the Saturday evening walk. The character of the city itself is notably different after dark (unsurprisingly), with the night time economy in full swing. Almost all of the venues were open, with patrons of the venues named on the tour making a noticeable difference to the busy-ness of the areas they were located in and to the type of people observed. In some of the venues, it was easy to walk in and become part of the activity in the space. At most venues, however, gigs and shows being held were ticketed, meaning people on the walk would either need to pay to enter or (in most cases) to have been organised in advance to purchase tickets to events that were sold out on the night. Despite this, the increased vibrancy in the vicinity of the venues still created a different experience than during the day. When venues could be accessed, or even outside venues in the midst of crowds, the prompts from the brochure to think about those important figures in music who had also occupied this space gained, in the author's mind, more immediacy, when surrounded by people in what might be a similar situation to these past events deemed important.

Of particular note was the experience in ACDC Lane on the evening walk. This lane is highlighted on the walk for two reasons: first, the laneway is of heritage value as 'the first street in Australia named after a rock band' and because of the way the name links this physical site with the idea of this band (see Strong et al. 2017); and second, it houses the rock venue the Cherry Bar. During the daytime walk, ACDC Lane was busy with tourists, mostly taking photos of and with the graffiti in the lane. At night, with a heavy metal show underway at the bar, it was filled with punters from the show (and still a few tourists). The experience a person doing the walk would have at this point could vary dramatically. Heavy metal fans on the walk may be unperturbed, whereas to someone completely unfamiliar with this subculture the scene in the laneway could be a novelty, or potentially even a frightening or threatening scenario. Regardless, there was still an effective combining of heritage discourse (in the name of the lane being that of a hard rock band) with the current activities taking place in the third place of the Cherry Bar (the playing of and listening to hard rock and heavy metal). What was being celebrated about the past was, in effect, also being enacted in the present. It was clear that for the show attendees spilling out into the laneway, they were inhabiting a third place where they were relaxing and socialising. In this instance, however, for the walker, watching others in their third place is all that can be experienced; the show is sold out so the Cherry Bar itself cannot be accessed.

Generally, the 'specialness' and non-everydayness of a walking tour means it would be difficult to describe it as a third place in itself. However, by focusing on venues, many of which are also bars and pubs that stay open regardless of whether a gig is being held, the Melbourne Music Walk's appeal is tied to third places. It also incorporates a number of actual third places into the tour, and, depending on when the walk is undertaken, gives those on the walk the possibility of interacting with these as third places rather than only as 'sites of interest' to be observed or intellectualised. This presents different possibilities for engaging with the heritage-related aspects of the walk, and for connecting these with the ongoing musical life of the city.

THE REUNION TOUR AS TEMPORARY THIRD PLACE?

Strong's research on music heritage tours demonstrates that third place can be evoked in interesting ways by popular music scholars that are in some cases removed from the original imaginary of Oldenburg. This is also the case for Driessen, whose work considers the reunion concert tour of heritage music acts as a site where aspects of third place are enacted. To do this Driessen explores these concerts as arenas for fans to revive past fandoms. The music fan has increasingly been considered as a collector and preservationist of popular music heritage (see Brandellero et al. 2015; Duffett and Löbert 2015). Although fans often invest in a tangible collection to illustrate their enthusiasm about a particular artist, for example by collecting records, concert tickets or T-shirts, some fan practices are intangible. While memories of a concert might be recollected through the viewing of photos, the feelings produced in that experience cannot be adequately captured by images or curated in a museum display. A reunion concert, a site to revive the past and reignite fandom, offers an interesting site for reliving and preserving these intangible memories. Differing from a typical third place in Oldenburg's (1999) conception, a reunion tour or concert does not have a permanent location – like a bar or a concert hall. However, the shows themselves are held in such places, making it possible to consider and thus examine the concerts as temporary third places. Characteristics of a third place are present, albeit for a fixed moment in time. Moreover, it can be argued that precisely due to their impermanent character, they deploy characteristics resembling a third place: the concert evening provides a place without obligations, in contrast to the work or family environment in which attendees might find themselves in everyday life. Consequently, this also means that status or rank is of no importance, everyone (who can afford it) is invited to join and relive the past at such concerts.

The reunion occasion highlighted here is The Big Reunion. In particular, The Big Reunion concerts, which extend Oldenburg's (1999) foundational notion as emblematic 'temporary third places'. The Big Reunion was initially created as a reality documentary TV programme aired by British commercial broadcaster ITV2 in 2013, followed by a second season in 2014. The show reformed mainstream popular music acts from the late 1990s to the start of the 2000s, for a second shot at fame. Its participants were once chart-topping boy bands like 5ive, 911 and 3T, and girl bands like Atomic Kitten, B*Witched and Eternal. The viewers are given a look behind the scenes of their reformation. A typical episode described how the band broke up, highlighted their past fame, after which a transition to the present was made. Then, the episode documents how the band 'finally' reconvened, talked through their (bad) break-up and what followed. After this reconciliation-footage, the hard work of the band (vocal training and dance lessons) to get back in shape for the reunion concert was presented. About a million viewers (and half a million for the second season) per week followed these physical and mental preparations to the bands' reunion concert. The high popularity of the television show led to a sold-out reunion performance at the Hammersmith Apollo in London. Due to this success, the concept transitioned from screen to stage and The Big Reunion Tour eventually hit fourteen music arenas across the United Kingdom and Ireland. This tour was followed by, The Big Pop Party (2013), The Christmas Party (2013), and The Boyband Tour (following season two in 2014).

The average audience member of The Big Reunion is someone who was a teenager in the late 1990s, and is now an adult (25 to 40 years old). Often, audience groups are among friends of the same age, or are paired with a parent. The Big Reunion is not aimed at a specific type of visitor, yet it is aimed at a specific cohort, the generation who came of age with these mainstream boy and girl bands. Further, being at a concert and enjoying music from the past, asks the participants to be playful and frivolous – elements belonging to and enacted in a third place (cf. Oldenburg, 1999). Concertgoers intend to have a good time, and to catch up with (old) friends, not to sit down and seriously listen to the music.

In December 2013, Driessen attended The Big Reunion Christmas Party-shows in Birmingham and London. The bands 5ive, B*Witched, Liberty X, The Honeyz, 911, and Atomic Kitten performed at these Christmas-themed concerts. Each of the bands was allowed to play three songs in the first half of the show, which were usually their biggest hits from the past; in the second part of the show, the bands played Christmas covers. The Christmas theme was visible via Christmas trees, Santa hats, and fake snow, which formed the stage decoration. Some concert attendees wore hats with blinking stars, or bought the Santa hat created for the occasion featuring the logo of The Big Reunion. Other visitors wore T-shirts of the tour, bought tote bags with the show's logo on it, or (older) T-shirts of the bands that played. Selina, one of the visitors met on site, bought glow sticks to wave around during the concert. She attended the gig because of 'childhood memories, because they're really the bands we grew up [with] when we were younger'.

Upon asking the concertgoers why they attended the reunion gig, Selina's answer appeared to be emblematic. Similarly, Reanne, who attended the concert with her friend and her mother, and had been to several of the shows after the initial performance in the Hammersmith Apollo, also mentioned how 'it just brings back memories of childhood'. However, for other attendees it was just a fun night out. Rachel and Lizzie had seen the programme on ITV2, and considered their trip to the music arena as a 'fun day out'. Another female visitor said that she was looking forward to dancing and singing along. Moreover, she was there not to see any of the bands in particular, but 'just to have a good time'. The audience did dance along; many of the bands had specific dance routines to their hit songs, which the band members themselves, their background dancers and the audience attempted to carry out exactly as they did in their heydays. Due to the artists being slightly older than when they originally performed these routines in their heyday, at times it was visible how they struggled with the routines, when they forgot a step or took a small break.

The concert was an opportunity to watch music acts perform who had not performed for over a decade. The Big Reunion moved beyond remembering music. Rebecca emailed after the concert how she 'was automatically taken back to my school discos . . . for just over 2 hours, [we] didn't have to worry about work, money or house work. We could sing, laugh and be silly. . . Brilliant!' The concert provided a site for the attendees to reform as well: they could travel back in time themselves, escape everyday adult life, or just get together with friends. Donna visited the concert after work, together with two friends. Afterwards, she emailed 'for me the only downside wasn't the concert itself, but the prices of things once inside like food and drinks'. This may be a challenge to consider future concerts as a temporary third place, since third places need to be low profile, accessible and accommodating. However, Donna's ability to see the concert with friends overruled this downside.

Although not complying with all features of a third place, the reunion concert does offer a neutral, levelling, playful and frivolous – albeit temporary – space for a community of interest to get together. As a site to remember and recollect intangible memories of popular music, the reunion concert is a place where both fans and bands reform.

CONCLUSION

These case studies highlight the variety of ways in which characteristics of third place are active in popular music heritage practices. Given its physicality and strong community focus, the more traditional space of the archive outlined by Baker aligns most easily with the idea of third place. The extension of this into the moveable (walking tours, band tours) and virtual (online archives) spaces further sees a renewed approach to contemporary iterations of the third place. Certainly, there are some caveats in their resemblance of third places. For example, 'accessibility' as one of Oldenburg's criteria is manipulated in terms of online forums (access is available easily only to those who have a computer and the Internet) and it could be seen as restricted in Driessen's appraisal of heritage act touring, in which tickets can only be purchased by those who can afford them. Similarly, the criteria that third places are a 'home away from home' could be contested in the above cases, though many spaces maintain a degree of neutrality. Music heritage activities often encourage conversation and invite regular participation within communities. In these examples, and perhaps in those beyond, heritage work or experience can engage people of all walks of life, thereby aligning with the idea of the third place as a 'leveler'.

Our contributions here are not exhaustive, for there are further activities of popular music heritage that extend or blend aspects of those already illustrated. One such example comes in the performance of 'heritage' popular music, as found in tribute acts (see Homan 2006; Bennett 2009), and localised 'cover' music. In simulating or remaking the sounds of well-known artists, bands, or genres, performers can also be seen as enacting characteristics of third place in both rehearsal spaces and venues. In these places of neutral territory, regular performers potentially contribute to elements of conversation, light mood, and enter into a space where roles are levelled. Using experience of popular music heritage within the concept of third place and vice versa allows for an expansion of the ways we consider third place to manifest in new and previously under-considered spaces of activity. This is particularly prevalent as communities move with developments in technology, which in turn change the ways we spend our leisure time, especially regarding music and its related heritages. To this end, considering popular music heritage as 'third place' enables a greater inclusion of physical, mobile, and online communities simultaneously engaging with others through the lens of music in the past and present.

REFERENCES

Aabø, S. and Audunson, R. (2012), 'Use of library space and the library as place', *Library & Information Science Research*, 34 (2), 138–149.

Baker, S. (2015), 'Affective archiving and collective collecting in do-it-yourself popular music archives and museums'. In S. Baker (ed.), *Preserving Popular Music Heritage: Do-it-Yourself, Do-it-Together*. New York: Routledge, pp. 11, 46.

Baker, S. (2017a), 'Learning, loving and living at the Australian Country Music Hall of Fame'. In H. Roued-Cunliffe and A. Copeland (eds), *Participatory Heritage*. London: Facet Publishing, pp. 47–56.

Baker, S. (2017b), *Community Custodians of Popular Music's Past: A DIY Approach to Heritage*. London, New York: Routledge.

Baker, S. and Collins, J. (2016), 'Popular music heritage, community archives and the challenge of sustainability', *International Journal of Cultural Studies*, first published on 9 March 2016 as doi:10.1177/1367877916637150.

Bennett, A. (2009), 'Heritage rock': Rock music, representation and heritage discourse', *Poetics*, 37 (5), 474–489.

Birmingham Music Archive (2008), About Us. Accessed 16 January 2017 at http://www.birminghammusicarchive.com/about-us/.

Brandellero, A., Van der Hoeven, A. and Janssen, S. (2015), 'Valuing popular music heritage: Exploring amateur and fan-based preservation practices in museums and archives in the Netherlands'. In S. Baker (ed.), *Preserving Popular Music Heritage: Do-it-Yourself, Do-it-Together*. New York: Routledge, pp. 31–45.

Cantillon, Z. and Baker, S. (2018), 'DIY heritage institutions as third places: Caring, community and wellbeing among volunteers at the Australian Jazz Museum'. *Leisure Sciences*, doi: 10.1080/01490400.2018.1518173.

Caswell, M., Cifor, M. and Ramirez, M.H. (2016), 'To suddenly discover yourself existing: Uncovering the impact of community archives', *The American Archivist*, 79 (1), 56–81.

Cheang, M. (2002), 'Older adults' frequent visits to a fast-food restaurant: Nonobligatory social interaction and the significance of play in a "third place"'. *Journal of Aging Studies*, 16 (3), 303–321.

City of Melbourne (2017), Melbourne Music Walk. Accessed 11 July 2017 at https://whatson.melbourne.vic.gov.au/visitors/Documents/Melbourne_Music_Walk_June2017.pdf.

Collins, J. (2015), 'Doing-it-together: Public history-making and activist archivism in online popular music archives'. In S. Baker (ed.), *Preserving Popular Music Heritage: Do-it-Yourself, Do-it-Together*. New York, Routledge: pp. 77–90.

Collins, J. and Long, P. (2014), '"Fillin' in any blanks I can": Online archival practice and virtual sites of musical memory'. In S. Cohen, R. Knifton, M. Leonard and L. Roberts (eds), *Sites of Popular Music Heritage: Memories, Histories, Places*. New York, London: Routledge: pp. 81–96.

Duffett, M. and Löbert, A. (2015), 'Trading offstage photos: Take That fan culture and the collaborative preservation of popular music heritage'. In S. Baker (ed.), *Preserving Popular Music Heritage: Do-it-Yourself, Do-it-Together*. New York: Routledge, pp. 151–164.

Facebook. (n.d.), The Golden Age of British Dance Bands. [Public Facebook Group] https://www.facebook.com/groups/282519584859/.

Flinn, A. (2007), 'Community histories, community archives: Some opportunities and challenges', *Journal of the Society of Archivists*, 28 (2), 151–176.

Harris, C. (2007), 'Libraries with lattes: The new third place', *Australasian Public Libraries and Information Services*, 20 (4), 145–152.

Homan, S. (2006), *Access All Eras: Tribute Bands And Global Pop Culture: Tribute Bands and Global Pop Culture*. London: McGraw-Hill Education.

Homan, S. and Newton, D. (2010), *The Music Capital: City of Melbourne Music Strategy*. Melbourne: City of Melbourne.

Kong, L. (1999), 'The invention of heritage: Popular music in Singapore', *Asian Studies Review*, 23 (1), 1–25.

Lashua, B. and Cohen, S. (2010), 'Liverpool musicscapes: Music performance, movement and the built urban environment'. In B. Fincham, M. McGuinness and L. Murray (eds), *Mobile Methodologies*. London: Palgrave, pp. 71–84.

Leonard, M. (2010), 'Exhibiting popular music: Museum audiences, inclusion and social history', *Journal of New Music Research*, 39 (2), 171–181.

Long, P. and J. Collins (2016), 'Affective memories of music in online heritage practice'. In J. Brusila, Johnson, B. and Richardson, J. (eds), *Memory, Space and Sound*. Chicago: University of Chicago Press, pp. 85–101.

Montgomery, S.E. and Miller, J. (2011), 'The third place: The library as collaborative and community space in a time of fiscal restraint', *College & Undergraduate Libraries*, 18 (2–3), 228–238.

Ohlandt, N.L. (2013), 'Creating a greater connection: Volunteer training in Seattle-area museums', Doctoral Dissertation, University of Washington.

Oldenburg, R. (1996–1997), 'Our vanishing third places', *Planning Commissioners Journal*, 25 (4), 6–10.

Oldenburg, R. (1999), *The Great Good Place: Cafes, Coffee Shops, Bookstores, Bars, Hair Salons, and Other Hangouts at the Heart of a Community*. Boston: Da Capo Press.

O'Reilly, T. (2005), Design patterns and models for the next generation of software. Accessed 12 January 2011 at http://www.oreillynet.com/oreilly/tim/news /2005/09/30/what-is-web-20.html.

Roberts, L. and Cohen, S. (2014), 'Unauthorising popular music heritage: Outline of a critical framework', *International Journal of Heritage Studies*, 20 (3), 241–261.

Robinson, S. and Deshano, C. (2011), 'Citizen journalists and their third places: what makes people exchange information online (or not)?', *Journalism Studies*, 12 (5), 642–657.

Rosenbaum, M.S. (2006), 'Exploring the social supportive role of third places in consumers' lives', *Journal of Service Research*, 9 (1), 59–72.

Schmutz, V. (2005), 'Retrospective cultural consecration in popular music: Rolling Stone's greatest albums of all time', *American Behavioral Scientist*, 48 (11), 1510–1523.

Slater, A. and Jung Koo, H. (2010), 'A new type of "Third Place"?', *Journal of Place Management and Development*, 3 (2), 99–112.

Soukup, C. (2006), 'Computer-mediated communication as a virtual third place: Building Oldenburg's great good places on the world wide web', *New Media & Society*, 8 (3), 421–440.

Steinkuehler, C.A. and Williams, D. (2006), 'Where everybody knows your (screen) name: Online games as "third places"', *Journal of Computer-Mediated Communication*, 11 (4), 885–909.

Strong, C. (2015), 'Shaping the past of popular music: Remembering, forgetting and documenting'. In S. Waksman and A. Bennett (eds), *The Sage Handbook of Popular Music Studies*. London: Sage, pp. 418–433.

Strong, C., Cannizzo, F. and Rogers, I. (2017), 'Aesthetic cosmopolitan, national and local popular music heritage in Melbourne's music laneways', *International Journal of Heritage Studies*, 23 (2), 83–96.

The Golden Age of British Dance Bands (n.d.), About. Accessed 16 January 2017 at https://groups.yahoo.com/neo/groups/british-dance-bands/info.

Wakimoto, D.K., Bruce, C. and Partridge, H. (2013), 'Archivist as activist: Lessons from three queer community archives in California', *Archival Science*, 13 (4), 293–316.

Wright, S. (2012), 'From "third place" to "third space": Everyday political talk in non-political online spaces', *javnost – the public*, 19 (3), 5–20.

Wynn, J.R. (2010), 'City tour guides: Urban alchemists at work', *City and Community*, 9 (2), 145–164.

8. Third places and social capital: case study community gardens

Joanne Dolley

INTRODUCTION

Community gardens, often designed, created and maintained by local residents, share many of the intentions and characteristics of third places. Community gardens can act as an informal neighbourhood meeting place outside of home (first place) or work (second place). This chapter focuses on the community aspect of community gardens, utilising the concept of third place to explore how community gardens have the potential to contribute to building social capital and a sense of community. It is apparent across community gardens studies internationally that third place characteristics are in evidence and several studies have made direct reference to community gardens being third places (Firth et al. 2011; Glover 2004; Thompson and Maggin 2012; Calderon et al. 2014; Veen et al. 2014; Galdini 2016).

There is evidence that unstructured social activity is declining in the US, a trend confirmed by Oldenburg (1997), who noted the disappearance of opportunities for informal social gatherings in what he labels 'the great good place' or the 'third place'. Social researchers have shown that increased isolation and alienation in cities in an increasingly globalised society lead to the demise of sense of community, which has implications for people's sense of place, their feelings of trust, safety, happiness and well-being (Jacobs 1996; Frumpkin 2003; Son et al. 2010; Sennett 2012; Easthorpe and McNamara 2013). Putnam lamented the demise of community in *Bowling Alone*, in which he described the decline of group participation activities through privatisation of leisure activities such as home theatres and corresponding isolation of individuals within neighbourhoods (Putnam 2000). Add to that the number of neighbourhood locales where we might have spoken to neighbours are reducing, with automated supermarket checkouts; the DVD store replaced by online movies; and on the local public transport, many of us stare down at our phones with earplugs in our ears. As urban populations densify and population mobility increases, solving problems of social isolation will become increasingly important to the creation and maintenance of healthy vibrant functioning cities.

The hypothesis in this chapter is that some community gardens act as third places, improving neighbourhood social capital in two ways. First, community gardens promote creation of weak ties (bridging capital) between members, neighbours, and visitors in the local vicinity. Second, for some members they also act as clubs which may strengthen weak ties into strong ties of friendship (bonding capital). Third places allow locals and newcomers to informally meet people in their neighbourhood. Planners and architects can design public places which encourage third place interactions. However, members of the local community itself usually design community gardens and have potential to activate its third place qualities.

The chapter first gives a brief literature review on community gardens and social capital. It then describes each of the eight characteristics of third place and uses an example from the community garden literature to illustrate each particular characteristic. The chapter then briefly discusses the research methodology and two case study sites from a larger study of seven community gardens. The study showed that not all community gardens are third places across all eight characteristics of third place. Data from two case study community gardens which act as third places across all eight characteristics is used to investigate if community garden participation leads to increased social capital, through building social ties within and beyond the garden setting. The chapter concludes by drawing together aspects of third place community gardens to envisage the utopian third place community garden.

COMMUNITY GARDENS

In the past two decades, there has been an upsurge of interest in community gardens in numerous countries, including Australia, the USA, Canada, Singapore, Denmark, Germany, New Zealand and Italy (Australian Community Gardens Network 2014; Birky and Strom 2013; Galdini 2016; Tan and Neo 2009; Firth et al. 2011). There are many different types of community gardens in practice today including indigenous gardens, kitchen gardens, garden clubs, re-vegetation projects (or native gardens), healing and therapy, school gardens, environmental restoration, demonstration and neighbourhood pocket parks and permaculture gardens (Ferris et al. 2001: Pascoe and Wyatt-Smith 2013). Some community gardens are place based, peopled by members who live within walking distance. Others are interest-based and may focus on activities such as work skill training, crime diversion, sustainability education and market days. A comprehensive systematic study of community garden literature conducted in 2012 found that very few studies defined the term 'community garden' (Guitart et al. 2012). Ferris et al., in defining community garden in their research, found the common factor was 'that specific communities actively support them' (Ferris et al. 2001 p. 562). Glover notes three important factors in defining a community garden, namely: located in an urban environment; produces food and/or flowers; and benefits individuals and communities (Glover 2003). The American Community Garden Association include in their definition that it is 'urban agriculture' gardened by a group (Birky and Strom 2013). This chapter applies Glover's definition of community gardens: 'An organised section of land located in an urban environment that is used to produce food and/ or flowers and benefits both individuals and communities' (Glover 2003 p. 265).

The literature indicates that community gardens are generally inclusive and informal, based around broadly common interests, attracting people of a range of ages and demographics. While clubs and societies may have a narrow focus, community gardens attract members motivated by a broad range of goals including growing organic food, social justice, charity, self-help, exercise, environmental action, education, socialising, civic engagement and skill building (Gaynor 2006; Guitart et al. 2012; Lyons et al. 2013; Ohmer et al. 2009; Turner 2011; Pascoe and Howes 2017). The benefits of community gardens are numerous and include enabling food security for political, economic and health reasons; enacting LA21 and the UN sustainability goals; crime prevention; beautifying an area; an alternative to modern food production and distribution; environmental activism; and protecting natural space (Draper and Freedman 2010; Hogan and Thorpe 2009; Walter 2013; Veen et al. 2014; Lyons et al. 2013; Zoellner et al. 2012; Ferris et al. 2001). Consensus in the literature indicates that community gardens are overall a positive initiative for those involved and the surrounding community.

Draper and Freedman (2010) suggested that as community gardens are a collective activity, they promote social interactions between members. Pascoe and Howes (2017) reported that numerous community gardeners indicated that the social aspect of the garden was not the primary reason for joining a community garden, however, many stated it as a benefit, or an unexpected bonus, often overtaking the initial motivation of growing food. Regular contact occurs in community gardens between members and volunteers at meetings and working bees, as well as informal encounters.

Community gardens combine nature with community. Planners recognise a need for public green space (Ferris et al. 2001). Yokohari and Amati note increasing demands for planners to restore nature in cities through parks and open spaces in urban areas to achieve a 'city in nature' (Yokohari and Amati 2005 p. 53). Access to nature in urban environments helps promote well-being in the community through generating positive feelings, sustained attention, relaxed wakefulness, and reduced anxiety (Shi et al. 2014; Shanahan et al. 2015; Yokohari and Amati 2005). Community gardens are viewed by those involved as 'important tools for improving communities, particularly for distressed neighbourhoods that often lack green space' (Ohmer et al. 2009 p. 398). Community gardens are a combination of a social landscape (community) and natural landscape (garden) in an urban landscape.

THIRD PLACES

The concept of third place, developed by Ray Oldenburg, can be summed up as 'informal public gathering spaces' (Oldenburg 1997 p. 6). Oldenburg generalises that compared to home (first place) and work (second place), third places provide opportunities for people to meet and interact on neutral ground and to develop a sense of belonging to place (Oldenburg 1989). Oldenburg describes third places as 'mediation between the individual and the larger society' which 'help to improve community spirit' (Oldenburg 1999 p. xxix). Both Oldenburg (1999) and Putnam (2000) argue that in the USA, society and socialising occurs almost entirely within private homes. Auge would argue that popular public places in the USA, such as airports and large shopping malls are impersonal 'non-spaces' (Auge 1995). Thompson and Maggin suggest that regular incidental interaction between people increases feelings of caring and safety (Thompson and Maggin 2012 p. 260). Third places provide opportunities for relaxed interactions and are inclusive across age, class and cultural backgrounds (Mele et al. 2015).

Third place offers a useful conceptual stance for investigating the community aspect of community gardens. Community gardens exhibit most, and in many cases all of the characteristics of third places in that they, to varying extents, have porous boundaries, where many people not involved in community gardens still show an interest and interact with gardeners. Interactions with the community can take place outside the garden where the garden is an opening topic of conversation. Community gardens which act as third places potentially strengthen weak ties and provide a sense of community well-being.

THIRD PLACE COMMUNITY GARDENS CREATING SOCIAL CAPITAL

Third place interactions provide an opportunity for the formation of weak ties, some of which may lead to strong ties of friendship and all of which contribute to building local social capital and forming of a sense of community. Third place acts to build social capital, particularly bridging capital (Putnam 2000). Social capital is an important indicator of the social well-being of a community (ABS 2004). For the purpose of this chapter, Putnam's (2000 p. 19) definition of social capital will be used: 'Social capital refers to connections among individuals – social networks and the norms of reciprocity and trustworthiness that arise from them.'

Firth et al. (2011) found that social capital provided a useful framework for investigating how community gardens function. 'Community gardens create social capital in that they create a meeting place, which enables people to interact and contribute to the creation of community. This helps to build bonding social capital through increasing ties between neighbours and like-minded individuals' (Firth et al. 2011 p. 565). An example of this kind of social capital building can be found in Kingsley and Townsend's research example of a community gardener in Portside, Melbourne, Australia who said that she had not met any neighbours in 15 years until she joined the community garden (Kingsley and Townsend 2006). Involvement in community gardening was found to increase residents' perception of bonding and bridging social capital in Flint, Michigan, USA (Alaimo et al. 2010). Such examples indicate that the effect of community gardens in some cases reach into the community.

This chapter utilises Granovetter's theory of weak ties, which are the loose ties between acquaintances and people who socialise together occasionally (Granovetter 1983). The theory of weak ties was developed in the 1960s by Granovetter when he investigated how people came to know about job opportunities (Easley and Kleinberg 2010). Granovetter's interview data showed that people were more likely to find out about a job opportunity from people they described as an 'acquaintance' rather than a close friend. He developed views of friendship across networks and described ties between friends as either weak or strong ties. Weak ties play an important role in creating feelings of safety, connection and well-being in communities (Chitov 2006).

Community gardens are usually open to the public and many people who are not involved in the gardens still show an interest in the garden. The results from Galdini's investigation of two community gardens in Berlin outline how they help build cohesion and vitality in a community, contributing to the 'generation of bonding and bridging social capital'

(Galdini 2016 p. 1). There is ample opportunity for over the fence conversations about the weather, plants and other neighbourhood matters. In addition, interactions with the community can take place beyond the community garden, where the community garden features as a point of conversation between gardeners and non-gardeners. Bende and Nagy's study of community gardens in Szeged, Hungary found that community gardens help people who are new to the area integrate into the community through forming connections with the gardeners' social networks (Bende and Nagy 2016). Draper and Freedman found that, 'The collective nature that differentiates community gardens from private gardens means that a social interaction is inevitable and the cultivation of meaningful relationships are likely to occur' (Draper and Freedman 2010 p. 484). Community gardens create opportunities for social capital development within the garden and the wider community.

EIGHT CHARACTERISTICS OF THIRD PLACES – COMMUNITY GARDEN LITERATURE

The characteristics of third place make an appearance in various forms across community garden research internationally. For the purpose of this chapter, the eight criteria used in Oldenburg's 1989 book are used to describe a third place. An example from the community garden literature will be given for each of the eight third place characteristics in this section.

Characteristic 1: They're Neutral Ground

Oldenburg described third places as open to all – places where everyone is free to come and go without obligations (Oldenburg 1999). Gaynor (2006) described community garden members as working cooperatively and the produce is often shared. In the Saldivar-tanaka and Krasny study of 20 Latino community gardens in New York City community gardens have been described as 'unique participatory landscapes' where the gardens were the locations for numerous neighbourhood social, educational, and cultural events (Saldivar-tanaka and Krasny 2004 p. 399). As one community garden participant indicated, 'It brings together people who might not participate in meetings, but would get together and get their hands dirty' (Ohmer et al. 2009 p. 390). However, the neutral characteristic is challenged in some community gardens with strong committee membership obligations, fees and locked gate access.

Characteristic 2: They're 'Levellers'

Third places are not dependent on participants' social or economic status as everyone is free to be there regardless. Third places bring together people of different ages, classes, ethnicity and skill levels. Community gardens create a mix of people interacting. Galdini said that community gardeners in Berlin noted the many different groups, ages, occupations and classes represented, described by one participant as, 'People from different milieus can come together here. That is not so much the case in other spaces around here' (Galdini 2016 p. 16). As Oldenburg said, 'One of the good feelings they experience is that stemming from the realization that they are accepted and liked by people from many different walks of life' (Oldenburg 1999 p. 45).

Characteristic 3: Conversation is a Main Activity

Third places enable routine social encounters and conversation is the main activity. In the third place literature, opportunities for conversation are enhanced when there is a reason for people to speak with each other. Oldenburg (1997) gives the examples of games such as boules in a park, or pool in a pub which help promote conversation. Third places 'should facilitate casual encounters as well as settings for sustained conversations' (Knox 2005 p. 8). Gardening in a community setting adds value to the third place notion, as gardening provides a common reason to initiate a conversation. People share information and participate in activities together or chat with non-members about the garden. In Dutch allotment gardening, participants noted the variety of conversations ranging from joking and teasing to very serious conversations amongst the gardeners. 'Working side by side, it's easy to talk because it creates an atmosphere of trust and togetherness' (Veen et al. 2014 p. 277). Studies in Sweden, Denmark and Australia noted the importance or benefits of the social aspect of community gardens as a motivation either to join, or to remain involved (Bonow and Normark 2017; Turner 2011; Pascoe and Howes 2017). Community gardens promote conversation as they provide authentic purpose for initiating conversations on broad topics of common interest (weather, plants, activities) requiring no specialist knowledge.

Characteristic 4: They're Easy to Access and Accommodating

Oldenburg's third place concept is place-based, as he argued that third places should be accessible by walking; they are open to everyone; and they are places where you see the familiar neighbourhood faces

(Oldenburg 1999). 'The nature and frequency of routine encounters and shared experiences depend a great deal on attributes of these spaces and places.' (Knox 2005 p.8). Bende and Nagy (2016) determined that the community gardens investigated in Szeged, Hungary became meeting places themselves. Galdini's study of community gardens in Berlin found that they play a role in placemaking where, 'it is not that gardens make communities, rather making gardens makes communities' (Galdini 2016 p.17). Most community gardens are broadly place-specific to weather, seasons, soil type and choice of plants relating to local diet. However, not all community gardens are place based, but can include interest-based communities, drawing people from beyond the local area (Firth et al. 2011; Easthorpe and McNamara 2013). Interest-based community gardens may exhibit club-like features, therefore may be less third place-like.

Characteristic 5: They Have a Core Group of Influential Regulars/Characters

Third places have a core group of influential regulars or characters who contribute to the friendly atmosphere and play a role in introducing newcomers. The regulars know people and keep an eye on the neighbourhood (Oldenburg 1989). Community garden regulars include organisers, plot holders and neighbours. Chitov's New York study found that community gardens such as the East New York gardens exist because of the work of particular 'characters'. 'It is primarily because of characters like Juanita that the East New York gardens exist. Bridging social capital is also reinforced by these characters' (Chitov 2006 p.454). The characters are often the ones who provide a homely, friendly atmosphere amongst organisers, plot holders and passers-by. However, when community garden regulars are burdened with too much responsibility, it can affect the longevity of the community garden. For example, Bonow and Normark (2017) cautioned, that in their observations of community gardens in Stockholm, Sweden, that gardens may rely heavily on only one or two organisers, which can affect their longevity.

Characteristic 6: They Have a Low Profile Instead of Being Showy

Oldenburg (1989) describes third places as homely, plain and tending to being wholesome. The community garden literature refers to community gardens as bringing 'authenticity' to urban environments (Zukin 2010 p.197). Third places are low key rather than showy. Galdini noted that Berlin community gardeners didn't mind getting their hands into the dirt in order to transform, 'uncared-for spaces into attractive gardens and places where neighbours and kids can meet, socialize and work together' (Galdini 2016 p. 14). Bende and Nagy (2016) talked about the handmade fixtures made by the community gardeners in Szeged in Hungary, including scarecrows, outdoor furniture and BBQs.

Characteristic 7: The Mood is Playful

The concept of third place is associated with incidental interactions. Third places are fun and 'the entertainment is provided by the people themselves' through lively conversation (Oldenburg 1997 p. 9). Third places are about enjoyment and exhibit a lively atmosphere. Ohmer et al. reported that community gardeners find it, 'really fun to get together with neighbours' in a community garden (Ohmer et al. 2009 p. 390). Bonow and Normark found that of 48 community garden interviewees in Stockholm, Sweden, 'Almost all of the gardeners answered that they were engaged in a community garden because it was fun' (Bonow and Normark 2017 p. 8).

Characteristic 8: They Feel Like Homes Away From Home

Third places are comfortable and people feel at home while they are there (but without the obligations which might come along with 'home' or 'work'). Hondagneu-Sotelo states that 'Gardens evoke Eden' and act 'as a sanctuary from the frenetic pace of public life, work, and competition' (Hondagneu-Sotelo 2010). Veen et al. spoke to gardeners who described the atmosphere as, 'Often it's sociable in the evenings, when you are at the canteen and you are with everyone else, you play cards and you talk but you also exchange experiences' (Veen et al. 2014 p. 270). Numerous community garden studies report the members saying that the act of gardening was relaxing compared to their regular daily stresses (Bonow and Normark 2017; Pascoe and Howes 2017).

METHOD AND FINDINGS

Reviewing the literature showed that community gardens had not been specifically studied in relation to 'third place', therefore very few articles contain data which is sufficient to demonstrate if community gardens of different types and locations all equally act as third places. The author collected and analysed data with the intention of determining if community gardens are third places. To do this a framework of the eight characteristics of third place was applied to case study data in Australia and Denmark. The author interviewed 29 community gardeners across seven case study sites including five community gardens in Australia (one Sydney, three Brisbane, one Gold Coast) and two in Denmark (one Albertslund, one Odense). Key stakeholders were interviewed, which included members and volunteers including at least one committee member at each site. Responses were analysed by coding the data into themes using NVIVO. The themes included the eight characteristics of third places. The sites cover a range of community garden designs, governance and urban environments.

The investigation found that individual community gardens fit on a scale between a club (with formal governance, membership obligations and common interests), to a third place (as described by the eight charac-teristics). All community gardens visited exhibited most, if not all, of the eight characteristics of third places. Community gardens which exhibit every third place characteristic are: open to the public at all hours; based in a walkable location in the neighbourhood it serves; have regulars – both members and visitors; and their activities and stories reach beyond the physical boundaries to local people who are not members. The community gardens show evidence of weak and strong ties of association amongst members and weak ties developing beyond the boundaries into the broader neighbourhood.

The community gardens which were more like a club than a third place tended to be interest-based rather than place-based, drawing members from further afield, for example to educate about sustainability. Some interest-based community gardens do play a role of introducing people to neighbourhood, however, the scale of 'local' is larger, that is, city-wide. Other characteristics contributing to the club-like description are the use of locked fences and key access; and adoption of formal membership roles, duties and obligations. Four of the seven community gardens investigated were found to be third places across all eight characteristics. Two of these, in the City of Sydney, Australia and Albertslund in Denmark, are discussed in this chapter to illustrate community gardens which are third places. It should be noted that the community gardens visited in the study may not be representative of all community gardens, which come in such a variety of places, purposes and designs. However, the case studies illustrate ways in which community gardens can act as third places.

Case Study 1: City of Sydney

The Australian community garden is one of several in the City of Sydney, hereafter referred to as 'Sydney' community garden. It is situated 1.5 km from the Sydney CBD in a park which is surrounded by apartments and terrace houses, many of which are owned by the government for public housing. The local council initially built the garden beds and continue to provide a community garden advisory service and oversee the other facilities in the public park, including a basketball court, tennis court, and children's play equipment. The low fence which surrounds the community garden is always open to the public. There is a combination of individual plots and common use areas which include paths, a community compost facility and fruit trees. The garden is run by the community garden members, some of whom have specific roles, such as the person who oversees the compost, or the first point of contact for enquiries. There is no hierarchy amongst the organisers and decisions about the garden are made by consensus at monthly meetings. The group welcomes new members, who are asked to attend at least two garden meetings and pay a minimal annual membership fee which is discounted for those on pensions. All members live within walking distance of the garden. Three members volunteer to assist with the neighbouring primary school food garden.

The Sydney garden is easy to access and accommodating, as it is open 24 hours a day to the public and all of the gardeners live within walking distance of it. The garden occasionally receives publicity, which attracts potential members from outside the local area, but members encourage them to find (or start) a community garden closer to their home. This emphasis on walkability is echoed throughout the membership as it promotes the usability of the produce and the neighbourhood composting facility. One participant said:

> I think if you had to drive, or if you lived more than 10 minutes' walk, you wouldn't bother, whereas for me it's always been around the corner. It's less than 5 minutes' walk. It is close enough that I can put my compost out. I'd come down and pick a few plants to cook with dinner. I think if it was further than that you just wouldn't visit. (Sydney, member, female)

The 24/7 accessibility to the unlocked community garden came at a cost. Problems of vandalism and theft arose for most of the gardeners interviewed. The current members expressed that the acts had discouraged the gardeners, but their talk demonstrated a level of tolerance for such negative events. One member explained that she keeps some weeds in her garden plot in order to hide her plants from theft and vandals:

> It is an open garden. We don't lock it. We have to trust the community to respect our space. We have to work too to make that respect too. We don't get a lot of produce. . . . If they take 1 or 2 leaves it is fine, but when they take whole plants or someone rips up your whole plot . . . I purposely don't pull out the weeds so people think it is weeds. Easy and not so disappointing. (Sydney, member, female)

The cover of weeds strategy protects the produce and contributes to the low profile atmosphere of the community garden, with one member describing it as, 'by no means a beautiful community garden' (Sydney, member, male).

Being open, the Sydney community garden acts as neutral ground where people of the neighbourhood join in. Some found out about the garden through neighbours while most came across it while walking through the neighbourhood. They have a noticeboard which explains the membership requirements and when the meetings are scheduled. However, as with a third place, there are local people who take an interest in the garden without being actively involved in it and some members try to encourage those visitors to join. One member told me:

> We do get a fair few (passers-by) stop and chat. Some people stop and pick stuff, so we make a point of saying, 'Hi, do you know how the garden works? If you want to pick, how about you contribute?' – Just join the garden rather than just picking. Or some people think that 'community garden' means they can pick what they want. It is not necessarily a bad intention. They just don't know, whereas some people do know and they come when they think no-one is watching (laughs). (Sydney, member, female)

The Sydney community garden acts as a leveller where age, occupation and other defining factors are irrelevant to visiting or participation. Members who were interviewed covered a variety of occupations including retirees, professionals, a university student and her small children and a (formerly) unemployed person. People of all ages, including children, join in. A participant explains:

> It's made up of, seems to be mostly university educated people in there, some in their 20s, 30s. I'm probably the oldest person in the group. But there is another set, there's about maybe four or five of us who are 60 plus. And then there's some people in their 50s, and then there's the rest of them. And I think there's about 20 members, 20 financial members. (Sydney, member, male)

The community garden actively encourages interactions with the broader neighbourhood. For example, three of the members help out with the neighbouring primary school garden. In addition, people from outside the garden take an interest in the garden as a topic of conversation at the local pub, or coffee shop. For example, the local coffee supplier took an interest in the garden's coffee trees and showed the members how to care for the trees and helped them to harvest and roast the coffee beans. One member noted there is a local pride in the garden even amongst non-members. Members recounted use of the garden by locals for such things as reading the paper, collecting grass for a pet rabbit, and regularly walking through it. The Sydney Community Garden has on occasion also been a place for homeless locals as one member explains:

> I remember at one of our gardening meetings there were these two young kids that were sort of standing just near where we were and someone said, 'You guys alright? You looking for something?' The kid said, 'No, I live here'. They don't live there very long. There are a lot of rough sleepers (here). (Sydney, member, male)

The role of community gardens in the provision of food and shelter for the homeless is a topic which merits future investigation.

Conversation is a main activity at the Sydney community garden, both between members, with visitors and outside the garden, as this person relates:

> Quite often if I'm down here I'll get people walking through and asking about it and, you know, whether they can join and you tell them about it and they might come or they might not. It tends to be word of mouth and blackboard that spreads information, so sometimes people chat. (Sydney, member, female)

There is a core group of influential regulars/characters who help to introduce new or potential members to each other. This was demonstrated by comments like:

> We met people down here, but we tend not to meet them except here and we've had some social activities over the period. Once or twice a year there will be some sort of meeting with food and everybody will bring some food and have a lunch. So there is a bit of social activity around it . . . there have been activities over time in a rather random and organic way. (Sydney, member, female)

The mood is relaxed and social with meetings taking place over a morning tea break. One woman related:

> I bring the cakes as well. It's a very important role. This is the right sort of meeting to have cakes at. People do a lot of work and then they have some cakes – I think that is very important. (Sydney, member, female)

The garden can also feel like homes away from home and include alone times for the enjoyment of gardening as related here:

> I'm not that chatty a person, so I'm quite happy to come down and pull weeds out for a while and it's cathartic and then I go away. Yeah, I find it's quite relaxing and it's not too much to, like, upkeep. (Sydney, member, female)

On occasion the core members encouraged activities beyond the garden boundaries. There is evidence that the weak ties of association which form in this community garden build to strong ties for some garden members. A member discovered the Sydney community garden by walking past it nine years ago and didn't know anyone when she joined. When asked if she had developed friendships through the garden she noted:

> Yes I do now. (J) teaches a yoga class. I go to that. Me, (S) and another gardener, we volunteer at the local school and help them get their garden going and the pre-school. Sometimes some of us get together for a meal. (F), an older lady, we've been to each other's houses for a cuppa or a meal or to check up on each other. Yeah sometimes we'll all have a meal together and we just look out for each other. (F) is getting a bit frail lately, so there is a sense of caring for each other. (Sydney, member, female)

The same gardener appreciated the sense of community brought about by the garden, noting that there were greater benefits than just the produce grown. She said:

> If it was a locked garden, it would be a lot easier, but then if it is locked, it is a lot more exclusive. Not so community minded. . . . Growing food and getting to know more people in the community because I think it is important to feel that sense of community in the neighbourhood and to learn to grow food. (Sydney, member, female)

Through this community garden's openness, accessibility and interactions between regulars, visitors and other locals, it can be determined that it is a third place in the neighbourhood. Informal interactions between regulars and the wider community both inside and beyond the boundary of the community garden illustrate its third place nature. The bonding and neighbourhood social capital building is evidenced through community composting, caring for members, developing friendships and assisting the local school.

Case Study 2: Albertslund, Denmark Library Community Garden

The library community garden is situated in Albertslund, which is is located 17 km west of Copenhagen in Denmark. The community garden was established on land owned by a private organisation which rents out residential apartments to individuals and rents community buildings to the municipality, including the library, youth club and a kindergarten. The housing area is connected to neighbouring housing areas via paths. The neighbourhood was listed by the Danish government as a 'Ghetto' according to their definition. The local population is reportedly comprised of approximately 50 per cent ethnic minorities from numerous language groups. In 2013, the librarians started decorating the entrance of the

Source: The author.

*Figure 8.1   Raised beds of the library community garden in Albertslund,
            September 2016*

library with plants as the area was grey concrete and stone and not inviting for people to sit. The local people were appreciative. In response, the staff of the municipal library initiated a community garden (see Figure 8.1), which was encouraged and funded by the private housing organisation.

The garden comprises a number of raised garden beds in boxes. The housing company provided all the equipment and garden boxes and agreed to plant numerous well-developed apple trees and provide the seeds and seedlings for the participants. Approximately 15 families are involved each growing season and each family can have two garden boxes; the youth club has a handful of boxes and the local school and the kindergarten also have some boxes. The librarians try to gather the participants every two weeks so that they help take care of the rest of the garden, though it is difficult to find a time which suits the library hours and the working adults.

The library community garden acts as a neutral ground, started in order to engage with the adults who live in the area by providing an attractive green place where they can get to know the library staff and each other.

The librarian noted: 'It is also a little bit about branding and about making people come and live more together and have places to hang out and meet each other.' As with the other case study community gardens, the openness of the garden 24 hours a day leaves it vulnerable to theft and vandalism. This was in evidence on a sign posted on the garden beds (translated):

> 'Please don't take the kid's vegetables' because they are supposed to be having a harvest party for the kids next week. Everything was just about ready for the harvest and then it was gone one morning. It is a sad little crying child on the poster there. (Librarian)

The community garden encourages participation of anyone who wants to join in and therefore acts as a leveller across ages, languages and ethnicity. The librarian told me:

> We have a group of women from Pakistan and we have some women from Turkey and we have an older Danish lady and a Danish family and we have one family from Somalia and we have a woman from Thailand, so it is actually representing this neighbourhood quite well. It is an opportunity to make people meet across age and cultures and languages.

Conversation is more authentic in the community garden because there is a purpose for initiating a conversation, evidenced by this comment: 'So these cultural meetings where you try to make people meet because then you have made a cultural meeting – it's uphill. This is better. People can see why they should participate' (Librarian).

Involvement in the garden is free, making it very easy to access and be accommodating. The librarians act as the core group of influential regulars/characters. The children from the school and kindergarten are also regulars.

The garden is low profile and not showy with casual seating and outdoor umbrellas provided for locals to enjoy the garden area. There is evidence that it feels like home away from home, with the librarian noting that locals are enjoying the seating at library closing time. The interviewee noted that it has vastly improved what was a 'boring' concrete area and that adults now congregate and socialise in the area.

The mood is playful and activities such as harvest festivals and regular meetings help to create a social atmosphere as described here:

> So we have these small individual meetings and then we have one day when we go and all plant together. So we make a bit of a party and we plant together. . ..

This community garden offers opportunities to develop weak ties and for those ties to grow into stronger ties as the gardeners get to know each other:

> The gardeners start to help each other.... Then they get to know each other. Then they help each other a little bit – 'I'm going on holidays these weeks can you water my boxes for me?' (Librarian)

The library community garden reaches beyond the members who have garden boxes and for people beyond the immediate neighbourhood by holding workshops about growing edible plants. Although this garden is well resourced, the coordinator said it would benefit from having a paid gardener who could advise and assist with the community garden, as the librarians note that they have a library to run.

The librarians had expected that the participants might like to cultivate plants from their own cultures. Saldivar-tanaka and Krasny (2004) determined that the Latino gardens in New York City 'provide a connection between immigrants and their cultural heritage'. The Albertslund library gardeners, however, perhaps because the seeds and plants are provided for free, all grow the same plants.

Overall the community garden builds on a well-known third place – the library. The fact that the gardening is free and participation is open to anyone and everyone who lives within walking distance makes this library community garden a third place. As such, the benefits to the neighbourhood are in evidence. The librarian related: 'I think in many ways this garden has made at least this part of the neighbourhood more friendly, more inviting, more social.'

CONCLUSION

Community gardens can act as third places when they are open to the public and are situated in a walkable location within a neighbourhood. Their advantage as a third place is that they provide an authentic purpose for people to interact and initiate conversations on broad topics of local common interest (weather, plants and activities). The plants and activities in them are points of interest and conversation starters – an important characteristic of third places.

The two case study community gardens discussed exhibit a number of characteristics of design, location and governance, which make them particularly effective third places. First, they open to the public. While the openness and accessibility led to some negative aspects of theft and vandalism in the community gardens, members seemed to cope with that challenge. Second, they draw their membership from within a walkable range. In addition, they have communal areas and regular working bees, where members get a chance to meet up. They have facilities which encourage social interactions, such as shaded seating areas. Also, both gardens are supported by the local council or land owner which means the cost and organisation are less onerous. The Sydney garden has a non-hierarchical management style, where informality of membership poses no burdensome obligation. Both gardens offer personal growing plots, which assists with enthusiasm and regular attendance to tend to plots. In addition, both gardens have formal and informal connections with the wider community. Finally, both community gardens are inclusive across age groups, ethnicity and socio-economic status. These factors can serve to inform the design of third place community gardens, which have potential to increase neighbourhood social capital.

Just as Oldenburg (1997) gave the example of bars which are friendly, local and inviting, compared to bars where nobody speaks to anyone, some community gardens do not entirely fit the third place definitions. Some community gardens are set up more like a club with membership fees; committee obligations; interest-based rather than place-based; and/ or they are inaccessible due to being locked, hidden away or exclusive. The design of the garden and the regularity of members attending the garden affect their third place-ness. Unlike a club, third place community gardens are a space in which locals are free to enter and browse. They also reach out into the neighbourhood, as noted in the Sydney garden, where people not involved with gardening have pride in the knowledge of it and talk to the gardeners. Small interactions centred in or about the community garden lead to people starting to recognise each other and feel a part of the neighbourhood. As per Putnam's (2000 p. 19) definition of social capital, third place community gardens connect individuals in a neighbourhood and build social networks. Community garden interactions provide weak ties which in some cases develop from weak ties to strong ties of friendship.

Drawing together the aspects of the case study community gardens which make them third places, the Utopian third place community garden would be:

- Walkable distance from most members' homes.
- Open to the public.
- Include activities which engage the neighbourhood (free herbs, classes, noticeboards, community composting); formal connections for example with local schools; and informal connections with for example the pub and local coffee brewer.

- Members exhibit a wide range of motivations for joining and remaining.
- Members not overly dispirited by negative interactions with the public (vandalism).
- Minimal or no barriers to entry – free or minimal joining fee.
- Design (such as inclusion of individual plots), and/or activities (such as working bees and community composting), which encourage regular attendance so people get to know each other.
- Inclusive by supporting diversity – introducing new locals and immigrants to the neighbourhood; and accommodating for mixed ages, aging people or those with disabilities (e.g. high rise garden beds).
- Space and/or infrastructure for socialising and casual meetings – shade, shelter, facilities, seats and water access.
- Offer different roles or levels of opportunity (casual volunteering, membership, allotments, passers-by, public events).
- Opportunities for communication – blackboard, signs and e-communication (emails, Facebook pages).
- Less onerous on the obligation and a non-hierarchical management style with consideration of longevity, where informality of membership poses minimal burdensome obligation.
- Citizen initiated, but supported by the local authority with advice and funding.

The third place characteristics form a useful framework for investigating community gardens and how they contribute to community by building social capital. The research illustrates the benefits of third place community gardens, including welcoming newcomers including international immigrants to the community; reducing loneliness and breaking down the self-selecting social interactions. Community gardens can act as third places improving neighbourhood social capital in two ways. First, community gardens promote creation of weak ties (bridging capital). The third place community gardens are visited by passers-by who stop to chat, or in the case of the Sydney garden, are a point of conversation at other venues such as the local coffee shop and pub. Second, for members, they also act somewhat like clubs, where strong ties of friendship are built (bonding capital).

Third places and community gardens share many of the same characteristics. Effective third places strengthen the social capital of the community, build people's sense of place, and improve their happiness and well-being. Community garden designers and advisors would benefit by incorporating the characteristics of third places into the design and placement of community gardens. Likewise, given the health and well-being benefits of community gardens through access to fresh food, physical activity and social interactions, it would make sense for local authorities to support community gardens and their members.

BIBLIOGRAPHY

Alaimo, K., Reischl, T.M. and Ober Allen, J. (2010) Community Gardening, Neighborhood Meetings, and Social Capital. *Journal of Community Psychology*, 38(4), 497–514.

Auge, M. (1995) *Non-Places. An Introduction to Supermodernity*. London: Verso.

Australian Bureau of Statistics (ABS) (2004) Information Paper: Measuring Social Capital. An Australian Framework and Indicators, Commonwealth of Australia.

Australian Community Gardens Network (2014) Australian Community Gardens Network: The Network. http://communitygarden.org.au/acfcgn/ (accessed 2 August 2018).

Bende, C. and Nagy, G. (2016) Effects of Community Gardens on Local Society – The Case of Two Community Gardens in Szeged. *Belvedere Meridionale*, 28(3), 89–105.

Birky, J. and Strom, E. (2013) Urban Perennials: How Diversification has Created a Sustainable Community Garden Movement in the United States. *Urban Geography*, 34(8), 1193–1216.

Bonow, M. and Normark, M. (2017) Community Gardening in Stockholm: Participation, Driving Forces and the Role of the Municipality. *Renewable Agriculture and Food Systems* https://doi.org/10.1017/S1742170517000734.

Calderon, R., Blackstock, M., Lea, R. and Fels, S. (2014) Supporting Conversation and Community Interaction With a Table-Top Community Garden Application. Paper presented at the Pervasive Displays, Copenhagen, Denmark.

Chitov, D. (2006) Cultivating Social Capital on Urban Plots: Community Gardens in New York City. *Humanity and Society*, 30(4), 437–462.

Draper, C. and Freedman, D. (2010) Review and Analysis of the Benefits, Purposes, and Motivations Associated with Community Gardening in the United States. *Journal of Community Practice*, 18, 458–492.

Easley, D. and Kleinberg, J. (2010) Strong and Weak Ties. In: Easley, D. and Kleinberg, J. (eds), *Networks, Crowds, and Markets: Reasoning about a Highly Connected World*. Cambridge: Cambridge University Press, pp. 47–84.

Easthorpe, H. and McNamara, N. (2013) Measuring Social Interaction and Social Cohesion in a High Density Urban Renewal Area: The Case of Green Square. Report, State of Australian Cities Sydney, Australia.

Ferris, J., Norman, C. and Sempik, J. (2001) People, Land and Sustainability: Community Gardens and the Social Dimension of Sustainable Development. *Social Policy and Administration*, 35(5), 559–568.

Firth, C., Maye, D. and Pearson, D. (2011) Developing 'Community' in Community Gardens. *Local Environment: The International Journal of Justice and Sustainability*, 16(6), 555–568.

Frumpkin, H. (2003) Healthy Places: Exploring the Evidence. *American Journal of Health*, 93(9), 1451–1456.

Galdini, R. (2016) Placemaking as an Approach for Innovative Urban Renewal Practices: Community Gardens in Berlin. *International Review of Sociology*, 2016, 1–21.

Gaynor, A. (2006) *Harvest of the Suburbs: An Environmental History of Growing Food in Australian Cities*. Perth: UWA (University of Western Australia).

Glover, T. (2003) 'Community Garden Movement'. In: Christensen, K. and Levinson, D. (eds), *Encyclopedia of Community*. Thousand Oaks: Sage Publications, pp. 264–266.

Glover, T. (2004) Social Capital in the Lived Experiences of Community Gardeners. *Leisure Sciences: An Interdisciplinary Journal*, 26(2), 143–162.

Granovetter, M. (1983) The Strength of Weak Ties: A Network Theory Revisited. *Sociological Theory*, V1, 201–233.

Guitart, D., Pickering, C. and Byrne, J. (2012) Past Results and Future Directions in Urban Community Gardens Research. *Urban Forestry and Urban Greening*, 11(4), 351–363.

Hogan, L. and Thorpe, S. (2009) Issues in Food Miles and Carbon Labelling. In Australian Bureau of Agricultural and Resource Economics (ABARE) research report (09.18 ed.). Canberra: ABARE.

Hondagneu-Sotelo, P. (2010) Cultivating Questions for a Sociology of Gardens. *Journal of Contemporary Ethnography*, originally published online, 39(5), 102–131.

Jacobs, M. (1996) *The Politics of the Real World. Meeting the New Century*. London: Earthscan Publications.

Kingsley, J.Y. and Townsend, M. (2006) 'Dig In' to Social Capital: Community Gardens as Mechanisms for Growing Social Connectedness. *Urban Policy and Research*, 24(4), 525–537.

Knox, P.L. (2005) Creating Ordinary Places: Slow Cities in a Fast World. *Journal of Urban Design*, 10(1), 1–11.

Lyons, K., Richards, C., DesFours, L. and Amati, M. (2013) Food in the City: Urban Food Movements and the (Re)-Imagining of Urban Spaces. *Australian Planner*, 50(2), 157–163.

Mele, C., Ng, M. and Chim, M. (2015) Urban Markets as a 'Corrective' to Advanced Urbanism: The Social Space of Wet Markets in Contemporary Singapore. *Urban Studies*, 52(1), 103–120.

Ohmer, M., Meadowcroft, P., Freed, K. and Lewis, E. (2009) Community Gardening and Community Development: Individual, Social and Community Benefits of a Community Conservation Program. *Journal of Community Practice*, 17, 377–399.

Oldenburg, R. (1989) *The Great Good Place*. New York: Paragon House.

Oldenburg, R. (1997) Our Vanishing Third Places. *Planning Commissioners Journal*, 25, 8–10.

Oldenburg, R. (1999) *The Great Good Place: Cafes, Coffee Shops, Bookstores, Bars, Hair Salons, and Other Hangouts at the Heart of a Community*. New York: Marlow & Company.

Pascoe, J. and Howes, M. (2017) A Growing Movement: Motivations for Joining Community Gardens. In: Brebbia, C. and Longhurst, J. (eds), *Sustainable Development and Planning IX, WIT Transactions on Ecology and the Environment Volume 226*. UK: WIT Press, pp. 381–389.

Pascoe, J. and Wyatt-Smith, C. (2013) Curriculum Literacies and the School Garden. *Literacy Learning: the Middle Years*, 21(1), 34–47.

Putnam, D. (2000) *Bowling Alone*. New York: Simon & Schuster.

Saldivar-tanaka, L. and Krasny, M.E. (2004) Culturing Community Development, Neighborhood Open Space, and Civic Agriculture: The Case of Latino Community Gardens in New York City. *Agriculture and Human Values*, 21(4), 399–412.

Sennett, R. (2012) *Together: The Rituals, Pleasures and Politics of Cooperation.* New Haven, CT: Yale University Press.

Shanahan, D., Lin, B., Bush, R., Gaston, K., Dean, J., Barber, E. and Fuller, R. (2015) Toward Improved Public Health Outcomes From Urban Nature. *American Journal of Public Health, January* (Online), 105(3),470–477.

Shi, S., Gou, Z. and Chen, L. (2014) How Does Enclosure Influence Environmental Preferences? A Cognitive Study on Urban Public Open Spaces in Hong Kong. *Sustainable Cities and Society*, 13, 148–156.

Son, J., Yarnal, C. and Kerstetter, D. (2010) Engendering Social Capital through a Leisure Club for Middle-Aged and Older Women: Implications for Individual and Community Health and Wellbeing. *Leisure Studies*, 29(1), 67–83.

Tan, L. and Neo, H. (2009) 'Community in Bloom': Local Participation of Community Gardens in Urban Singapore. *Local Environment*, 14(6), 529–539.

Thompson, S. and Maggin, P. (2012) *Planning Australia: An Overview of Urban and Regional Planning.* Cambridge: Cambridge University Press.

Turner, B. (2011) Embodied Connections: Sustainability, Food Systems and Community Gardens. *Local Environment: The International Journal of Justice and Sustainability*, 16(6), 509–522.

Veen, E., Derkzen, P. and Visser, A (2014) Shopping Versus Growing: Food Acquisition Habits of Dutch Urban Gardeners. *Food and Foodways: Explorations in the History and Culture of Human Nourishment*, 22(4), 268–279.

Walter, P. (2013) Theorising Community Gardens as Pedagogical Sites in the Food Movement. *Environmental Education Research*, 19(4), 1–19.

Yokohari, M. and Amati, M. (2005) Nature in the City, City in the Nature: Case Studies of the Restoration of Urban Nature in Tokyo, Japan and Toronto, Canada. *Landscape and Ecological Engineering*, 1(1), 53–59.

Zoellner, J.R.D., Zanko, A.M.S., Price, B., Bonner, J. and Hill, J.L. (2012) Exploring Community Gardens in a Health Disparate Population: Findings from a Mixed Methods Pilot Study. *Progress in Community Health Partnerships*, 6(2), 153–165.

Zukin, S. (2010) *Naked City. The Death and Life of Authentic Urban Places.* New York: Oxford University Press.

9. Third places in the ether around us: layers on the real world

Dmitri Williams and Do Own Kim

INTRODUCTION

The 2016 US Presidential election will be remembered for many things, but for sociologists and communication researchers, the most glaring aspect will no doubt be the mainstreaming of the idea of 'filter bubbles.' Heavy partisans – whether conservative or liberal – used social media to find comfort in the notion that sensible people agreed with them. Our technological systems were only too happy to comply, supplying the country with an endless stream of agreement from within the tribe and vilification for those outside. Knowledge of these filter bubbles became common in the aftermath (Hess 2017), but they were of course not new phenomena. Political scientists had been sounding alarm bells about 'cybercascades' (Sunstein 2001) and 'cyberbalkanization' (VanAlstyne and Brynjolffson 2005) since the Internet became a public space, with several noting negative correlations (Kraut et al. 1996; Nie and Hillygus 2002) between time spent online and anything resembling the good stuff we associate with social capital (Coleman 1988).

Surely this was Oldenburg's worst nightmare: a technology that took our already weak social connections and fragmented them into homogeneous, siloed-off, angry echo chambers. And while it's easy to see red (or blue, depending on your political persuasion), it's usually an oversimplification of things to look at a new technology as purely good or purely bad.

We start from the point of view that neither a Luddite nor a utopianist perspective is going to do anything other than (ironically) confirm our false assumptions and feelings about technology. Histories of technology teach us that their effects require time and distance to be seen clearly, and in their proper context (Pinch and Bijker 1999).

Theories of computer-mediated communication are a lens to help us find that context, and to absorb the fast pace of change that whips past us daily. Indeed, whenever you read this chapter, it will probably feel out of date to the extent that we focus on any modern technology. Better then to figure out the theory, and the criteria, to decide on how new technology should be viewed as either helping build or destroy the structures and benefits of third places.

This chapter attempts to do that with the following steps: First, we briefly review Oldenburg's criteria, with a focus on his framework of architectures and physical neighborhoods. Second, we introduce concepts from computer-mediated communication and political communication that directly mimic these ideas for non-physical places. Third, we revisit recent technologies for test cases. Finally, we attempt to use this framework to bridge to new and emerging technologies with a neutral, but critical eye. We introduce the concept of 'layering,' which is simply looking at everyday spaces, places and functions, and asking what happens when their elements are changed by new media. Our conclusion is that some technologies can help third place development, while others can hinder it. A rough generalization is that there are many mixed effects. Looking forward, we envision a society where technology layers information on top of our regular lives. The extent to which these layers will be built in support of third place functionality will have a large impact on our communities and quality of life.

THE ARCHITECTURE OF THIRD PLACES OFFLINE

Oldenburg's (1997) third places are those that do not fulfill the space or the role of our traditional first and second places – home and work. In his view, it is critical to have a place outside of those two for a healthy life and a strong community. In a sense, this is not a new idea, and scholars have for a very long time been pointing out the importance of mixing with others out in the public sphere (Habermas 1998). However, Oldenburg's critique came in a historical moment when our civic institutions seemed to be under attack by the twin forces of media and urban planning. Putnam is probably the most well-known example of those arguing that media have displaced our critical, human, social interactions, documenting that for example, the time spouses spend watching TV comes at the expense of the time they talk to each other (Putnam 2000). Both he and Oldenburg have focused on the immense zoning and urban transformations that radically changed community life in the twentieth century. As cities birthed more private suburbs, our boisterous cheek-by-jowl communities were increasingly replaced by separate, quieter, and often homogenous neighborhoods. Mixed-use spaces were increasingly zoned away in favor of strictly commercial or residential uses. The upshot of all of this was an increase in personal space at the expense of daily conversations and regular, serendipitous interactions with people unlike ourselves. For those fleeing to the suburbs, comfort and privacy increasingly drove out noise and interaction. It's a stepping stone to a science fiction future in which we don't interact with each other at all unless it's mediated – a scenario depicted in Asimov's (1957) *The Naked Sun*, which doubtlessly was written in reaction to the Levittown movement and rise of television. The argument isn't that people changed their preferences or needs, but that we architected and zoned ourselves away from each other, not realizing the social price we were paying for our convenience and luxuries.

What's implicit in this argument – and in the balance of this chapter – is that architectures drive behavior (also see Chapter 1 this volume). Some readers and scholars may take issue with this highly structuralist approach in that it gives short shrift to human agency. However, it's inescapable that the same people placed into a differently architected neighborhood will behave differently. For example, a neighborhood with porches will have more interactions than one without. A neighborhood where residents can walk to a grocer will have more interactions than one that requires cars regardless of how personable they were before moving in.

The stakes in this dynamic are extraordinarily high. Our social capital – whether it's the 'bridging' kind that gives us access to new ideas and people, or the 'bonding' kind that gives us strong social support – is critical to our lives (Putnam 2000). And more recently, demographers have discovered an irrefutable connection to our actual health. In a comprehensive review of the world's healthiest and longest-lived communities, Buettner (2015) has found that longevity is directly tied to community. Although the food eaten in these 'Blue Zone' areas gets the headlines, Buettner takes care to point out that these communities are all marked by strong social ties, and often by the kinds of rituals and places that Oldenburg called out as essential.

Table 9.1 provides a quick review of the criteria of ideal third places. As we consider the impact of new media technologies, these same criteria should be adapted and applied. Just because a new technology isn't in a bar or coffee shop doesn't mean these criteria can be, or should be, ignored.

As we move into an ever-more technologically mediated future, we assume that our human needs are unchanged, although our awareness of the effects of technologies isn't always strong. We want love, connection, opportunities, and human contact. And since we collectively haven't given up our suburbs, our cars, and our zoning laws, it stands to reason that our unmet needs are not going away. In other words, despite the supply changing, the demand remains. So, do new technologies meet those needs? We need frameworks to think this through.

Table 9.1   Oldenburg's third place criteria (1997)

Characteristic	Definition
Neutral Ground	Third places are neutral grounds where individuals are free to come and go as they please with little obligation or entanglements with other participants.
Leveler	Third places are spaces in which an individual's rank and status in the workplace or society at large are of no import. Acceptance and practice is not contingent in any prerequisites, requirements, roles, duties, or proof of membership.
Conversation is Main Activity	In third places, conversation is a main focus of activity in which playfulness and wit are collectively valued.
Accessibility & Accommodation	Third places must be easy to access and are accommodating to those who frequent them.
The Regulars	Third places include a cadre of regulars who attract newcomers and give the space its characteristic mood.
A Low Profile	Third places are characteristically homely and without pretension.
The Mood is Playful	The general mood in third places is playful and marked by frivolity, verbal word play, and wit.
A Home Away from Home	Third places are home-like in terms of Seamon's (1979) five defining traits; rootedness, feelings of possession, spiritual regeneration, feelings of being at ease, and warmth.

FRAMING THEORIES AND ONLINE ARCHITECTURES

Computer-mediated communication (CMC) has a raft of theories that might help us connect the third place idea to new technologies. We focus on two related theories as most applicable. The first is the simplest: media richness theory (Daft and Lengel, 1984). It posits that humans convey a wide array of cues in our face-to-face communication. When we interact we have the content of our speech, but also the tone of that speech, and a host of non-verbal cues such as our posture, eye contact, facial expressions, etc. Communications media that convey those cues well are considered 'richer,' while those that are unable to convey them are 'poorer' (Walther, 2006). In a case of extremes, Skype video would be on the richer side, while texting would be on the poorer side. Face to face communication (FTF) is the gold standard, with the most cues.

The second theory, and the most cited and supported in the CMC literature, is SIDE or the 'social identity model of deindividuation effects'

(Postmes et al. 2001), which focuses on how we get cues and act in mediated situations. In other words, it predicts how we will act and feel when those cues are removed. The premise of SIDE is that whenever we enter a social situation we look to others for models of how to behave. If we enter a loud party with dancing or a quiet library, it's the actions of others that tell us how we should act. SIDE takes this concept online where these social cues are often weaker or fewer. Its main hypothesis is that the few cues we do see become more powerful because they are all we have to go on. We are 'deindividuated' by circumstance, and become less individual and more reliant on social proof and the actions of others. And online or not, we are still humans who want to feel connected, included and together. So, we will seek those few cues we can find, and they will have an outsized influence on our behavior. This is especially important for groups of people trying to emotionally connect, or to accomplish some task (Altschuller and Benbunan-Fich 2010). Evidence of this is that many online functions that aren't intended to form communities do so anyway, as is the case with many bloggers (Dennen 2014). Now we consider how different communication technologies do or do not provide those cues.

This is where 'architecture' comes back into the picture. Obviously in places that aren't the 'real world,' there can't be real architecture, even if sometimes a virtual place mimics a real one. Instead, we are focusing on architecture as an analogy. In what we might call the 'social architecture' of an online place, it isn't the walls or the doors or the zoning laws that push us into some actions and not others. Instead it's the code of the technology that enables or prevents behaviors. This code is the online equivalent of those forces – in an online place, a wall may not be a real wall, but it still prevents you from 'moving' freely across an area.

Lessig (1999) was the first to crystallize this idea, noting that the code of an online place was essentially its law and its architecture (more recently, see Couldry and Hepp 2016). If the code allows you to talk to anyone, you can. If it allows only some people to talk to only some others, that's the way it is. Likewise, it may allow you to – or prevent you from – flying, sending files, talking verbally, identifying yourself, or a thousand other things. Lessig's idea that 'code is law' is value-neutral, and is often applied and enforced by engineers and developers who are not thinking about Oldenburg, social capital, filter bubbles or life offline. Much like builders and architects, their choices have ramifications on the social lives of those who use their products. And, arguably, computer programmers as a group are less aware of the social implications of their design choices than architects. Thus, there are frequently social architectures coming out of their code that enable or stymie community entirely by accident. Conversely, there are also those sets of code that are the carefully considered result of developers or governments who want to encourage or prevent a particular behavior (Gillespie 2017). Lessig invokes the 'Great Firewall of China' as an example of a set of code that regulates information, access and behavior for an entire country. It is his fear that such architectures have and will become tools of control (Lessig, 1999).

Most architectures aren't quite as obvious, or political, but they still impact behaviors. Many scholars have begun investigating and critiquing these fundamental structures and algorithms as awareness of these potential impacts has become more apparent (Ananny 2016; Napoli 2014) and as the lack of visibility into the code becomes a problem (Ananny and Crawford 2016).

EARLY INVESTIGATIONS INTO MEDIATED SPACES

So, how do new places compare to the classical in-person experience? It's tempting to paint with a broad brush, but we should instead be very careful to consider the features and affordances of each place as potentially different. Video games and virtual worlds, for example, may seem like all one kind of thing, but each can have radically different social architectures. One early example of research into such worlds provides an example.

Steinkeuhler and Williams (2006) investigated two early virtual worlds specifically focusing on their third place characteristics. These are large-scale always-online games called 'massively multiplayer online games,' or 'MMOs' for short. Newer generations of these games persist today as an active niche in the extraordinarily large and profitable medium of online gaming. To have some context for the impact of gaming, consider that as an industry in 2017 it drew more than 250 percent more revenues than the movie business (Games, 2017) and now rivals or exceeds the worldwide revenues of all sports (Taylor, 2017). Drawing on a wide array of ethnographic, experimental, survey and data-based methods, Steinkuehler and Williams concluded that these places had strengths and weaknesses compared to their equivalents in Oldenburg's ideal 'real world' places.

Most obviously, these online games fell short on the physical and the intimate aspects of the in-person tavern or coffee shop ideal. To put it simply, if you can't physically hit or have sex with a person in a virtual space like you can in a real one, it changes the stakes in any interaction. The costs and benefits are simply different. Thus, the depth of relationships that were formed in these games were initially relatively shallower than in the corresponding 'real' place (although it is notable that even here the authors found real, substantive relationships form, some of which even lead to real-world connections and marriages). On the other hand, these game places offered the opposite of the 'zoning' effect that Oldenburg argued transformed the country. By removing the barriers of space, travel and inconvenience, virtual worlds created massive analogs to the corner tavern. In his framing, a game must be thought of as a tavern with tens of thousands of patrons inside, all with similar interests, but less likely to share their demography. Even the most idealized third place in Oldenburg's thinking was subject to some form of demographic clustering in the real world. Yet in a cheap online space, the only barrier to entry tends to be interest. Thus, there is potentially more mixing than in a traditional third place, even as it falls short on some other criteria. What's more, these game places are competitive and fulfill the 'leveler' function that Oldenburg valued. Games are almost always meritocracies, and so wealth and status rarely make a difference (Shen 2014). As Herz (1997) put it bluntly but eloquently, 'It didn't matter what you drove to the arcade. If you sucked at Asteroids, you just sucked.' Games can mix CEOs with janitors, men with women, Jews with Arabs, children with adults, and on and on, in ways that real-world places rarely do.

At least initially, these relationships were seen to lack depth. We normatively assume that is a bad thing, but let's be value-neutral for a moment. Depth is also value-neutral. Deep affinity and deep hate both require depth. With relatively poor media, we see fewer cues, and so depth takes longer to occur. Relationships are instead built on personalities and common interests (Schwämmlein and Wodzicki 2012), and can form where they wouldn't otherwise form offline. The term 'discrimination' applies here: When you don't have all of the cues, it is much harder to discriminate. As those cues are introduced, or architected in, players learn who the people are and the relationship deepens. Deep doesn't automatically mean good. Bridging and bonding can both increase. It can reinforce stereotypes at the same time as it can introduce people to diversity of thought and demographics (Hansen et al. 2015). In an echo of SIDE theory, Kim (2011) found that groups coalesce better when they hide their actual identities in favor of uniform conformity.

More advanced work following those early studies has delved deeper into the social architectures of game places, finding the ones that promote better identity politics and community. For example, Harrell (2010) and Harrell and Harrell (2012) have created and studied systems that play with representation as an architectural feature.

This is a quickly evolving area, in which new technologies and companies are sprouting up and altering social architectures all the time. For context, we have moved through what Couldry and Hepp (2016) call the 'media-tization' phase, where technology has become ubiquitous and intertwined in our daily lives. What was at first merely mechanizing communication later moved to electrify it and most recently and impactfully to digitize it. This digital phase has been rapid and seemingly total. Communication has become so mediated that what was once considered to be standard is now just part of a larger, digitized mix. Online communication is no longer a supplement but an essential and basic part of relationships, making face-to-face one of many modes we must take seriously.

Couldry and Hepp's framework suggests that our relationships with space and place have profoundly shifted, and will continue to. To paraphrase their thinking, it is as if there is a set of layers now imposed upon reality, each of which has social and third place implications. These layers can be rich with connection and opportunity, or the equivalent of gated communities: 'Just beneath the spatial surface of everyday reality are developing new topologies: networks that link one set of persons into certain possibilities for action, but cut off another set of persons from those same possibilities' (Couldry and Hepp 2016 p. 99).

LAYERS

Today, you can occupy a multitude of on- and offline places through a variety of devices and media platforms concurrently. You can snicker at your friends' constant exchange of quips on social media, co-watch your favorite show with hundreds of anonymous others online in the comfort of your bed, or scroll through shopping apps before purchasing a new laundry detergent at your local supermarket. It would not be an exaggeration to say that we can now be theoretically anywhere and everywhere yet never exclusively somewhere. In other words, technologically enhanced connectivity enables us to shift among multiple information and social layers. Thus, the question of how new technology will affect communities and human interaction is not only a question of what new off- or online places will be created, but what their confluences will mean. Couldry and Hepp (2016 p. 90) argued, 'within . . . a context of deep mediatization and the media manifold it is meaningful to ask "where people are" with and through media.'

The rise of social media 'detox' practices – such as the phone stack game in which the first one to lose to the urge to check one's phone (usually stacked among others in the middle of the table) during a group activity is required to pay the bill – illustrate a growing understanding of the power and potential threats present in this context of deep mediatization. With the help of communication technology, one can experience total transportation to virtual social environments or radical re-encoding of one's situated physical environment. Are these new layers a social good or an ill? Some argue this technologically-enabled accessibility is beneficial for social networks (K. Hampton et al. 2011; K.N. Hampton et al. 2015) while others like Turkle (2012) warn against the dawning of being 'alone together.'

Adding onto the complexity, breakthroughs in Augmented Reality (AR) and Virtual Reality (VR) technologies take us even further down this road of complicated multi-existence. How can we unpack this through the lens of Oldenburg's third place? One starting point could be to re-approach 'reality' through an analogy of layers. This begins with the presumption that reality is not a fixed, monolithic space. Depending on who you are, how you experience it, and how you interpret such past, present, and future experiences and expectations, 'reality' can be infinitely redefined. In other words, reality can be understood as a gestalt of layers that are connected by its interpreter/re-presenter (self) as well as the web of interpreter/re-presenters (the society). The benefit of this frame of thought is that it does not impose normativity on one type of experience over another; they are layers. Offline interactions are no more 'real' than online or any other mediated interactions, and no one person's experiences should be more or less 'real' than those of others. Under this perspective, even if there exists some form of 'real' reality, it will forever be evasive to human beings. Thus, the central concern becomes what has been experienced how by whom. Simultaneously, because the layers can coexist and are connected, it puts emphasis on the communicative processes that occur both within an individual and among collectives. In order to unpack all of this, we must first identify which layers are involved and then analyze how these layers are structured in relation with one another.

To discuss how this conceptualization may help with our task, let us start stacking from the basic layer all humans co-occupy: the layer of physical reality. Humans necessarily exist through bodies that are situated in a material context no matter whatever mediated reality or interpretive reality we have access to. This is an ineradicable tie unless a Science Fiction-like future of eternity in circuits awaits us. In other words, we, as beings that live with bodies, are bound to the imminent physical reality and its material conditions. This means physical location and its accompanying material conditions (still) matter. On the flip side, this also means we can meaningfully analyze 'where people are' by grounding the metaphysical concept of reality on physical reality.

Are our third places bounded to the physical realm? As we've noted, they can exist beyond it, but we should also consider the converse: can layers turn physical spaces that weren't third places into them? Consider Oldenburg's classic first and second places of home and work. New communication technologies are already layering information into these places, enabling office workers to be mixing with others elsewhere, or family members at the kitchen table to be mixing in Minecraft. This offers the ability to give access to groups and places that weren't possible, even in our idealized notions. Consider the Habermasian coffee house, allowing for the mixing of merchants and the exchange of ideas. It's all well and good if you were a male merchant, but not for the majority of people. Yet with layers, the exchange of that coffee house need not be tied to class, place, or involve coffee. Liberated from the confines and velvet ropes of society, what matters would be to be able to create and make accessible third place layers, and pay attention to the ways they can affect physical reality, which is one layer all human beings necessarily have to share.

The notion of layering, and anchoring of the layers through the material layer can ease the task of understanding both existent and emerging communication technologies regarding different spaces. For instance, AR and VR are often grouped together because they both deal with technologically mediated reality or realities. However, as Williams (2016) argued, AR and VR experiences are qualitatively different. In VR worlds, the user 'leaves' their immediate surroundings and 'goes' somewhere else. On the other hand, AR, by definition, provides layers that are to be placed on top of one's immediate surroundings. In short, VR attempts to maximize the immersion component of media experience whereas AR aims to fully acknowledge and utilize the imminent surroundings of the user. For example, AR has been applied in factories to augment assembly instructions for workers (Levy 2017) and by furniture companies to help the customers test the look and feel of their products in their home or office without requiring the actual product (Castellanos 2017).

In contrast, VR can flourish in fields that require complete and persuasive transportation from the immediate reality. For example, VR has been used to alleviate pain and fear in surgeries to decrease the use of anesthetic drugs (Marchant 2017), as well as in campaigns to raise awareness through vicarious experience such as Amnesty International's interactive 360-degree video that captured the devastation from bombing in Syria (Nudd 2016). However, because VR can convincingly transport the users to a different layer, it may also increase the weight of returning to one's physical conditions. This may be what will make VR's trajectory different from AR, as the latter attempts to use our local, physical spaces. Thus, it is possible to speculate that VRs, whether social or non-social, can be successful in a different context than ARs, which has the better capacity to fit into our everyday lives. Do third places need to be physical or present? As noted above, prior work suggests not. However, the code, mechanics and the intent of the developers always plays a critical role. VR developers will need to work harder to leverage third place characteristics (see Chapter 8). And, thus far VR developers have not been focused on the social side of their experiences.

One strategy to think about new technology through Oldenburg's third place would be to focus on specific layers. For instance, one approach would be to reevaluate whether certain physical places that have been deemed as third places continue to qualify via Oldenburg's criteria. However, a more fruitful task would be to consider two or more layers at the same time. A seemingly disintegrating community in a singular layer may be vibrant on a second, or when two or more layers are considered in conjunction with one another. No new technology makes these issues as unavoidable as virtual and augmented reality.

APPLYING LAYERS: VR AND AR

Virtual reality (VR) is the use of graphic technology to transport your mind somewhere else while your body stays in one place. It is currently used with a headset or goggles. While it has great potential for immersion, it's less clear if it is an inherently social technology that would help recreate third place conditions. The immediate applications of VR include travel, fantasy, games, and of course pornography. Some developers are passionate about VR's potential for social connectivity (Brightman 2017), but the lessons from MMOs suggest that the relative lack of depth of relationship will be similar with VR because it keeps people highly mediated and at a physical distance. There is also the base issue that VR goggles block eye contact and make simple movements in space dangerous, rendering any social interactions virtual-only. In contrast, Williams (2016) finds augmented reality (AR) to be the technology with more potential for recreating Third Place functions. AR is technology that adds some new information on top of what you see in daily life. It's an exact fit for the concept of layers. At the time of this chapter, AR layers are largely filtered through phones, using their cameras to see real space, but with new information superimposed on it. This allows for mixed reality experiences, which have a broad array of potential applications. For example, theme parks have added AR features to thrill ride experiences, dating applications allow people to see those nearby who are interested in relationships (Blackwell et al. 2015), shoppers can 'see' what furniture would look like in their home (Martindale 2017), foodies can overlay restaurant reviews on eateries as they walk past (Roberts 2016), and tourists can overlay guides as they explore a new city (Simpson 2017) (Figure 9.1). All of these concepts make sense for businesses looking to capture interest and guide consumers to clients (Barrett 2017). And, there is little doubt

Source: iStock by Getty Images.

Figure 9.1   An AR app, using a phone as a window into overlaid information

that employees with AR filters could be more productive, with so much information at their fingertips (Gavish et al. 2015; Levy 2017). We might imagine that as phones give way to glasses (e.g. Google Glass), that we will eventually see this technology more seamlessly embedded through implants or contact lenses (Figure 9.2).

But will this technology be social? If we follow Lessig's provocations, there is a potential tension between forces that will seek to capture our attention and redirect it for commerce and those forces within us that will seek to use it to connect with each other. And of course, by layering actual imagery on top of reality, there is immense potential for change, both good and bad. The technology could be used to block or alter real-world objects or people. The code will matter, and the choices made in it will have legal, ethical and social implications. 'It could mean the difference between truly helpful tools – that provide time saving guidance through daily tasks – and new art forms, versus highly distracting and confusing experiences that create greater tensions and barriers within communities' (Ranen 2017). Consider a filter bubble that would visually block out stimuli you find politically, socially, or religiously undesirable (Metz 2017). On

Source: iStock by Getty Images.

Figure 9.2   *Augmented design making layers appear literal*

the positive side, consider how AR could foster the kinds of connections that MMOs did, but with more substance because they would occur in real places. While it is still subject to the kinds of discrimination we see in any rich environment, AR could turn any location into a third place. A park need not be just a park – it could via AR become an Athenian agora, a beachfront, a trivia show, or (in a nod to Putnam) a giant bowling alley. This opens up the potential for layers to augment not just what we see, but how we can connect with each other through technology.

What will always be critical will be the values that are knowingly (or accidentally) coded into the experience. As Lessig used a constitution as his guiding light for good code, so too will AR developers need to have a set of values to help them create architectures and experiences that bring us together rather than separate us. Oldenburg's criteria are an excellent fit as a North Star for these creators. If AR experiences can layer in these values, then our third places can expand from those handful of nostalgic corner taverns to literally anywhere. What will be critical will be a new kind of media literacy in which everyday people are aware of the value encoded into their technologies. There is reason to be skeptical that everyone will know, or care, but educating ourselves and others is the very role of the people who are likely to read a chapter like this.

REFERENCES

Altschuller, S. and Benbunan-Fich, R. (2010). Trust, Performance, and the Communication Process in Ad Hoc Decision-Making Virtual Teams. *Journal of Computer-Mediated Communication*, 16(1), 27–47. doi:10.1111/j.1083-6101.2010.01529.x.

Ananny, M. (2016). Toward an Ethics of Algorithms: Convening, Observation, Probability, and Timeliness. *Science, Technology, and Human Values*, 41(1), 93–117. doi:10.1177/0162243915606523.

Ananny, M. and Crawford, K. (2016). Seeing Without Knowing: Limitations of the Transparency Ideal and its Application to Algorithmic Accountability. *New Media and Society*. doi:10.1177/1461444816676645.

Asimov, I. (1957). *The Naked Sun*. New York: Doubleday & Company.

Barrett, B. (2017). In Facebook's Future, You Live Through Your Phone. *Wired*, April 18.

Blackwell, C., Birnholtz, J., and Abbott, C. (2015). Seeing and Being Seen: Co-Situation and Impression Formation Using Grindr, a Location-Aware Gay Dating App. *New Media and Society*, 17(7), 1117–1136. doi:10.1177/1461444814521595.

Brightman, J. (2017). VR Criticism 'A Little Unfair,' Fargo, July 13. Retrieved on July 20, 2017 from http://www.gamesindustry.biz/articles/2017-07-13-vr-critic ism-a-little-unfair-fargo.

Buettner, D. (2015). *The Blue Zones Solution: Eating and Living Like the World's Healthiest People*. Washington, DC: National Geographic Books.

Castellanos, S. (2017). IKEA Readies Augmented Reality App for Shoppers, Using Apple Tech. Retrieved on July 19, 2017 from https://blogs.wsj.com/cio/2017/06/21/ ikea-readies-augmented-reality-app-for-shoppers-using-apple-tech/.

Coleman, J.S. (1988). Social Capital in the Creation of Human Capital. *American Journal of Sociology*, 94, S95–S121.

Couldry, N. and Hepp, A. (2016). *The Mediated Construction of Reality*. London: Polity.

Daft, R. and Lengel, R. (1984). Information Richness: A New Approach to Managerial Behavior. *Research in Organizational Behavior*, pp. 191–223. Homewood, IL: JAI Press.

Dennen, V.P. (2014). Becoming a Blogger: Trajectories, Norms, and Activities in a Community of Practice. *Computers in Human Behavior*, 36, 350–358. doi:10.1016/j.chb.2014.03.028.

Games, N. (2017). Nielsen Games 360 report 2017. Retrieved on October 24, 2017 from https://www.nielsen.com/content/dam/corporate/us/en/reports-downloads/2017-reports/nielsen-games-360-report-2017.pdf.

Gavish, N., Gutiérrez, T., Webel, S., Rodríguez, J., Peveri, M., Bockholt, U., and Tecchia, F. (2015). Evaluating Virtual Reality and Augmented Reality Training for Industrial Maintenance and Assembly Tasks. *Interactive Learning Environments*, 23(6), 778–798. doi:10.1080/10494820.2013.815221.

Gillespie, T. (2017). Governance Of and By Platforms. In J. Burgess, T. Poell, and A. Marwick (eds), *Sage Handbook of Social Media*. London: Sage, pp. 254–278.

Habermas, J. (1998). *The Structural Transformation of the Public Sphere: An Inquiry into a Category of Bourgeois Society*. Cambridge, MA: The MIT Press.

Hampton, K., Goulet, L.S., Rainie, L., and Purcell, K. (2011). Social Networking Sites and our Lives. Retrieved on August 22, 2017 from http://cn.cnstudiodev.com/

uploads/document_attachment/attachment/46/pew_-_social_networking_sites_
and_our_lives.pdf.

Hampton, K.N., Goulet, L.S., and Albanesius, G. (2015). Change in the Social
Life of Urban Public Spaces: The Rise of Mobile Phones and Women, and
the Decline of Aloneness Over 30 Years. *Urban Studies*, 52(8), 1489–1504.
doi:10.1177/0042098014534905.

Hansen, M., Fabriz, S., and Stehle, S. (2015). Cultural Cues in Students' Computer-
Mediated Communication: Influences on E-mail Style, Perception of the Sender,
and Willingness to Help. *Journal of Computer-Mediated Communication*, 20(3),
278–294. doi:10.1111/jcc4.12110.

Harrell, D.F. (2010). Designing Empowering and Critical Identities in Social
Computing and Gaming. *CoDesign*, 6(4), 187–206. doi:10.1080/15710882.201
0.533183.

Harrell, D.F. and Harrell, S.V. (2012). Imagination, Computation, and Self-
Expression: Situated Character and Avatar Mediated Identity. *Leonardo
Electronic Almanac*, 17(2), 74–91.

Herz, J.C. (1997). *Joystick Nation*. Boston: Little, Brown and Company.

Hess, A. (2017). How to Escape Your Political Bubble for a Clearer View. *The
New York Times*, March 3. Retrieved on September 12, 2017 from https://www.
nytimes.com/2017/03/03/arts/the-battle-over-your-political-bubble.html.

Kim, J. (2011). Two Routes Leading to Conformity Intention in Computer-
Mediated Groups: Matching Versus Mismatching Virtual Representations.
Journal of Computer-Mediated Communication, 16(2), 271–287. doi:10.1111/
j.1083-6101.2011.01539.x.

Kraut, R., Patterson, M., Lundmark, V., Kiesler, S., Mukhopadhyay, T., and
Scherlis, W. (1996). Internet Paradox: A Social Technology that Reduces Social
Involvement and Psychological Well-Being? *American Psychologist*, 53, 1011–1031.

Lessig, L. (1999). *Code and Other Laws of Cyberspace*. New York: Basic Books.

Levy, S. (2017). Google Glass 2.0 Is a Startling Second Act. *Wired*, July 18.

Marchant, J. (2017, 2017/01/31/). Virtual Reality Can Make the Pain of Surgery
Easier to Bear. *The Atlantic*, January 31.

Martindale, J. (2017). Ikea Shopping Experience Will Be Augmented With AR
App for iOS 11. *Digital Trends*, July 19.

Metz, C. (2017). The Rise of AR Will Recreate Your Filter Bubbles In the Real
World. *Wired*, April 20.

Napoli, P.M. (2014). Automated Media: An Institutional Theory Perspective on
Algorithmic Media Production and Consumption. *Communication Theory*,
24(3), 340–360. doi:10.1111/comt.12039.

Nie, N.H. and Hillygus, D.S. (2002). The Impact Of Internet Use On Sociability:
Time-Diary Findings. *IT and Society*, 1(1), 1–20.

Nudd, T. (2016). Amnesty International Unveils Incredible VR Experience
Showing the Devastation in Syria. Adweek, March 14.

Oldenburg, R. (1997). *The Great Good Place: Cafés, Coffee Shops, Community
Centers, Beauty Parlors, General Stores, Bars, Hangouts, and How They Get You
Through the Day*. New York: Marlowe & Company.

Pinch, T. and Bijker, T. (1999). The Social Construction of Facts and Artifacts: Or
How the Sociology of Science and the Sociology of Technology Might Benefit
Each Other. In W.E. Bijker, P. Hughes, and T. Pinch (eds), *The Social Construction
of Technological Systems*. Cambridge, MA: The MIT Press, pp. 17–50.

Postmes, T., Spears, R., Sakhel, K. and deGroot, D. (2001). Social Influence in

Computer Mediated Communication: The Effects of Anonymity on Group Behavior. *Personality and Social Psychology Bulletin*, 27, 1243–1254.

Putnam, R.D. (2000). *Bowling Alone: The Collapse and Revival of American Community*. New York: Simon & Schuster.

Ranen, M. (2017). We've Not Thought Through the Legal and Ethical Disruption of Augmented Reality. Retrieved on December 17, 2018 from https://shift.newco.co/2017/10/26/weve-not-thought-through-the-legal-and-ethical-disruption-of-augmented-reality/.

Roberts, D. (2016). How Pokémon Go could have a big impact on Yelp. *Yahoo Finance*, July 29. Retrieved on July 20, 2017 from https://finance.yahoo.com/news/pokemon-yelp-nintendo-augmented-reality-000000062.html.

Schwämmlein, E. and Wodzicki, K. (2012). What to Tell About Me? Self-Presentation in Online Communities. *Journal of Computer-Mediated Communication*, 17(4), 387–407. doi:10.1111/j.1083-6101.2012.01582.x.

Seamon, D. (1979). *A Geography of the Lifeworld*. New York: St. Martin's Press.

Shen, C. (2014). Network Patterns and Social Architecture in Massively Multiplayer Online Games: Mapping the Social World of EverQuest II. *New Media and Society*, 16(4), 672–691. doi:10.1177/1461444813489507.

Simpson, C. (2017). Meet Bixby: Samsung's Vision For The Future of AI. *Gizmodo Australia*, March 30.

Steinkuehler, C. and Williams, D. (2006). Where Everybody Knows Your (Screen) Name: Online Games as 'Third Places.' *Journal of Computer-Mediated Communication*, 11(4), 885–909.

Sunstein, C.R. (2001). *Republic.com*. Princeton, NJ: Princeton University Press.

Taylor, H. (2017). Global Gaming Revenue on Par with Sports at $149bn for 2017. Retrieved on December 17, 2018 from http://www.gamesindustry.biz/articles/2017-11-28-global-gaming-revenue-on-par-with-sports-following-2017-estimates.

Turkle, S. (2012). *Alone Together: Why We Expect More from Technology and Less from Each Other*. New York: Basic Books.

Van Alstyne, M. and Brynjolffson, E. (2005). Global Village or Cyber-Balkans? Modeling and Measuring the Integration of Electronic Communities. *Management Science*, 51(6), 851–868.

Walther, J. (2006). Nonverbal Dynamics in Computer-Mediated Communication, or:(and the Net:('s with You,:) and You:) Alone. In V. Manusov and M. Patterson (eds), *The Sage Handbook of Nonverbal Communication*. Thousand Oaks, CA: Sage, pp. 461–480.

Williams, D. (2016). Community is the 'killer app' missing from virtual reality. Los Angeles Times, December 27. Retrieved on August 29, 2017 from http://www.latimes.com/opinion/op-ed/la-oe-williams-virtual-reality-20161227-story.html.

10. Third places in transit: public transport as a third place of mobility

Daniel O'Hare

THE RISE AND RISE OF COMMUTING: SHIFTS IN WORKPLACES, URBAN FORM AND LIFESTYLES

This chapter considers whether the public transport commute, historically a linear experience between the workplace and home, can be a third place rather than a soulless shuttle to be bracketed with 'work' as the opposite to 'home'. In the context of this book, this topic is important because work is frequently separated from home. Suburban dwellers therefore spend considerable time moving between the two, with many travelling by public transport such as trains, trams, buses and ferries. As we shall see, the separation between home, transit and work is not as simple as it was once conceived to be, and this makes third places of mobility both interesting and complex.

This exploration of public transport as a third place draws mainly on a literature review that is shaped and informed by knowledge and experience of public transport in cities in Australia and around the world that I have either lived in, visited, heard of or read about. It is not based on original research; instead it is hoped that it will inspire others to pursue research and implementation of more humane public transport systems that will enrich the lives of communities and individual commuters using public transport to experience their first, second and third places.

Oldenburg's alternative description of third places as 'the great good place' sets a high bar for public transport to aspire to. Oldenburg himself has set a huge hurdle for any consideration of public transport as a third place. He writes (Oldenburg 1997, p. 7) that 'Life without community has produced, for many, a lifestyle consisting mainly of a home-to-work-and-back-again shuttle. Social well-being and psychological health depend upon community'. For workers, students and others who spend time on public transport, much could be gained by cultivating community in transit vehicles and stations. Oldenburg's evocation of third places was a reaction to the period of peak suburban sprawl, whereby daily life in North American cities was dominated by a long car-commute – the daily shuffle – between low density residential-only suburbs (or small towns and villages) and workplaces. By this time, workplaces were becoming less concentrated in city centres or 'downtowns'. Through the suburbanisation process of 'making a middle landscape' (Rowe 1992), workplaces were becoming dispersed through the rise of office parks and standalone major employers. These isolated, monocultural working environments lacked the diversity and richness of city centres, depriving employees of the access to a variety of third places that a worker might find within a short walk during their lunchbreak in a city centre – places such as a park, a gallery, a hidden-away café. In the new middle suburban landscape, the office park provided only an alternative form of lack of diversity, so commuters' lives could be split by an unrewarding drive between a residential desert and an office desert where few other human needs could be met or interests stimulated.

Oldenburg seems to write more of the office worker's commuter lifestyle than that of the blue collar worker. White collar workplaces had been concentrated in city centres, but by the 1990s there were increasing signs that major cities were developing into polycentric city regions (Garreau 1991; Simmonds and Hack 2000) or that they should be restructured to do so (Calthorpe and Fulton 2001).

Emerging 'edge cities', new clusters of economic activity noted by Garreau (1991), initially lacked the diversity of traditional city centres and it has taken decades for some of them to be 'refined' into genuine town centres with attractive streets and good public transport. The literature traces the transition of Tyson's Corner, outside the Washington DC beltway, from incremental unplanned urban fringe automobile stop-off to integrated town centre over the past half-century. Connection of this former 'non-place' to the Washington DC Metro, combined with dense redevelopment and the insertion of a walkable street grid is described by Levy (2017).

Although there is widespread agreement that public transport is important to the social and environmental sustainability of our cities, public transport use is comparatively low in Australian cities, being the chosen mode for only 27 per cent of all trips to work in Sydney at the 2016 census, and below 20 per cent in Australia's other major cities (Charting Transport 2017). Only 11 per cent of all trips in Sydney are by public transport. This is low by comparison with the mode share of public transport (all journeys, not just to work) in world cities in 2011: Hong Kong 80 per cent, Seoul 63 per cent, Paris 62 per cent, Tokyo 51 per cent,

Singapore 44 per cent (Anon. 2011). In some cities with similar public transport mode shares to that of Sydney's journey to work (i.e. around 27 per cent), similar or greater percentages of trips are by walking (for example in Bangalore, London, New York) rather than the majority being by private car as in Australian and North American cities, where densities are generally lower and a century of zoning has restricted mixed use development until recently.

Oldenburg's implied binary distinction between home and work was arguably at its most pronounced during the mid-twentieth century. Earlier, in the industrial revolution, work became separated from home as large numbers of workers became employees of large companies. Rather than artisans working below their homes, or shopkeepers 'living over the shop', these industrial workers left home each day to work in their mines or factories of employment. But home was often nearby, for example down the street or around the corner, and walking was a dominant transport mode for employees to get to work.

The rise of health problems for families living too close to these 'satanic mills' led to the suburbanisation of housing. At the same time, new forms of energy and technology enabled the introduction of mass public transportation by train and tram. The consequence was that work and home became separated, and commuting became a feature of daily life. With the growth of private car ownership in the second half of the twentieth century, the commute became less communal and more individualised.

Many commuters choose to use their private car rather than public transport for reasons including privacy, security and lack of tolerance for travelling with people of different socioeconomic status. The average car commute in Sydney is 26 minutes while the average public transport commute is considerably longer at 61 minutes per day (BITRE 2016). These minutes are valuable to the individual, so their commuting space has the potential to be a third place, whether it is a shared mass transit vehicle or an individual private car.

Young adults in Western countries are driving less than their parents. In the Australian state of Victoria, the proportion of 17–25-year-olds having a driver's licence fell from 77 per cent to 67 per cent between 2000–2001 and 2011–2012, while the proportion of licence-holders in the 25–64 years age group remained steady at 95 per cent (Delbosc and Currie 2013b). Similar falls in young age groups attaining licences were recorded in nine developed countries, most notably in Sweden and Norway, 'where licensing of young adults dropped by over 10% between the mid-1980s and the late 1990s (Berg, 2001)' (in Delbosc and Currie 2013a, p. 272). In the UK, males aged 17–20 holding a driver's licences fell from a 1993 peak of 54 per cent to fluctuate between 30–40 per cent in the years 2004–2012. In the same period, the equivalent statistics for UK females aged 17–20 fell from 41 per cent in 1993 to 25 per cent in 2004, recovering to 30–35 per cent between 2009 and 2012 (Berrington and Mikolai 2014).

A survey of 200 young Australian adults reveals that, while the high cost of motoring is the biggest reason for the decline in licence-holders, other major reasons include the ability to get around without a car and the desire to keep in contact with friends using social media (Delbosc and Currie 2013b). There are strong signs that this generation values their time, the experience of walkable neighbourhoods, and staying connected to friends and the world through their Internet-connected devices, which cannot be fully utilised while driving. The private car is no longer regarded by young urban people in developed nations as the primary means of establishing an independent lifestyle or symbolising status. As discussed later, trends towards less driving are predicted to persist because new communication technology substitutes for driving and supports alternative transportation (Davis and Dutzik 2012). The alienating daily auto shuttle decried by Oldenburg is being rejected, and so lively walkable neighbourhoods with good public transport are likely to be in greater demand.

THIRD PLACE, OR MOBILE SECOND PLACE FOR WORK?

The division between work and other activities – and other places – is no longer as definitive as when Oldenburg first wrote on third places. New technology and changing labour practices have made work more portable, so that it is not unusual for some work to occur amongst other activities at home, on holiday or at your kid's sporting match. Or while you are travelling on public transport to your official workplace. In their study of 'travel time use in the information age', Lyons and Urry (2005) acknowledge the blurring of previous distinctions between 'travel time and activity time' (Lyons and Urry 2005 p. 263) and between 'home and away', so that 'people can be said to *dwell* within mobilities' (Lyons and Urry 2005 p. 267). New information and communications technology enables passengers to be 'at home' on public transport because of the ability 'to make more flexible and extensive use of their time on the move' (Lyons and Urry 2005 p. 263). People thus increasingly make productive and enjoyable use of their time while travelling, rather than passively enduring the journey as they await arrival at the destination.

For long commutes, intercity rail services are reportedly beginning to rival everyday commuter public transport services, due to quality, convenience and price competitiveness (Rose 2012). On-board digital services make intercity commuter trains in Europe, North America and Asia ideal mobile workplaces (Lauber 2018). Plamondon (2009), a consultant engineer and writer, provides great detail on his 200 km twice-weekly commute from his home in central Oregon to a client's workplace in Portland's outer metropolitan area across the state border in neighbouring Washington. He found the train well-equipped to support what we would call third place activities as well as work activities: it was comfortable, seats had tray tables and AC jacks for his laptop, mobile phone reception was good, he could walk around and stretch his legs during the journey, and there was a dining car for use as an alternative workspace or for eating, drinking, relaxing or socialising. He used the uninterrupted travel time to complete concentrated bursts of writing. If he was tired on the homeward journey he could watch an onboard movie or stream a podcast. The crew were friendly and got to know him; the railway station staff were also friendly: they advised him of the best place to park his car and kept an eye on it for him while he was away. Plamondon's experience, rich in third place options, is one that many commuters on regular, shorter everyday services would like to have available to them (including this author).

Hustle Juice, a website established to support footloose workers, describes well-equipped intercity trains as ideal co-working spaces, where location-independent workers can work in comfortable and convenient surroundings while seeing the countryside and meeting new people for friendship and potential business collaboration or exchange (Lauber 2018). Some of these high-speed intercity trains are more like replacements for intercity flights, rather than regular public transport routes for any but the most mobile or highly-paid workers who live in one city and work in another.

TRAVEL TIME AS A GIFT RATHER THAN A COST?

A big part of the public transport experience is waiting: the wait at your stop or station and at any interchange points along the journey. And the journey itself may take a long time (cf. the average 61 minute commute in Sydney). While there is a long tradition in transportation policy and research of portraying travel time as a cost or penalty to commuters, there is emerging knowledge that travel time can be 'perceived and experienced as a gift rather than a burden' (Jain and Lyons 2008 p.81). While this reconceptualisation seems to accord with third place thinking regarding public transport, the debate indicates that the issue is far from settled.

News and social media exchanges in 2013–2014 show the diversity of opinion, with some supporting third place arguments and some supporting speed and convenience. A member of the Portland Streetcar Citizens Committee, quoted in a local newspaper, defends an 18-minute service frequency with the opinion that '... frequency is an overrated thing. Let's say there's a 20-minute [wait]. You can look on your phone, wait inside and have a beer' (Fry, requoted in humantransit.org 2013). This drew some strong reactions, including "I'm glad Mr. Fry has such a forgiving employer, spouse, extended family, dining companions, clients ... who don't mind him being late, but also a little drunk' (humantransit. org 2013). Others note how real-time knowledge of the location and timing of your streetcar gives passengers freedom to manage their time.

Another essential requirement for third place outcomes is that public transport allows the passenger some freedom. Information technology via mobile phones and real-time digital display boards is giving people more information on services and more ability to make their own choices about the times, routes and experiences offered for their trips. Access to real-time information on the location and timing of a bus lets us know how much time we have available to either rush or enjoy our walk to the station (Walker 2012). This can have a liberating effect that is beneficial to the workings of our local streets as third places, particularly allowing spontaneity to be accommodated. For example, we would know if we have time to stop and talk following a chance meeting with a friend or acquaintance in our community on our walk to our bus. User control, over their travel and environment, contributes to higher levels of satisfaction and even enjoyment of commuting (Paez and Whalen 2010).

A THIRD PLACE FOR WINNING FRIENDS AND LOVERS

Bus stop, bus goes, she stays, love grows
Under my umbrella. (The Hollies 1966)

The young lovers in the Hollies' 1966 pop song (Gouldman 1966) found the bus stop the ideal place to initiate a spontaneous romance during an everyday activity, confirming that a bus stop could bring people together in a neutral space where accidental life-changing encounters were possible. High school students also have a record of using bus stops, railway stations, trains and trams as venues for embarking on their romantic lives. Half a century after the Hollies' bus stop song, Zoe Folbigg's (2014) article, 'How I found love on the 8.21' confirms that life-enriching encounters on public transport are still possible. For Folbigg and the Hollies' opportunistically courting couples, public transport delivered on its potential to be a special place: 'a great good place' in Oldenburg's words.

Although there is very scarce refereed literature on public transport romances and friendships, there is a rich vein of ephemeral literature on such third place companionship encounters. The *Sydney Morning Herald*, over several decades, has published 'Column 8' contributions from readers who travel from the Blue Mountains to Sydney daily in friendship groups formed spontaneously on the train. Some just sit and read their books and newspapers after exchanging friendly greetings, while others play cards or board games, and celebrate birthdays or Christmas with a cake.

Russell's (2012) research into Wellington (New Zealand) commuters gives the researcher's own eyewitness account of small groups of passengers enjoying carefully prepared Christmas celebrations around the tables between the facing seats in their train carriages. The seating configuration is supportive of commuter choices in favour of social interaction. Given the importance of cafés and bars to relaxation and sociability, as noted in the third place literature, it is arguable that such facilities should be a standard inclusion in stations and longer-distance commuter trains.

Jensen (2015) describes the mobile communities of public transport in a paper entitled 'The making of Multiple Mobile Places in everyday train commuting'. She observes how Danish commuters produce what Oldenburg calls third place through 'the routines and rhythms of the train' (Jensen 2015 p.7). As well as 'individual practices of regeneration, relaxation, daydreaming and sleeping' (Jensen 2015 p.9), commuters make acquaintances and develop a range of classifications of intensity of interaction, ranging from '*mobile others*' (with little or no interaction), through to increasing degrees of interaction classified as '*mobile withs*' (whom we might call 'friends on the train') to '*mobile friends*' (where the friendship becomes extended into life beyond the train) (Jensen 2015 p.8, Jensen's italics).

COURTESY: CUSTODIANS AND CURATORS OF THE MOBILE THIRD PLACE

Public transport as third place requires an atmosphere of 'civility', whereby 'the rider feels respected as a customer, as a citizen, and as a human being' (Walker 2012 p.29). The basic conditions of civility are provided by the operator, including a quality service, timeliness, value for money, safety, security, cleanliness and comfort (Walker 2012).

Oldenburg and others write of the role of the staff of third places in creating a congenial atmosphere to enable people to feel at home. The staff who historically 'curated' the public transport experience have been disappearing for several decades due to cost-saving and replacement by technology. The shedding of station staff and on-board staff has changed the travel experience. We rarely encounter a ticket seller as we buy our tickets from a machine or top up our travel card automatically by direct debit from our bank account. Guards and conductors on trains, trams and buses have joined the ranks of obsolete occupations. Until their abolition in the 1990s, Melbourne's tram conductors – the 'connies' – created a welcoming atmosphere and provided travel directions and other information to passengers on 'their' trams. Automation has replaced these hospitality services, enabling efficiencies but also reducing security.

Urban transit authorities show support for the sociability and civility of public transport with behaviour management campaigns to encourage passengers to avoid anti-social behaviour (Russell 2012). These include Transport for London's 'considerate traveller' campaign, Philadelphia's 'dude it's rude' posters and Queensland Transport's 'super simple stuff' etiquette poster series, and similar campaigns in Perth, New York, Vancouver, Toronto, Tokyo, Singapore and many other cities.

Trains in some cities have introduced identified 'quiet' carriages in which passengers are expected to socially enforce the absence of loud conversations and other noise such as listening to music without headphones. Whether or not voluntary quiet carriage compliance is observed depends very much on the social characteristics of the particular train line and the culture of the particular city. Sydney's quiet carriages are strictly enforced by the passengers while 'quiet carriages' on South East Queensland's Gold Coast line are routinely ignored by both passengers and rail staff.

The ability to personalise a public space enables the user to feel more comfortable by exercising choices over their environment. The appeal and social value of movable seating in public open space has been noted as far back as Whyte's (1980) study of the social life of small urban spaces, and reinforced by Gehl (2010) and others. Such 'personalisation' could be put to use in public transport stations, but also apply to public transport vehicles. Some trains, such as Sydney's double-deckers, enable passengers to choose a more or less sociable setting, and a forward or rear-facing view, by offering reversible seating in the carriages.

Public uproar greeted an announcement in 2018 that Sydney's new intercity trains, servicing longer-distance commuters travelling up to four hours return each day, would not have reversible seats (also known as 'flip seats'). A media report (one of many) stated that 'internal documents released under freedom of information laws show why the state's lead transport agency chose fixed seats for the new intercity trains despite its own research revealing 'a strong customer appeal and usage of reversible seating' and a perception that fixed seating was a 'backward step' (O'Sullivan 2018 n.p.). Costs, weight, maintenance requirements, capacity, safety and procurement issues were cited among the reasons for the change. Opposition was not mitigated by the transport agency spokesperson citing several new benefits that support 'third place' performance at both an individual and social level, including 'wider seats, arm rests and wider aisles, [and] amenities like tray tables and charging outlets for mobile devices' as well as 'two sets of seats . . . at either end of each carriage which would allow passengers travelling in groups to face each other' (cited by O'Sullivan 2018 n.p.). Selling the new seating arrangements to the public, with 'half the seats facing in one direction and the rest in the other' is clearly a public relations challenge. The 235 public comments on the online story, interestingly did not give much attention to issues that might be considered 'third place' concerns, with the risk of motion sickness (from rear-facing travel) being the only consistent substantive point advanced. The limited scope of public comments indicates that the community of commentators has not been educated in relation to the third place values and potentials of public transport.

Another issue relating to user control over their transit space is that public transport passengers might appreciate the ability to raise or lower blinds to suit their preferences for sunlight and shade. Mehta and Bosson (2010) point out that personalisation is also affected by people's observation of whether a public space is well maintained, clean and free of vandalism. The other aspect of 'personalisation' is the individual touch that traders bring to their shop's presentation to the street, something that the research noted made these small businesses stand out in contrast to corporate conformity. In the case of a railway station, this type of personalisation tends not to be present as there is usually a standardised corporate identity for the transit service. Personalisation – and custodianship – can be imparted in smaller ways, however, by amusing notices posted by station staff or by dryly humorous announcements made by quirky station and train staff.

CONNECTING TRANSIT WITH WALKABLE PEOPLE PLACES

Public transport, and in particular public transport stations and stops, could offer more third place experiences by adoption of some of Mehta and Bosson's (2010) findings regarding third places and the social life of streets. In the research of three Massachusetts main street centres around transit stations, they found that four physical characteristics facilitated human interaction in an urban third place: personalisation, permeability, seating and shelter (Mehta and Bosson 2010).

Permeability, an important urban design quality (Bentley et al. 1985), influences how connected a station feels within a local street. Although ticket barriers may be a practical requirement, it is possible to influence the visibility and openness of the station through visual permeability. Visual connectivity offers advantages for crime prevention through environmental design (CPTED) and enhances passengers' feelings of safety while awaiting their service (also see Chapter 6 this volume). Shelter is essential to the climate comfort and protection of people awaiting public transport. In winter, solar access and protection from wind and rain may be the priority, while in summer shade via awnings and trees will be needed, together with protection from tropical storms in tropical cities.

Mehta and Bosson's (2010) research of main street centres gives clues to the types of 'third place' businesses that might be encouraged within or immediately adjacent to public transport stations: coffee shops, bars, restaurants, bookshops and convenience stores. Their observations and interviews found that these places acted as 'meeting places or community gathering places', 'places where [people felt] welcome and the people were friendly and where they spent time in active and passive socializing (i.e. sitting in the presence of other people, watching people and their activities, etc.) with their neighbours, friends, and acquaintances' (Mehta and Bosson 2010 p. 788).

To attract passengers and to have a chance of being sociable third spaces, public transport nodes need to be highly walkable. Lavadhino (2017 pp. 170–171) stresses that 'public transport never happens on its own; it is sparked by walking, and it needs walk-enabled environments to thrive.' Citing efforts by public transport operators in Grenoble and Bordeaux to boost patronage by upgrading pedestrian catchments, she proposes 'a new paradigm of a pedestrian-driven multimodal city, a city where the *comfort of the walking experience* plays a key role in choosing public transport over other modes of transportation' (Lavadhino 2017 p. 171, emphasis added). She notes that pedestrian-supportive public transport precincts may result in movement about the city being seen as a *pleasure* rather than an obligation (Lavadhino 2017 p. 171).

Travel by public transport includes more than the time spent on each public transport vehicle between the passenger's origin and destination. Walking and waiting time are part of the overall trip. In an impoverished urban environment, time spent walking and waiting can be seen as 'lost' or 'wasted' time. Alternatively, walking and waiting can be seen as personal leisure providing the social opportunity to 'grab a coffee, catch up with friends, do some shopping or simply connect with the city through walking. . ... If well equipped with amenities that add value to these break times, public transport nodes stop being dull places where captive people kill time while waiting, and become places in which people actually enjoy spending time' (Lavadhino 2017 p. 173).

Lavadhino's 'in-between mile approach' in Grenoble sought to extend the attractive walking catchment of public transport and the acceptable modal interchange distance to a 10–15 minute walk by creating an experiential setting 'designed to empower people to create their own meanings to the acts of waiting and switching between travel modes while bringing *joy and delight* in the process' (Lavadhino 2017 p. 174, emphasis added). Temporary physical interventions were supported by mobile phone apps to improve people's knowledge of the area and the opportunities it offered. Functional walking corridors to and between public transport nodes, Lavadhino argues, need to be 'blend[ed] together to coalesce into a unified sense of place in the minds of the users', and this is achieved through combining 'three core ingredients . . . things to do, people to meet and comfortable places to dwell' (Lavadhino 2017 p. 174). An important element of the 'nearness dynamics' of public transport nodes is 'serendipity, the capacity of hosting chance encounters between diverse people' (Lavadhino 2017 p. 182 citing Merton and Barber 2003). The Grenoble experiment identified a wide range of such chance encounters between diverse people. A newly created parklet above the railway station became a rendezvous place for commuters, a picnic spot for nearby office workers, a play space for children after school, and a social space for formerly isolated middle-aged women living in nearby public housing. Each of these activities is a 'third place' activity. Lavadhino (2017 pp. 182–183) proposes a 'habitability paradigm' in which the 'economy of place' is more important than the 'economy of speed' framework within which public transport is technically viewed.

THE EMERGENCE OF THE DIGITAL THIRD PLACE

There is a long tradition of public transport passengers, particularly solo travellers, relaxing by spending their time reading books and newspapers. Now it is commonplace to listen to podcasts of radio programmes, recorded music and watch movies via mobile phones and tablet computers. Social networking via Facebook enables people to keep in touch with friends and family while they commute. With this technology we can manage our social interactions while we are on public transport.

The ubiquity of mobile phones greatly increases the opportunity for commuters to participate in social networking while on their journey. The passenger's seat even in a crowded train, provides them with a base from which to connect into a 'placeless' digital third place that is beyond the mobile third place in which they are travelling.

Mobile social networks provide a means for public transport users to meet up with friends, while also assisting accidental travelling companions to develop friendships. The operation of such networks in the third places of urban areas, investigated by Humphreys (2010), can be transferred from fixed urban spaces such as bars, to the public transit spaces of public transport. Humphreys' (2010) research studied the use of Dodgeball, since superseded by other location services including the Google Maps app and Snapchat's Snap Maps feature. The location-sharing capability of mobile social media provides a means of being automatically alerted to and then connecting physically with your social network when in geographic proximity. If you choose, time spent in stations and on transit vehicles can therefore be shared with people in your circle of acquaintances and friends. Lofland (1998, in Humphreys 2010 p. 768) calls this the 'parochialisation' of public space. In this way, the public spaces of public transport can take on a more intimate and welcoming character in which people are more connected with their friends.

The founder of Dodgeball illustrates how location services and New York City's fine-grained street grid combine to enable subway users to readily adjust their walk home from the station in response to alerts that friends are walking nearby:

> Everyone walks [in New York City], so the paths we take are so fluid. . .. So it's kind of like we can change the way they experience a city, if only in a small way.. . . I can't tell you how many times I've had the experience where it's an average Tuesday and I get out of the subway and my phone starts to get some signal and I'm walking home and someone is a block north so I walk that way instead of walking this way. . .. it's helping me meet up with people I normally wouldn't meet. . .. (Dennis Crowley, cited in Humphreys 2010 p. 769)

These examples (also see Chapter 9 this volume) show how the public transport experience is able to be transformed into a third place by social media. These services could also be used by public transport users who wish to check the locations of, and make a side trip to, potential 'great good places' near their station or walking route. These services can also be used to avoid acquaintances, for example if you are aware that a friend or work colleague is at a particular end of the train platform, you might choose to go to the other end and board a different carriage if you wanted to just read rather than socialise.

It is becoming very common for public transport providers to provide free Wi-Fi to support the digital life of the train commuter. Free Wi-Fi access can make the public transport stop or station more enjoyable while waiting, and make the trip on the transit vehicle productive or pleasurable, according to the experience desired by the commuter. Many of these providers only allow very restricted bandwidths, meaning that passengers might not be able to download videos and other visual content. Some, such as South East Queensland's Translink, terminate the passenger's access after a certain time or when a certain amount of data is used up. Similarly 'most Amtrak trains provide free Wi-Fi but do not support high-bandwidth actions such as streaming music, streaming video or downloading large files' (Lauber 2018). Other train systems, as in the UK and Europe, have more bandwidth available but charge the passenger according to use (Lauber 2018).

The accelerating pace of digital technology promises to transform the public spaces of public transport into more socially-oriented 'hybrid spaces' in which social connections, digital information, and physical space are increasingly merged (Frith 2013 p. 250). Just as location-based mobile games (LBMG) can 'operate as an encouragement for people to engage in non-gaming behaviors like going to bars and historical sites' (Frith 2013 p. 249), gamification could be used to enhance the passenger experience of public transport by making it a more playful experience.

PUBLIC TRANSPORT AS PUBLIC SPACE: LEARNING FROM DISNEYLAND AND REKINDLING DESIRE FOR THE STREETCAR . . . AND TRAIN, TRAM, BUS AND FERRY

Nordahl (2008, 2012) argues that public transport should be fun (and therefore appealing and enticing to potential riders) and that public transport systems constitute an important part of the civic space of a city. He notes how designers and marketers make automobiles desirable and says that public transport should be designed and marketed in similar ways. Nordahl (2008) emphasises the experience rather than the efficiency and speed of public transport: most of the public transport vehicles he depicts are old rather than new, or forms of technology that were never taken up seriously for mass transit, such as monorails. His exemplar for captivating the public's interest in using public transport is Disneyland and some of the places and transit systems he extolls would not be out of place in Disneyland, for example San Francisco's iconic cable cars, which are noted elsewhere as more suited to tourists than to everyday commuters (Walker 2009).

The experiential focus needs to be balanced, nevertheless, with the practical need for speed and reliability of service: 'the romantic impulse towards slow transit wears away quickly if you have no choice but to rely on it all the time!' (Szarkowski, in Walker 2014). It seems unnecessary for us to have to choose between efficiency and experiential qualities like charm or 'sexiness', as if they were mutually exclusive. They are not, and we do not need to exclude one by prioritising the other.

The emphasis in much of the research on public transport user experience is focused on the individual public transport user and their individual experiences. Factors highlighted typically include the punctuality of service, perceived security, and the comfort and cleanliness of vehicles and waiting areas. But 'the opportunity to meet people' is also valued by some public transport users (Hine and Scott 2000 p. 222). A study of work commuters using public transport in Sweden's three largest urban areas found that talking to other passengers on the homebound commute attracted high levels of satisfaction (Ettema et al. 2012). The sociability of the transit experience is critical to whether public transport can truly be a third place.

The more important argument that Nordahl (2008) makes is that public transport vehicles are civic space, as acknowledged by Walker (2009), a major critic of the 'Disneyland theory of transit':

> Transit vehicles are not just transportation, they are civic space, and they must be designed as such. Most of the values that [Nordahl] elucidates and defends – such as scale, style, transparency, lighting, and connection to place – should be considered in every decision about the design, procurement, and fitting of transit vehicles. But these experiential values cannot expect to rule on matters such as frequency, speed, and staffing . . . because those factors are the dominant cost-drivers of transit; they will always be governed largely by what provides the greatest possible mobility at the least possible cost. (Walker 2009 blog post)

We have seen in other chapters that public spaces are important third places in our cities, towns and suburbs. Public transportation systems are worthy of attention in this book because public transport stations and vehicles are public places associated with mobility (Nordahl 2008). Hence public transport stations and vehicles are critical opportunities for third place activities to flourish.

CREATING DISTINCTIVE, PERSONAL AND SOCIABLE PUBLIC TRANSPORT 'PLACES'

Public transport systems – the networks of stations and fleets of vehicles – contribute greatly to the sense of place of a city or locality. Sydney Harbour Ferries, San Francisco's trolley cars, London's Underground and many other public transport systems internationally, offer a distinctive experience of the city at the same time as contributing significantly to the character of the city. The modern London Underground logo, almost unchanged since 1918, projects a highly legible corporate identity as well as making a major contribution to the local and regional identity of the metropolis (Meggs and Purvis 2016). Butina-Watson and Bentley (2007, pp. 101, 124) argue that the high quality modern graphic design of the Underground extended far beyond legibility, to create a distinctive 'cultural landscape', 'presenting the Underground not just as a means of transport, but rather as a life-enhancing source of varied experiences' (Butina-Watson and Bentley 2007 p. 105). In this way, public transport users were encouraged to identify themselves as belonging to 'a public transport community' (Butina-Watson and Bentley 2007 p. 101). The design approach sought to develop a 'coherent place-identity' for each line (Butina-Watson and Bentley 2007 p. 109), while the consistency in overall system design 'helped to bind together the "city of villages" which many felt London to be' (Butina-Watson and Bentley 2007 p. 124). All of these points can be related to third place ideas, because they all focus on creating a system for people to identify with and to make it the setting for daily life experiences beyond merely transit.

When new public transport lines are being designed, design decisions are made between the legibility and character of individual stations versus the corporate identity of the whole system. This was the case in recent additions to South East Queensland urban public transport infrastructure, where after some consideration of alternatives the decision was made in favour of consistent rather than individual design treatment of stations on (respectively) the Brisbane Busways that commenced in 2000 and the Gold Coast Light Rail that commenced in 2014. Such decisions follow the example set by the strength of the London Underground. The Paris Metro is a slightly different example, where there is a subtler balance between the consistent identity of the system and the variations seen in different locations and different eras of development. Purely by being maintained through the mid-twentieth century when other cities were tearing up their tram lines, Melbourne's extensive tram system has continued to contribute significantly to the city's identity. Its role in place attachment was even greater before the tram conductors ('the connies') were abolished in a 1990s labour-saving and cost-cutting move.

In other more recent systems, efforts are made to differentiate particular public transport lines, as in the different coloured lines of the Boston Subway (the Blue, Green and Red Lines). While being differentiated in colour for legibility and passenger wayfinding reasons, the distinctiveness enhances the identity of different corridors in the city. When Sydney's Eastern Suburbs suburban rail line opened in 1979, it established a line identity distinct from others in the system and this was further enhanced by each station being differentiated by its own boldly coloured signage so that passengers could recognise their stop at a glance.

It is a well-established urban design principle that people like to be able to control their environment (Whyte 1980; Lynch 1984). Many cities have introduced movable street furniture that enables the users of urban space to arrange it to meet their needs and to be physically and socially comfortable (as first established in Whyte's 1970s research on the social life of small urban spaces). Adoption of movable urban furniture seems not to be growing at the same pace in public transport vehicles, even being removed in the case of Sydney trains, as discussed above.

PLANTING SOCIAL CAPITAL IN A PERENNIAL THIRD PLACE

A breakfast radio interview describes how a stationmaster-initiated garden built community pride in a Brisbane suburban railway station (Begley 2017). Feelings of ownership and belonging are expressed by the stationmaster, local train passengers and community members. Establishment of the garden gives the stationmaster a sense of custodianship of a significant public place and his pride communicates that to passengers and community members, who may either assist in the garden's establishment and maintenance or share in the sense of place while catching or disembarking from trains at the station. The interview reveals enthusiastic participation by passengers and other local community members who bring in plant cuttings from their own gardens and provide advice on what to plant where or on when to prune particular plants. The stationmaster notes other benefits such as people getting to know each other and the station staff, and the opportunity for social interaction, including having someone to confide in during times of trouble. It is clear that, through custodianship of the station, this stationmaster plays the role of third place host described by Oldenberg. Devoting a daily 30–45 minutes to gardening activities before and after his basic duties, the stationmaster reports that the results include reduced vandalism, including passengers intervening to deter intending vandals (Begley 2017). Given the recognition of this station garden in a state-level community award nomination, and the stationmaster's endorsement by his local Member of Parliament, the Queensland Rail Chief Executive, his regional supervisor, passengers and local community members (Begley 2017; Bennion 2017), it is surprising that this effective means of social capital building is not endorsed as a system-wide programme (see also Chapter 8 this volume).

A British example illustrates the challenges of community gardening at railway stations. A Somerset village station was known for its distinctive community garden for a quarter of a century until its elderly volunteer carers were defeated by old age and 'officialdom', finally abandoning the garden when required by the authorities to wear high-visibility vests and helmets while gardening on the platform (Kington 2007). After the garden became derelict, a local committee was formed to recreate it with volunteer work, dedicating it with a plaque to the original retired gardeners. Within weeks, contractors 'with strimmers and chainsaws' completely destroyed the garden in an incorrect interpretation of a maintenance contract. Examples such as this are not widely reported, but they show that the property management practices of the large transit companies can be incompatible with local values such as custodianship of sense of place.

Changes in public transport infrastructure may provide resources for other community uses that may deliver third places to a community over time. When a railway station is superseded by new lines or falling patronage, the station buildings can be (and are) used as community centres, craft rooms and other activities that invite in the local community. Disused railway yards may become available for community gardens. A formal example is the development of a high standard public garden in Brisbane's former Roma Street railyards. The Roma Street Parklands have been professionally designed, built and managed, but volunteers assist in their running and maintenance, and nearby residents, workers and citywide users find this a valuable community space to meet, play and enjoy nature.

A less formal example is the Railway Park Community Garden established in the former Queanbeyan railyards, near Canberra, in 2002 (Parsons 2017). Under the current management arrangements, 26 community members lease separate garden plots from the head lessee, Queanbeyan Sustainability Group, which in turn leases from the local council. 'Many people who garden at Railway Park live in small units or townhouses with little or no outdoor space suitable for growing food. The garden provides a place for them to grow food for themselves and an opportunity to mix with neighbours they might not meet in the ordinary course of their lives' (Parsons 2017). Plot holders and the broader community invite greater community participation through working bees and harvest and spring time open days. This public transport infrastructure is used as a new kind of third place – the community garden – that is separate from its public transport use.

New York's Highline is perhaps the best known example of a disused urban railway line being reborn as a community garden, walkway and meeting place. Beyond the garden and beyond the city, other disused railway lines in many countries provide a stimulus to community through rebirth as rail trails for walking and cycling, opening up nature and countryside for the enjoyment of local people and tourists travelling slowly by bicycle or on foot.

PIXELATING THE PERSON-TO-PLACE ATTACHMENT

The view from the passenger seat is a taken-for-granted priority for many public transport passengers. As an infrequent traveller on Sydney Harbour Ferries over many years, I have been surprised that regular commuters could take their eyes off the spectacular view of the cityscape on the water and concentrate on a newspaper, book or mobile device. When the Gold Coast was selecting optimal routes for its new light rail system, a section of the community expressed a strong preference for a waterfront route because of the views of the beaches, rather than the selected route a block or so inland that services more people and connects into local centres. Brisbane's Citycat waterbuses also offer very enticing views of the city from its broad river, while smaller cross-river ferries bob along providing a very sensory experience appreciated through sight, sound, maritime smells and the feel of the subtropical breeze.

A clear view out of the public transport vehicle adds to the visual interest of the journey and connects passengers to the physical and social places through which they travel. Passengers need to be able to see out so that they know when their stop is coming up. In some neighbourhoods, a passenger might also need to be able to see out to ascertain whether it is safe for them to alight at a particular stop. In the case of school children or young adults, there may be a need for them to see if there is someone they wish to avoid at the stop or station, and a social decision may be made to 'stay on the bus' until the next stop. Equally, passengers feel safer and more comfortable when boarding public transport if they can see the people and behaviour on-board.

Public transport passengers are among the 'eyes on the street' (Jane Jacobs' timeless term) that provide safety through their passive surveillance of public places. In a notorious criminal case of child abduction in South East Queensland in the early 2000s (the Daniel Morcombe case), it was passengers' views from a bus window that contributed vital evidence that assisted the identification and conviction of the main suspect, because he and his car were sighted near the boy at the time of his disappearance from a bus stop. Had this event occurred five years later, the passengers might not have been able to see clearly through the advertising wrap that is now common on the region's Translink bus windows. Would the caring observations of these bus passengers be possible in today's buses screened in by advertising film?

Advertising wrap is now commonly seen on the windows of public transport vehicles in cities around the world. Usually the reason given for applying the wrap is that the advertising revenue helps to subsidise the cost of public transport provision. Yet on some services, such as Brisbane's Citycat waterbuses and City Glider high-frequency buses, the wrap merely advertises the vehicle itself.

The public transport authorities who sign the contracts with the advertisers apparently believe that the reverse-dot-matrix film is see-through. In the brightest light it is largely transparent, appearing like a thin veil over the view. But in dull weather, at night time or in rain, it appears opaque. This deprives passengers of an outward view and makes it difficult for them to see when their stop is coming up. The advantages of the passenger view, ranging from the pleasure of the journey to the passive surveillance of the streets, are lost in return for a relatively small advertising revenue.

CONCLUSION

This chapter demonstrates that the public transport experience – in trains, trams, buses, ferries, stops, stations and station locales – is, and remains, central to the concept of third place. Public transport has continued to constitute a very important element of the public places of our cities throughout the major changes in urban structure that have accompanied globalisation. Since Oldenburg introduced the third place concept in the 1980s, there have been major changes in the shape of cities and in the nature of work as a result of changing work practices and technological development. Cities have continued to evolve into polycentric city regions that offer more than the simple contrast between the central city workplace and distant suburban homes implied by Oldenburg. At the same time, the distinction between work and other activities has become blurred and technology enables – and employer and employee expectations demand – that many people undertake work activities away from the workplace, including while on their public transport journey. Neat distinctions between first, second and third places are less applicable now. Through all of this change, the need for work-related and study-related travel has not abated.

We have seen that commuting by public transport can be much more than the dehumanising shuttle decried by Oldenburg. Examples have been provided of commutes that are enjoyed rather than merely endured, where public transport travel time is more of a 'gift' than a penalty in commuters' daily lives. Given the time that so many people spend commuting, it is essential that such positive experiences become the norm rather than the exception. There is much work to be done for this to become reality. This is an exciting time for public transport research and development, particularly as the potential of information and communications developments is only beginning to be realised. Greater recognition of the potential of public transport to be a 'gift', to be enjoyed rather than endured, presents design opportunities for transforming public transport vehicles, stops, stations and neighbourhoods into truly enriching third places of mobility. It is essential that we design and manage them in a way that contributes to 'the great good life' that people deserve from their cities.

REFERENCES

Anon. 2011 Passenger transport mode shares in world cities, *Journeys* (November) pp. 60–70. Accessed 25 April 2018 at http://studylib.net/download/7972629.

Begley, T 2017 Community spirit grows in train station garden, ABC Radio Brisbane, 6 June. Accessed 30 April 2018 at http://www.abc.net.au/radio/brisbane/programs/breakfast/train-garden/8593258.

Bennion, B 2017 Station master nominated for Queensland Day award for garden work, Quest Newspapers 2 June. Accessed 30 April 2018 at https://www.couriermail.com.au/questnews/southeast/station-master-nominated-for-queensland-day-award-for-garden-work/news-story/b26eba26e15a2348420ac83e9eb9280c

Bentley, I, A Alcock, P Murrain, S McGlynn and P Smith 1985 *Responsive Environments: A Manual for Designers*. Oxford: Architectural Press.

Berrington, A and J Mikolai 2014 *Young Adults' Licence Holding and Driving Behaviour in the UK: Full Findings*. London: RAC Foundation.

Bureau of Infrastructure, Transport and Regional Economics (BITRE) 2016 Five facts about commuting in Australia, information sheet no. 77. Canberra: BITRE.

Butina-Watson, G and I Bentley 2007 *Identity by Design*. London and Burlington: Butterworth-Heinemann.

Calthorpe, P and W Fulton 2001 *The Regional City: Planning for the End of Sprawl*. Washington DC: Island Press.

Charting Transport (blog) 2017 Trends in journey to work mode shares in Australian cities to 2016 (2nd edition). Accessed 25 April 2018 at https://chartingtransport.com/2017/10/24/trends-in-journey-to-work-mode-shares-in-australian-cities-to-2016/.

Davis, B and T Dutzik 2012 *Transportation and the New Generation Why Young People Are Driving Less and What It Means for Transportation Policy*. Published by Frontier Group and US PIRG Education Fund. Accessed 30 April 2018 at https://uspirg.org/sites/pirg/files/reports/Transportation%20&%20the%20New%20Generation%20vUS_0.pdf.

Delbosc, A and G Currie 2013a Causes of youth licensing decline: a synthesis of evidence, *Transport Reviews* 33(3), 271–290.

Delbosc, A and G Currie 2013b Exploring attitudes of young adults toward cars and driver licensing, Australasian Transport Research Forum 2013 Proceedings, October. Brisbane.

Ettema, D, M Friman, T Garling, L Olsson and S Fujii 2012 How in-vehicle activities affect work commuters' satisfaction with public transport, *Journal of Transport Geography* 24, 215–222.

Folbigg, Z 2014 How I found love on the 8.21, *Daily Mail* 4 January. Accessed 30 April 2018 at http://www.dailymail.co.uk/femail/article-2533460/How-I-love-8-21-A-dreary-daily-commute-handsome-stranger-aisle-story-make-heart-soar.html.

Frith, J 2013 Turning life into a game: Foursquare, gamification, and personal mobility, *Mobile Media and Communication* 1(2), 248–262.

Garreau, J 1991 *Edge City: Life On The New Frontier*. New York: Doubleday.

Gehl, J 2010 *Cities for People*. Washington, DC: Island Press.

Gouldman, G 1966 Bus Stop [Recorded by The Hollies]. On *Bus Stop*. Los Angeles: Imperial Records.

Hine J and J Scott 2000 Seamless, accessible travel: users' views of the public transport journey and interchange, *Transport Policy* 7, 217–226.

humantransit.org 2013 Quote of the week: the portlandia streetcar, Human Transit: the professional blog of public transport consultant Jarrett Walker. Accessed 6 December 2018 at http://humantransit.org/2013/02/quote-of-the-week-the-portlandia-streetcar.html.

Humphreys, L 2010 Mobile social networks and urban public space, *New Media and Society* 12(5), 763–778.

Jain, J and G Lyons 2008 The gift of travel time, *Journal of Transport Geography* 16, 81–89.

Jensen, H 2015 The making of Multiple Mobile Places in everyday train commuting. Paper presented at the RC21 International Conference on 'The Ideal City: between myth and reality: representations, policies, contradictions and challenges for tomorrow's urban life' Urbino (Italy) 27–29 August. Accessed 7 May 2018 at http://www.rc21.org/en/conferences/urbino2015/.

Kington, M 2007 The railway station garden that set a rival village apart, *The Independent* 16 September. Accessed 30 April 2017 at https://www.independent.co.uk/voices/columnists/miles-kington/miles-kington-the-railway-station-garden-that-set-a-rival-village-apart-464377.html.

Lauber, K 2018 It's time to book a train as your next coworking space, Hustle Juice. Accessed 25 April 2018 at https://www.thehustlejuice.com/travel/2018/2/13/railway-train-for-coworking.

Lavadhino, S 2017 Public transport infrastructure and walking: gearing towards the multimodal city. Chapter 9 in Mulley, C, K Gebel and D Ding (eds) Walking: connecting sustainable public transport with health, *Transport and Sustainability* 9, 167–186. ISSN: 2044-9941 doi 10.1108/ S2044-994120170000009011. Accessed online 9 October 2017.

Levy, J 2017 *Contemporary Urban Planning*. New York and London: Routledge.

Lofland, L 1998 *The Public Realm: Exploring the City's Quintessential Social Territory*. New York: Aldine de Gruyter.

Lynch, K 1984 *Good City Form*. Cambridge, MA: MIT Press.

Lyons, G and J Urry 2005 Travel time use in the information age, *Transportation Research Part A* 39, 257–276.

Meggs, P and A Purvis 2016 *Meggs' History of Graphic Design* (6th edn). Hoboken, NJ: Wiley.

Mehta, V and J Bosson 2010 Third places and the social life of streets, *Environment and Behavior* 42(6), 779–805.

Merton, R and E Barber (2003) *The Travels and Adventures of Serendipity: A Study in Sociological Semantics and the Sociology of Science*. Princeton, NJ: Princeton University Press.

Nordahl, D 2008 *My Kind of Transit: Rethinking Public Transportation in America*. Chicago: Center for American Places at Columbia College in association with The Elizabeth Firestone Graham Foundation.

Nordahl, D 2012 *Making Transit Fun! How to Entice Motorists from their Cars (and onto their Feet, a Bike, or Bus)*. Washington, DC: Island Press (126 pp) (e-book). ISBN: 9781610910446.

Oldenburg, R 1997 Our vanishing 'third places', *Planning Commissioners Journal* 25 Winter 1996–1997, 6–10. Accessed 18 December 2018 at plannersweb.com/wp-content/uploads/1997/01/184.pdf.

O'Sullivan, M 2018 Cost, safety trumps passengers' desire for flip seats on new trains, *Sydney Morning Herald* 15 March. Accessed 30 April 2018 at https://www.smh.com.au/politics/nsw/cost-safety-trumps-passengers-desire-for-flip-se ats-on-new-trains-20180302-p4z2ib.html.

Paez, A and K Whalen 2010 Enjoyment of commute: a comparison by different transportation modes, *Transportation Research Part A* (44) 537–549.

Parsons, S 2017 The community garden at Queanbeyan Railway Station, *Canberra Times* 9 January. Accessed 30 April 2018 at https://www.canberratimes.com.au/national/act/the-community-garden-at-queanbeyan-railway-station-20170109-gto0ft.html.

Plamondon, R 2009 Commuting by train on the Amtrak Cascades, high-tech writing and engineering blog. Accessed 25 April 2018 at http://www.hightechwriting.com/amtrak_commute/.

Rose, J 2012 Amtrak gaining popularity among commuters who ride between Portland, Oregon City and Salem, *The Oregonian/Oregon Live* 5 March. Accessed 25 April 2018 at http://www.oregonlive.com/pacific-northwest-news/index.ssf/2012/03/amtrak_gaining_popularity_amon.html.

Rowe, P 1992 *Making a Middle Landscape*. Cambridge, MA: MIT Press.

Russell, M 2012 Travel time use on public transport: what people do and how it affects their wellbeing, unpublished PhD thesis, University of Otago.

Simmonds, R and G Hack (eds) 2000 *Global City Regions: their Emerging Forms*. London and New York: Spon.

Walker, J 2009 The Disneyland theory of transit. 17 April. Accessed 28 April 2018 at http://humantransit.org/2009/04/the-disneyland-theory-of-transit.html#more-24693.

Walker, J 2012 *Human Transit*. Washington DC: The Island Press.

Walker, J 2014 Blog post, 28 July. Accessed 28 April 2018 at http://humantransit.org/category/philosophy.

Whyte, W 1980 *The Social Life of Small Urban Spaces*. New York: Project for Public Spaces.

11. Third places and their contribution to the street life

Leila Mahmoudi Farahani and David Beynon

INTRODUCTION

Commercial service establishments such as cafés, restaurants, pubs and bars play a key role in the social life of communities and contemporary urban life. They are often considered 'anchors of community life' (Lukito and Xenia 2017) as they can provide opportunities for social engagement (Bookman 2013; Oldenburg 2013). Oldenburg's (1989) theory of 'third places' provides a useful account of how cafés and other similar eateries can perform as a neutral ground for social interaction, as they 'accommodate the regular, voluntary, and informal gatherings of individuals beyond the realms of home and work' (Lukito and Xenia, 2017).

Previous studies have mainly focused on how third places as 'indoor' public or semi-public venues can accommodate social engagements and act as sites of 'care' (Warner et al. 2012; Rosenbaum et al. 2016) or provide an opportunity for people who want to be 'alone in the company of others' (Walters and Broom, 2013). However, what happens outside third places and how they may contribute to the street life has not been fully investigated. To address this gap, this chapter focuses on how third places contribute to the vitality of their surroundings and encourage social interactions on streets or how they can constitute the 'heart of urbanism' (Stenseth 2013).

Drawing on careful observations of three commercial streets in City of Greater Geelong, Victoria, Australia, this study aims to define the physical and urban design qualities of third places which break the indoor-outdoor boundaries and encourage vitality and social life in commercial streets.

This chapter is structured as follows. The next section gives a brief overview of third places and their importance for contemporary community life. After this, two sections explore how third places can contribute to pavement dining and their role in the social life of suburban neighbourhood centres. The following section then contextualises the research by exploring the study area and methods used for this study and two further sections describe the analysis and findings from nine case studies in three commercial streets in the City of Greater Geelong. The conclusion reflects on the findings and what they mean for future suburban development.

THIRD PLACES

According to Oldenburg (1989), a third place is a place of refuge, where people can eat and drink, relax, commune and interact beyond first place of 'home' and the second place of 'work'. Eating venues that perform as third places not only can satisfy consumption needs but also customers' needs for companionship and emotional support especially for the elderly (Rosenbaum 2006). The frequency of receiving emotional support is cor-related with customers' loyalty to such venues (Rosenbaum 2006).

Within this context, third places become places where social needs can be satisfied, one can meet friends, colleagues, neighbours and even strangers, fulfilling desires for relaxation, social contact, entertainment and leisure. They present as neutral, inclusive and accessible settings where conversa-tion is the main activity and the mood is playful (Oldenburg 2009). Because of this, third places are often considered as second homes and settings that can provide psychological comfort (Lukito and Xenia 2017).

Third places can be semi-public or privately owned spaces such as cafés, pubs, local stores, bookshops, post office and restaurants or public spaces such as residential streets or a bench in a local park (Oldenburg 1989). Commercial service establishments such as cafés and restaurants are pri-vate spaces as they are privately owned but they have a public dimension as they accommodate a variety of customers from the public (Warner et al. 2012). Such third places are not entirely public, being privately owned, but still have a semi-public nature. However, more than public third places, these commercial third places are designed to appeal to a target group, and so, if successful, project themselves into the public realm as an invitation to this target group. Such third places are often places of meeting, though this meeting is enabled through consuming. They create social networks and tap into them for business. In bars and cafés the strength of the networks can be connected to the perceived publicness of the place.

'The best third places are locally owned, independent, small-scale, steady-state businesses and both government and incorporated chain operations have wreaked havoc upon them' (Oldenburg 2009, p.4). Although social interactions occurring in third places might be considered as weak ties (Granovetter 1973), Rosenbaum et al. (2016) have shown that many consumers find the support received in third places similar to the ones they receive from family members.

Third places that accommodate outside dining can contribute to the vitality of streets. According to Banerjee (2001), in the contemporary society, it is the appropriate mix of flânerie and third places that dictates the script for a successful public life. Flânerie, following Walter Benjamin's (1999) earlier definition of the flaneur, someone who took their recreation by moving casually through urban space (in particular the shopping arcades of the early twentieth century), refers to 'hangout' places such as new shopping centres that are designed to encourage lingering activities. Benjamin sensed the presence of alternative knowledges of the city derived by those inhabited or moved through its spaces. As such, one of his interests was in how flaneurs were critical to city life as those politically or hegemonically in control, and whose engagement with the city needed to be recognised. Taking this into the twenty-first century, Banerjee refers to third places and the streets that promote hanging-out as 'reinvented streets' (Banerjee, 2001). These streets can be located in the heart of the city, serving city dwellers, or in the heart of neighbourhoods serving locals.

Third Places and Pavement Dining

Cafés and similar eateries and drinking venues can enhance social activities occurring in commercial streets. Many cities are encouraging the private and for-profit use of public spaces as a strategy to encourage social life. For instance, 'New York city that once disallowed open sidewalk cafés now has nearly a thousand of them with about 80 per cent of them in Manhattan' (Oldenburg 2013, p. 18).

According to Oosterman (1992), drinking, relaxing and enjoying fresh air are not the only activities pavement dining facilitates. One of the most favoured activities is to 'watch people go by, to be entertained by street life and to inhale the atmosphere of the city' (Oosterman 1992, p. 90). According to Whyte (1980), watching others is the most popular activity in successful urban spaces. Oosterman (1992) compares the street to a stage where café chairs are placed towards it. Pavement dining also offers the opportunity to meet inadvertently or to meet strangers (Oosterman 1992).

Montgomery (1997) argues that pavement dining particularly, pavement cafés, have positively impacted the urban life in British cities. Pavement cafés are places of interaction and meeting new people. Cafés are inclusive as they are not associated with particular ethnic traditions as are pubs or clubs. Additionally, they are not alcohol-centred and thus can attract a diverse group of customers.

Pavement cafés are places of great interaction with the street and improved visibility. They enhance perceptions of safety by 'natural surveillance' and 'eyes on the street' (Oldenburg 2013). Compared to the pubs and bars, cafés are able to attract a more diverse age-group of people. They are also places where a great deal of business is transacted, and pavement dining is perhaps one of the few remedies to the fully privatised public realm. Pavement dining can also contribute to businesses along the streets where they are located and beyond that by attracting customers and encouraging lingering activities (Oldenburg 2013).

However, not all cafés and restaurants equally contribute to the social activities on the street. Mehta and Bosson's (2009) study of three commercial streets in the US showed that only the third places that are relatively high in personalisation and permeability and offer seats and shelters on the footpath contribute to the sociability of streets.

This implies that certain spatial and compositional qualities are needed for successful third places, and there is a relationship between the design of such places and their use that can and should be understood. As a basis for this, Henri Lefebvre's conceptions of space (1991) might be considered. In *The Production of Space*, Lefebvre defines three ways of dealing with space: spatial practice (espace perçu, perceived space); representations of space (espace conçu, conceived space); and spaces of Representation (espace vécu, lived space). 'Perceived space' is that which can be measured and analysed objectively; the perception of order within space. 'Conceived space' is that which is planned, designed and subdivided; the imposition of order on space, and finally 'lived space' is the space of direct experience. Considering this, there is the question of the degree to which space is the repository of 'creative energy', 'stored in readiness for new creations' (Lefebvre 1984 p. 14) and how honing particular characteristics of spaces might make places successful.

Third Places in Suburbia

Such a consideration might then be applied to suburbia, as both the prevalent condition in Australia and many other locations, but one which is often viewed pejoratively. The suburban lifestyle is associated with a lack of vitality and social life (Davidson and Cotter 1991; Richards 1994). According to Richards (1994), living in suburbia is the 'dream' achieved at the price of deprivation and isolation. Low-density suburbs are the most challenged areas regarding social life in suburban nations such as Australia.

Taking Lefebvre's idea that the city is capable of 'exposing' meanings, whether political, philosophical or religious, through its physical features; buildings, streets and monuments have the capacity to 'voice' these meanings (Lefebvre 1996 pp. 113–114). They do this by playing theatre to the

life that happens within them; sometimes staged events such as festivals
and ceremonies, but more importantly they frame everyday life. Whether
considered at the level of the neighbourhood, the street or the individual
café, physical/spatial elements within a built environment are not neutral
or filled only with the meanings that their designers ascribe to them, but
draw their meanings performatively, most specifically in this case from
how they perform as third places.

What has been recorded by researchers is that neighbourhood activity
centres are important within this context, as they provide opportunities for enhancing social life in low-density settlements, and scholars
commonly interpret their commercial activities as being central to local
community life and identity (Deener 2007; Jacobs 1961; Oldenburg 1999).
Researchers have viewed commerce as the source of neighbourhood
safety (Jacobs 1961), the core of democratic participation and community
vitality (Oldenburg 1999). Cafés in nations such as Australia where more
than one billion cups of coffee are consumed in commercial services every
day can significantly enhance lingering activities around neighbourhood
centres (Walters and Broom 2013).

The image of cities such as Melbourne and Geelong in Australia is
associated with café culture enhancing their tourism and destination
marketing. Until the Second World War, Australians, in the tradition
of their British forebears, were mostly drinking tea and beer and pub
culture was more dominant. An influx of Southern European migrants to
Australia brought with them a love of coffee, and the social rituals that
accompany it (Walters and Broom 2013). One might understand these
spaces as simultaneously real and imagined (Soja 1996), both the outcome
of human activity, and a frame and guide for it. Social rituals imply that
understanding space as 'lived' is most important, because only by paying
attention to it can the rhythm and tenor of everyday life be enhanced for
communities who socialise in cafés and other suburban third places.

To address these questions in relation to the social life of suburban
developments, this study will take three low-density suburbs into consideration as a representative of a wider context of Australian suburbs. The
case studies were chosen because of their different character and type of
social life.

STUDY AREA AND RESEARCH METHODS

Three commercial streets in the City of Greater Geelong have been chosen
as the case studies: Separation Street in Bell Park; Pakington Street in
Geelong West and Belle Vue Avenue in Highton. The case studies have

been fully described in previous publications from this project (Farahani et al. 2017; Farahani and Beynon 2015). About 300 metres of each street was chosen for a comprehensive investigation of activities.

The primary tool or method for studying everyday life in public spaces has been a direct (yet discreet) observation of behaviours, with a particular focus on how it relates to spatial features (Gehl and Svarre 2013; Stevens 2014). Direct observations provide an avenue to understand why and how some spaces are frequently used, while some others are quite underused. The analysis of people's use of public spaces is identifying links between observed activities and the physical environment, where they occur (Stevens 2014).

For this study, data was collected through unobtrusive observations of activities naturally occurring in the three commercial streets. There was no interaction with individuals or manipulation of the environment. Data was collected on the same day for each street on four days (Monday, Tuesday, Saturday and Sunday) with similar weather conditions, from early November till early December in 2014. On each day, the temperature was between 15°c and 27°c, which is considered as suitable for being outside. The selected suburban commercial streets were divided into eight identifiable sections.

Each section was video recorded for 30 seconds, every two hours, from 8:00 am to 10:00 pm. The short movies were inspected carefully and mapped in the format of visual tables registering the type of activities, the placement of activities, approximate age group and the time of the activities (Figure 11.1).

Identifying the Zones of Activity

The activities observed on the three streets were registered through mapping based on the time and type of activities and place of occurrence. We have identified where the agglomeration of the activities was highest on each street (shown in grey rectangles in Figure 11.2). These sections, which are considered as the zones of activity in this chapter, can be classified in three groups (number one, two and three in Figure 11.2). The first zone is inspired by pavement dining encouraged through popular third places. Not only do several activities happen around the cafés and restaurants, but also the duration of these activities is the longest. The most eventful spaces on the pavements are the ones claimed by the cafés' and eateries' temporary chairs and shade structures.

The second zone of activity occurs around popular shops and facilities that serve residents on a frequent basis. Everyday uses and services such as supermarkets, butcher, bakery, and grocery stores usually attract a high

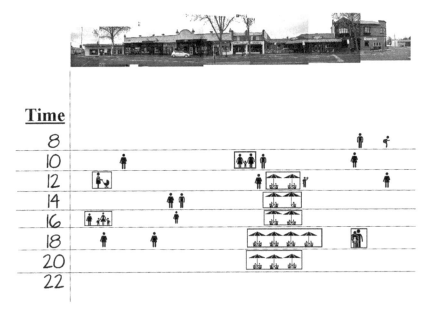

Source: The authors.

Figure 11.1   Observation mappings at Bell Park on Monday from 8:00 am to 10:00 pm

level of frequent coming and going activities. This zone is noticeable in the section of Belle Vue Avenue where, a butcher, bakery, grocery store and newsagent have been placed next to each other, attracting a great number of activities. The third zone, which might not be clearly visible, forms around the connecting points of the popular zones, such as everyday food stores. For instance, in Highton, a pedestrian alley, followed by a pedestrian crossing, connects the supermarket to the other side of the street, where the second activity zone is located (number three in Figure 11.2).

As the mapping shows, this zone is mostly occupied by coming and going activities which are the shortest in terms of time spent on the street, and consequently the street has the least number of social activities.

Figure 11.3 shows all the activities that occurred on a Saturday on the three selected streets. Social activities (people observed in groups) are shown in rectangles and people in cafés are highlighted in grey. Over 46 per cent of activities observed on streets were in the format of pavement dining around cafés and eateries (Table 11.1). Therefore, this study considers third places, in particular pavement dining, as a potential solution to strengthening the social atmosphere of commercial streets.

Table 11.1   Number of activities, café users and people in groups observed in four days

Street	Number of activities	Café and eateries	Activities in groups
Belle Vue Ave	1171	486 (41%)	748 (64%)
Pakington Street	1074	571 (53%)	863 (80%)
Separation Street	368	157 (42%)	174 (47%)
TOTAL	2613	1214 (46%)	1785 (68%)

Source: The authors.

Not only can third places such as cafés and bars inspire a considerable number of activities on streets but also the majority of activities occurring around cafés and eateries are social (Figure 11.3). In fact, about 68 per cent of activities observed are social activities and a considerable proportion are lingering activities in third places' pavement dining.

The social atmosphere facilitated by pavement dining is not the same on every street or for every café and restaurant. Many third places do not use pavements as a dining area and therefore the activities they generate are limited to customers entering and exiting their premises. Cafés and restaurants may adopt different approaches to communicate their social presence on the street. The degree of transparency and permeability impacts the way cafés and third places share their social activities with the street. Some cafés have completely open fronts crossing the boundaries of public and private and some only invite customers through their entrances.

Cafés and eateries can provide opportunities for outside dining in different ways: they might use their backyards where customers do not have a direct engagement with the street; they might use their front yards where customers are within the private boundaries of the commercial space but have visual contact with the street; and they may use footpaths for pavement dining which contributes the most to the vitality of the street.

This study's investigation of the physical qualities of third places (cafés, restaurants and bars) indicates how they contribute to the vitality of commercial streets. There are 24 eateries in all the case studies (eight on each street). Based on the observations, we have selected the nine most successful cafés or restaurants (three on each street). The affordances of streets in hosting pavement dining have been investigated through the comparison of these cafés and the result of observations mappings.

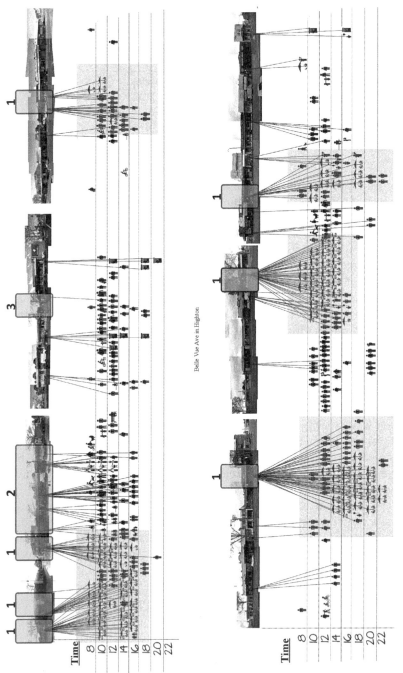

Belle Vue Ave in Highton

Pakington St in Geelong West

204

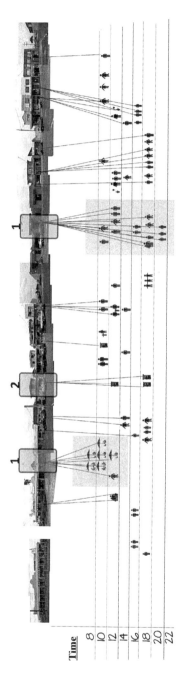

Separation St in Bell Park

Source: The authors.

Figure 11.2   Highlighted activities have occurred in relation to the pavement cafés and restaurants

205

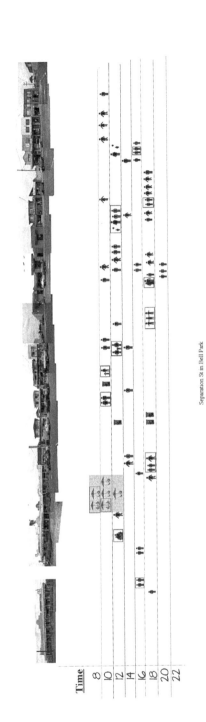

Separation St in Bell Park

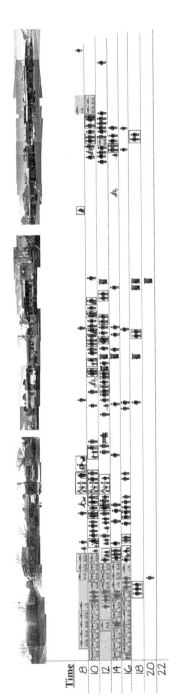

Belle Vue Ave in Highton

206

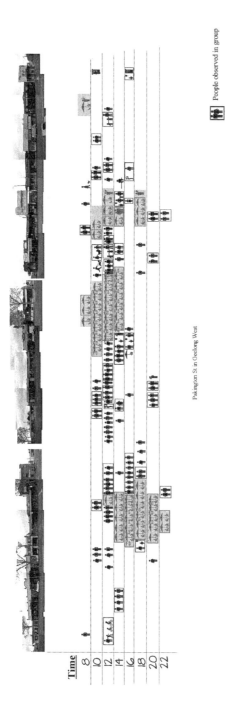

Pakington St in Geelong West

People observed in group

Source: The authors.

Figure 11.3   Highlighted activities have occurred in relation to the pavement cafés and restaurants on Saturday

Physical Qualities of Third Places and the Social Life of Commercial Streets

Our research has shown that third places may contribute to the social life of commercial streets in different ways and to various extents. As mentioned above, pavement cafés and restaurants with a higher number of enduring and stationary activities are more efficacious than the indoor cafés, which merely add to the number of coming and going activities. Previous studies have investigated physical qualities that may concern the social life on commercial streets (Farahani and Lozanovska 2014; Farahani et al. 2017; Farahani et al. 2015; Mehta 2013). Among these characteristics, we have selected the ones that may directly contribute to the success of pavement dining and contribute to the commercial streets vitality.

These qualities include the width of footpaths or outdoor sitting areas in eateries' front yards, the area available for outside dining, personalisation of shop fronts and footpaths, and softness of edges and landscaping. Although measuring the width of footpaths and the area of outside seating is straightforward, the three remaining characteristics are complex to quantify. Therefore, to assess personalisation, softness of the edges and greenery, a rating of low or high has been given to each third place by the first author based on the definitions of these terms in the literature.

Personalisation: Personalisation is the act of modifying the physical environment toward an expression of claiming a territory (Mehta 2009). Personalisation is usually accompanied by territorialisation or creating an identity. Kopec (2006) describes personalisation as a physical marker used to identify personal identity, mark territories and hence regulate social interaction. According to Abu-Ghazzeh (2000), personalisation is a way for people to modify their environment and make it distinctly theirs by being different to others. Based on the observations of third places' shop fronts, five types of personalisation were identified: advertisement boards, decorative features, shading structures and chairs, flower box and vertical filters (barriers for defining territory and separating the sitting area from streets or car parks). In order to assess personalisation, a value of 'high' is given to the third places with three or more types of personalisation. Third places with two or less types of personalisation are given a score of 'low' (Figure 11.4).

Soft edges: 'Soft edges' is a term coined by Gehl to describe indistinct boundaries between public and private spaces. According to Gehl (2010), the characteristics that contribute to the softness of edges are: scale and rhythm, transparency, appeal to many senses, texture and fine details, diversity of functions and vertical facade rhythm. Gehl (1987) argues that soft edges encourage feelings of safety through communicating with

Source: The authors.

Figure 11.4   Personalisation of shop front by a few third places

people. However soft edges need particular qualities to be successful. Mehta (2013) uses the term 'dull facades' to describe soft edges without these characteristics and argues that such dull and unwelcoming building facades create dead spaces. The quality of public spaces within the city is therefore of vital importance to creating a vibrant and lively city.

Soft or active edges contain many details that add to the quality of public spaces. A clear demarcation between public and private, active facades and appropriate urban furniture encourages people to stay in public spaces. Active facades refer to those facades where the inside and the outside uses are 'connected visually and thus can enrich and inspire each other' (Gehl and Gemzøe 2004). Gehl argues that no other element has a greater impact on the life and attractiveness of city spaces than active, open and lively facades (Gehl 2010). Based on this study's observations, three items that contribute to the softness of edges have been identified: level of details, visual connection of inside and outside and permeability. In order to quantify soft edges, a value of high has been given to third places with two or more items contributing to the softness of edges. The remaining third places have received a score of low.

Landscape and greenery: Landscape and greenery is believed to have contributing effects on the social life of neighbourhoods and commercial streets (Whyte 1980). A study of neighbourhoods' common spaces indicated that the presence of trees and grass is related to the degree of use of outdoor spaces, the amount of social activity that takes place within them, and the proportion of social to non-social activities they support (Sullivan 2004). For instance, Nasar and Julian (1995) found easy access to common outdoor green space can enhance a sense of community. Greenery and landscaping not only encourage activities by tempering the atmosphere, but also they may function as traffic barriers or shading. Therefore, in regard to the role that the landscape plays and based on our observations, five items have been identified: beautification, defining territory, traffic barrier, maintenance and shading (Figure 11.5). A value of high has been given to third places with landscaping and greenery that have three or more of the five identified roles. The remaining third paces have received a score of low for their landscaping.

Table 11.2 summarises the physical attributes of the nine most successful third places in the case studies. The physical attributes have been assessed in order to generate a clear picture of how they might encourage pavement dining and contribute to the vitality of the commercial streets.

Table 11.2 illustrates how the number of activities generated by cafés correlates with the width of pavements and seating area, personalisation, softness of edges and landscape. Although analysing nine cases will not

Source: The authors.

Figure 11.5   Landscaping and greenery

Table 11.2 *Comparing the number of observed activities in relation to the physical characteristics of cafés*

Third place	Suburb	Number of activities	Number of stationary activities	Width of footpath or front yard (m)	Area (m²)	Personalisation	Softness of edges	Greenery
1	Highton	39	38	5–8	140	High	High	High
2	Highton	30	26	4.5–12	100	High	High	High
3	Highton	9	5	3.5	30	High	High	High
4	Geelong West	61	60	7	90	High	High	Low
5	Geelong West	28	26	6	60	High	High	High
6	Geelong West	25	7	3.5	35	High	High	Low
7	Bell Park	14	8	4	50	High	Low	Low
8	Bell Park	12	0	2.5–4.6	25	Low	Low	Low
9	Bell Park	9	0	4	25	Low	High	Low

Source: The authors.

Source: The authors.

Figure 11.6   Some third places use their front yard for outdoor dining

provide enough data to prove the exact effect of these characteristics, the table generates a pattern of how and to what extent these features have encouraged pavement dining in the studied third places. According to the table, cafés with more than 25 patrons had a sidewalk or seating area of more than five metres wide, and a seating area of larger than 60 square metres. Popular pavement cafés were usually located in the widest section of the footpath (café number one, two and four in Table 11.2). However, sometimes the pavements are not wide enough to accommodate outdoor dining. Therefore, some cafés (number four and five) have allocated an outdoor space from a part of their lot and interior space (Figure 11.6).

The width of footpaths is not the only prerequisite for successful outside dining. The personalising and defining of the outdoor dining area also seems to be very critical for the popularity of outdoor dining. For instance, third place number five contains two separate outdoor dining areas: one is on the footpath separated from the street by flower boxes and the other is a semi-public open area within the lot surrounded by walls and separated from the footpath by a short fence. The observations showed that the space surrounded by walls is full of customers throughout the day, while the space on the footpath is hardly used.

Third places may define and personalise the dining space by different elements, including shades, flower boxes, awnings, columns, panels, and greenery. Popular pavement cafés (all the third places, except eight and nine in Table 11.2) use different elements to personalise outside space. As the table shows, all the third places have at least utilised three types of personalisation.

Facades may achieve softness through transparency, permeability and the level of detail. Softness of edges seems to positively correlate with the number of outside activities. Based on the observations, the five cafés with the highest number of activities had the highest ranking for softness. The softness of edges not only provides the interior with a view of the outside, but also benefits third places in linking the inside space to the footpath area. It also facilitates the flow of service for customers sitting outdoors.

Although greenery may provide a pleasant atmosphere to encourage outside activities, it does not seem to be a prerequisite for successful pavement dining. For instance, third place number six with no greenery, still encourages a considerable number of patrons dining outside. However, most third places use greenery as a means of beautification, defining boundaries and also as a traffic barrier.

Source: The authors.

Figure 11.7   Third places with hard edges

Among the case studies, there are two cafés in Geelong West with a branch in Highton (third places number three and four and third places number two and six). The cuisine and menu, the quality of food, style and non-physical features among these branches are the same. However, the affordances of the built environment has caused one of the cafés to have a more successful street life in Geelong West, while the other has a more successful Highton branch. These two third places and their branches make a good case for the significance of the built environment in encouraging pavement dining and the social life of commercial streets. Wherever the environment affords, these cafés have benefited from the outdoor area for dining patrons outside.

Third places can interact with the footpath in three ways. First, if the footpath is wide enough and the environment is desirable, they might claim the footpath with their outdoor chairs and shades. Second, if the footpath is insufficiently wide, they may sacrifice a part of their own lot for an outdoor space to accommodate a shaded or semi-shaded area that performs as a pavement café and contributes to the social life of the street. And if there is not enough space for outdoor dining, blurring the boundary and using transparency with an open front can be a solution for integrating the interior to the footpath.

However, when the outside environment is not entirely desirable, third places seek hard edges to minimise the interaction between the interior and the exterior, for instance with third place number eight (Figure 11.7).

CONCLUSION

Australian suburbs are associated with a lack of vitality and third places as 'hearts of urbanism' can be a solution for encouraging social interactions in neighbourhood centres. Certain features of the built environment and qualities of third places may encourage social activities and mitigate this lack of social life. Based on our observations, we have identified three zones of activity on commercial streets. The behavioural mappings showed that third places such as cafés, restaurants and bars are the first zone of activity which engender most of the stationary activities on commercial streets. Pavement cafés with a high number of staying activities create a sociable atmosphere and are vital to the image of their neighbourhood centres.

As Benjamin (1997) has suggested; 'living means leaving traces', suggesting that the physical elements of these environments provide a kind of casing for human action (in this case pavement dining). The collective act of creating these spaces is therefore an integral part of what Bourdieu

(1977) has called the habitus, a network of predispositions that reinforce and tacitly inform everyday action, and so a potent means by which identity can be formed and socialisation encouraged. Each third place makes concrete the set of conditions that has produced it, from specific meanings such as the provision of coffee or meals, or the reproduction of familiar elements such as tables and shade umbrellas, to economic and socio-political factors that drive the viability of such places and the broader neighbourhood around them.

More specifically, our research has found that there are several physical qualities of third places that may affect the social life of commercial streets. Of these characteristics, the ones that directly contribute to the success of pavement dining have been selected, such as the width of footpaths or front yards (outdoor sitting area), the area available for outside dining, the extent of personalisation, softness of edges and landscaping. These qualities have been investigated for the nine most successful third places in the three case studies and the results have been summarised for analysis.

In conclusion, cafés as third places seem to be successful in neighbourhood terms when they can claim the storefront, where footpaths are wide and there is enough room for a dining area. Beyond this, the personalisation or defining the boundaries of the dining area through physical elements such as panels and shades are critical factors in the popularity of pavement dining. A soft facade with permeability and transparency is another physical quality that may affect the success of outdoor dining. On streets where these qualities are lacking, people avoid outdoor dining and third places are drawn into their interior, meaning less visible activation of the neighbourhood.

The findings improve and broaden our understanding of the physical characteristics that influence the social life and patterns of activities in commercial streets and provide evidence that pavement dining plays an important role in creating vital neighbourhood centres.

REFERENCES

Abu-Ghazzeh, T.M. 2000. Environmental messages in multiple-family housing: territory and personalization. *Landscape Research*, 25, 97–115.
Banerjee, T. 2001. The future of public space: beyond invented streets and reinvented places. *Journal of the American Planning Association*, 67, 9–24.
Benjamin, W. 1997. *Charles Baudelaire: A Lyric Poet in the Era of High Capitalism*. London: Verso Books.
Benjamin, W. 1999. The return of the flâneur. *Selected Writings*, 2. Cambridge, MA: Harvard University Press, pp. 1927–1943.
Bookman, S. 2013. Brands and urban life. *Space and Culture*, 17, 85–99.

Bourdieu, P. 1977. *Outline of a Theory of Practice.* Cambridge: Cambridge University Press.

Davidson, W.B. and Cotter, P.R. 1991. The relationship between sense of community and subjective well-being: a first look. *Journal of Community Psychology,* 19, 246–253.

Deener, A. 2007. Commerce as the structure and symbol of neighborhood life: reshaping the meaning of community in Venice, California. *City and Community,* 6, 291–314.

Farahani, L.M. and Beynon, D. 2015. Pavement cafes as the activity zone in the social life of neighbourhood centres. 49th International Conference of the Architectural Science Association. Melbourne: The Architectural Science Association.

Farahani, L.M., Beynon, D. and Freeman, C.G. 2017. The need for diversity of uses in suburban neighbourhood centres. URBAN DESIGN International, 1–16.

Farahani, L.M. and Lozanovska, M. 2014. A framework for exploring the sense of community and social life in residential environments. *International Journal of Architectural Research: ArchNet-IJAR,* 8, 223–237.

Farahani, L.M., Lozanovska, M. and Soltani, A. 2015. The social life of commercial streets. 8th Making Cities Liveable Conference 2015 Melbourne, Australia.

Gehl, J. 1987. *Life Between Buildings: Using Public Space.* Washington, DC: Island Press.

Gehl, J. 2010. *Cities for People.* Washington, DC: Island Press.

Gehl, J. and Gemzøe, L. 2004. *Public Spaces–Public Life.* Copenhagen: Arkitektens Forlag.

Gehl, J. and Svarre, B. 2013. *How to Study Public Life.* Washington, DC: Island Press.

Granovetter, M. 1973. The strength of weak ties. *American Journal of Sociology,* 78(1), 78–84.

Jacobs, J. 1961. *The Death and Life of Great American Cities.* New York: Vintage.

Kopec, D.A. 2006. *Environmental Psychology For Design.* New York: Fairchild.

Lefebvre, H. 1984. *Everyday Life in the Modern World* (1950), translated by Sacha Rabinovitch. New Brunswick, NJ: Transaction Books.

Lefebvre, H. 1991. *The Production of Space,* translated by Donald Nicholson-Smith. Oxford: Blackwell.

Lefebvre, H. 1996. *Writings on Cities.* Oxford: Blackwell.

Lukito, Y.N. and Xenia, A.P. 2017. Café as third place and the creation of a unique space of interaction in UI Campus. IOP Conference Series: Earth and Environmental Science, 2017. IOP Publishing, 012028.

Mehta, V. 2009. Sense of place in everyday spaces: lessons for urban design. In: Rashed-Ali, H. and Roff, S. (eds), *Leadership in Architectural Research.* Lulu. com pp. 379–386.

Mehta, V. 2013. *The Street: A Quintessential Social Public Space.* New York: Routledge.

Mehta, V. and Bosson, J.K. 2009. Third places and the social life of streets. *Environment and Behavior,* 42, 779–805.

Montgomery, J. 1997. Café culture and the city: the role of pavement cafés in urban public social life. *Journal of Urban Design,* 2, 83–102.

Nasar, J.L. and Julian, D.A. 1995. The psychological sense of community in the neighborhood. *Journal of the American Planning Association,* 61(2), 178–184.

Oldenburg, R. 1989. *The Great Good Place: Cafés, Coffee Shops, Community Centers, Beauty Parlors, General Stores, Bars, Hangouts, and How They Get You Through the Day.* New York: Paragon House.

Oldenburg, R. 1999. The character of third places. In: Oldenburg, R., *The Great Good Place*, New York, Marlowe & Company, pp. 20–42.

Oldenburg, R. (ed.) 2009. *Celebrating the Third Place: Inspiring Stories About the 'Great Good Places' at the Heart of Our Communities*. Chicago: Da Capo Press.

Oldenburg, R. 2013. *The Café as a Third Place*. Dordrecht: Café Society. Springer.

Oosterman, J. 1992. Welcome to the pleasure dome: play and entertainment in urban public space: the example of the sidewalk cafe. *Built Environment* (1978–), 155–164.

Richards, L. 1994. Suburbia: domestic dreaming. In: Johnson, L. (ed.) *Suburban Dreaming*. Geelong: Deakin University Press, pp. 114–128.

Rosenbaum, M., Ward, J., Walker, B. and Ostrom, A. 2016. A cup of coffee with a dash of love. *Journal of Service Research*, 10, 43–59.

Rosenbaum, M.S. 2006. Exploring the social supportive role of third places in consumers' lives. *Journal of Service Research*, 9, 59–72.

Soja, E.W. 1996. *Thirdspace: Expanding the Geographical Imagination*. London: Blackwell.

Stenseth, B. 2013. *Heart of Urbanism. The Café: A Chapter of Cultural History*. Dordrecht: Café Society. Springer.

Stevens, Q. (2014). Public space as lived. In: Carmona, M. (ed.) *Explorations in Urban Design: An Urban Design Research Primer*. Farnham: Ashgate Publishing, pp. 277–287.

Sullivan, W.C. 2004. The fruit of urban nature: vital neighborhood spaces. *Environment and Behavior*, 36, 678–700.

Walters, P. and Broom, A. 2013. *The City, the Café, and the Public Realm in Australia*. Dordrecht: Café Society. Springer.

Warner, J., Talbot, D. and Bennison, G. 2012. The cafe as affective community space: reconceptualizing care and emotional labour in everyday life. *Critical Social Policy*, 33, 305–324.

Whyte, W.H. 1980. *The Social Life of Small Urban Spaces*. Washington, DC: Conservation Foundation.

Index

Rethinking third places